THE STORY OF THE
SUPERCAR

FROM MIURA TO McLAREN

A **car** BOOK

PUBLISHED BY EMAP NATIONAL PUBLICATIONS LTD

CONTENTS

WHAT DOES 'SUPERCAR' MEAN TO YOU? IF YOU'RE more than a certain age – over 40, say – it might once have meant a supersonic single-seater car-cum-plane, a pre-Fireball XL5 and Thunderbirds Gerry Anderson creation with impossibly small wings and a pilot called Mike Mercury. To most of us, though, it simply means something sensationally fast and powerful, with that speed and power absolutely central to its being.

Asked to imagine a typical supercar, your brain's first image will probably be of something mid-engined and muscular with two seats, a low and sleek roof, and a strong feel of the racetrack. Probably Italian, too. That's been the convention since Lamborghini's Miura set today's template in 1966. But siting the engine directly behind the occupants is not the only way to interpret the supercar idea. Pre-Miura, engines were invariably front-mounted under a long, assertive bonnet. A Ferrari 250 GTO, a Mercedes 300SL (gull-wing coupé or slinky sports car), a Blower Bentley, a Bugatti Type 35: these were supercars too.

And there was still room for the old guard even after that 1966 watershed, for no-one would deny supercar status to a Ferrari Daytona or an Aston Martin Vantage. In the hit list of desirable attributes, colossal power more than makes up for an engine bolted in at the old-fashioned end. Such cars, though, were of the past. The future was a new era of Miuras and Boras, Countachs, Boxers and Testarossas.

In this book you'll find the pick of CAR's supercar stories through the years. They're arranged decade-by-decade, from the metamorphosis of the 1960s (when CAR was born), through the power games of the 1970s and 1980s, to the sky's-the-limit technology of the 1990s. And we've included the Ferrari F50 and 550 Maranello, born after the McLaren, to bring the story up-to-date. You'll discover the unofficial emergence of the 200mph club (Ferrari F40, Lamborghini Diablo, Ferrari F50, McLaren F1), and you'll see that despite a climate of pervasive political correctness, the supercar is hardly extinct.

Quite the opposite, in fact. If there's one thing as true today as it was in the 1960s, it is that you're never alone with a supercar. Almost whenever you park, someone will stare in awe and admiration, and engage you in conversation. Such cars seem to transcend envy and green-tinged tut-tutting. They are appreciated for what they are, items of visual and aural excitement. Beauty, too, if the beholder has the right eyes.

It is arguably easier to design a supercar than to create the next Volkswagen Golf, because the constraints aren't so tight. The Golf will be better made, too, although today's supercars aren't the trouble their ancestors often were. But nothing can thrill so completely, so viscerally, as something with huge tyres, huge grip and even huger power. The next 206 pages will show you how.

John Simister

Road test editor, CAR Magazine

PLEASE NOTE: A FEW OF THE CARS APPEARING IN THE PHOTOGRAPHS ARE NOT THE EXACT MODELS DRIVEN IN THE FEATURE

SUPERCARS HAVE BEEN AROUND SINCE MOTORING BEGAN,
for that was when the line between fast road car and race car was
thinnest. If we look at the 1920s and 1930s, we find blown Bentleys and
Mercedes-Benz SSKs, beautiful Bugattis, pre-GM Vauxhall 30/98s,
Alfa Romeo 8C 2300s; all of these, in their day, fulfilled the supercar brief
of being more than just a sports car, but more road-ready than a racing
car. All were fast, all were created with passion, all existed for the twin
purposes of going hard and exciting the eye of the beholder.

   All, too, were front-engined, with engines of large capacity, many cylinders
or both of these attributes. That front-engine layout stayed the norm right
through to the mid-1960s, long V12s lurking under the longer bonnets of
a Ferrari 250 GTO or 275 GTB, a simple but monstrous V8 hidden under the
bursting curves of an AC Cobra, straight-sixes powering a Mercedes-Benz
300SL or an Aston Martin DB5 with James Bond mythically at the wheel.
High-end grand tourers or steroidal sports cars, these were the old guard, still
flourishing. Then something happened.

   What happened was that the supercar breed became redefined as a distinct entity.
Endurance races of the Le Mans variety were why, because some of the entrants
started apeing what was going on in Formula One, and put the engine behind the driver.
No longer was a top Le Mans car just a stripped-out, souped-up grand tourer; suddenly
it was a whole new breed of racing car: compact, mid-engined, devastatingly efficient.

   Picture those new-look Le Mans pace-setters. Picture a Ferrari 250LM, a Ford GT40, a
Chaparral 2F, a Ferrari P4. Le Mans cars were never as brutally beautiful before, nor have they
been since, but what they gained in track-worthiness they had now lost in road-friendliness. You
could drive them on the road, but that was no longer a part of what they were for. Ford did make a
roadgoing GT40, the plushed-up and watered-down Mk3, but to drive it was to feel a spell breaking.
Better to let a GT40 stay in the land of your auto-dreams.

   The rôle model had been redefined. With the redefinition came a longing for a new breed of supercar – compact,
mid-engined, devastatingly efficient, of course. But the first car-maker to latch on to this new future was not
Ferrari but Lamborghini, a tractor-maker from Sant'Agata Bolognese with
absolutely no race-track connections. In 1966, as the Ferrari-versus-Ford
battle notched up hitherto uncharted degrees of deadliness in the World
Championship of Makes, Ferruccio Lamborghini launched his Miura. Its shape
took on the new Le Mans norm: low and sleek, oozing power and agility. As
much as blastability along straights, it promised prowess in bends. After this,
the world's fastest, most glamorous cars would never be the same again.
All the stranger, then, that the only other mid-engined exotic to emerge
before the decade's end was Ferrari's Dino 206. Calling this little
2.0-litre beauty a supercar was stretching a point, though, despite its
genes and the fact that its line would sire a series of compact Ferraris of
undoubted supercar quality. If we're talking real supercars, only the
Miura looked to tomorrow, while rivals ignored the signs. Swinging the
'60s may have been, but in supercar evolution terms they were near stagnant.
Not until the 1970s would the front-engined dinosaurs start to die off.

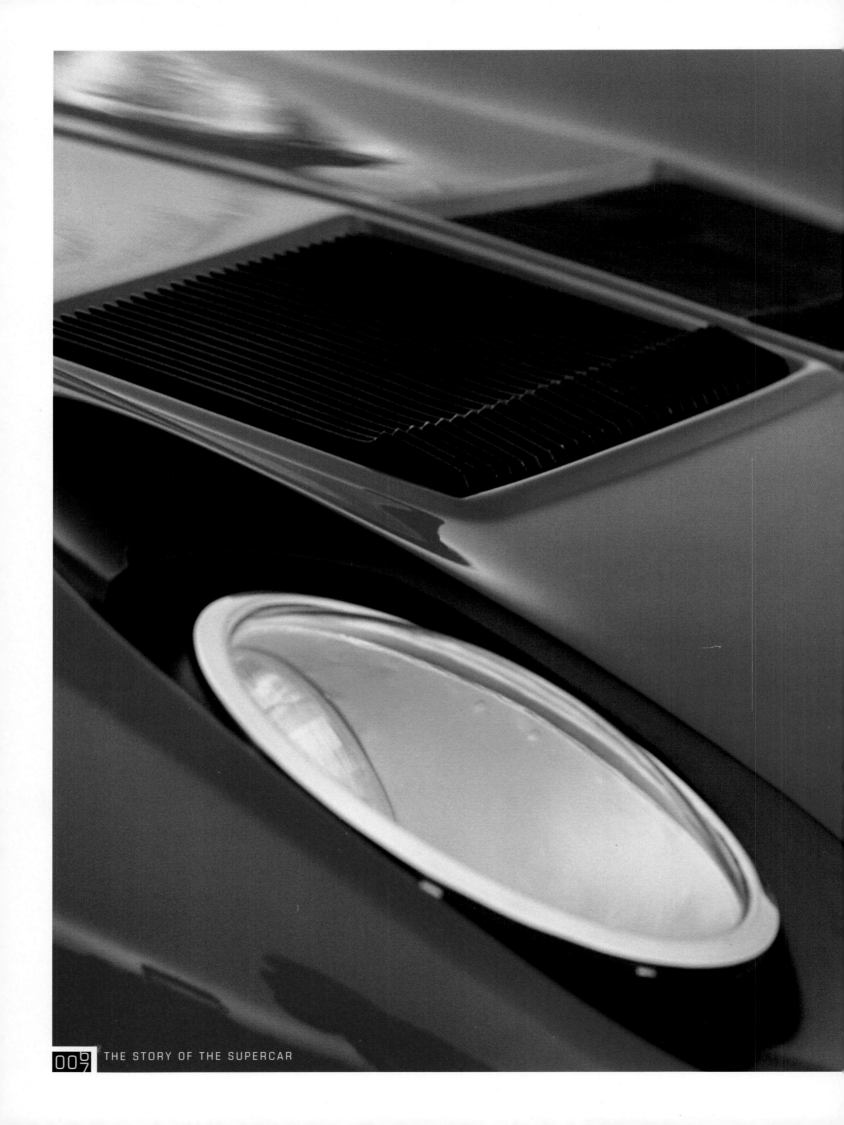

This beautiful car startled the sports car world not only with its sheer beauty, but with the ingenuity of its mechanicals too. Its essence would inspire supercars right into the 1990s

LAMBORGHINI
Miura

By LJK Setright

THE SWISS CUSTOMS MAN SMILED indulgently when I told him the Miura was simply a Mini Cooper turned back to front. Perhaps he did not altogether believe me – perhaps I was not altogether telling the truth. The Miura is really rather special.

There are other cars whose rear wheels are driven by an engine mounted transversely in the tail, and some of them have nicely shaped and streamlined two-seater coupé bodies – but none of them can do anything like 180mph, and none of them costs anything like £8050.

If all this isn't enough to make the Miura special, there is the tantalising thought that there are only three or four in Britain. So when the time came last September for our East End friends Lamborghini Concessionaires to go and fetch another one it seemed that the occasion should be marked in some way. What better way – from my point of view, at least – than for me to go to Italy and help drive the thing back to England? Providence, I must say, was looking after me very well inasmuch as (a) Mr Assistant Daniels was infernally busy because (b) Mr Editor Blain was on holiday and (c) nobody else had been let into the secret. Little persuasion was needed to get me on a plane for Milan, little encouragement for me to hustle a Hertz-hired Fiat 125 down the *autostrada* to Bologna. The *autostrada* was not very busy and the folk using it were excellent mirror watchers, so the Fiat could maintain a noble 95mph all the way while I sought to get my eye in for the fast motoring expected on the morrow.

Hunger is supposed to be the best sauce, and I must admit that I was mentally slavering in anticipation of the way the Miura would eat up the roads on my return journey. There is so much to look forward to with a Miura: that legendary V12 engine by Bizzarrini, the reputedly brilliant chassis by Dallara, the spellbinding sculpture of the body by Bertone, and the final sorting and tweaking by Wallace. And think of it: £8050! The most expensive thing I had ever driven before cost a mere £8025 – but there, I suppose I just have to admit that my life hitherto had been humdrum and lacklustre...

There is another way of looking at the price-tag: on a basis of pounds sterling per pound avoirdupois, the Miura is just about 50 percent more expensive than anything else I have driven before. Or again. £4025 per seat does seem rather a lot – especially when the seats are not very comfortable. However, I do not think it was reflections such as these that caused such a crowd of excited Italians to cluster round the Miura as it stood outside our hotel (the sadly misnamed Jolly) in Bologna next morning. They weren't crowding round it because it was so expensive or because it was particularly well made, for parked right behind it was a more expensive and in many ways better made Series T Rolls-Royce with special coachwork which never attracted a second glance. Maybe the Miura's colour scheme had something to do with it: it was a particularly virulent lime green, with the details picked out in matt black – not a trace of brightwork anywhere on the car except for the little Bertone insignia on the flank. But surely this is the most exciting thing on the roads today, with that blind-looking and heavily slatted rear window so much part of the roof as to be almost horizontal, with those vast and obviously functional air intake scoops on the rear quarters, that vast windscreen and right up at the front those retracted Minnie Mouse headlamps pointing resolutely skywards. The thing looks magnificently absurd, expensive, expansive: it is 3ft 5in high, 5ft 9in wide, 14ft 2in long and it weighs the best part of a ton. It develops 350bhp, wears its own special Pirelli radials and has synchromesh on reverse gear (yes – really).

Maybe it was a bit too much to expect luggage space as well. There is in fact a bit of a boot in the extreme tail, but the Lamborghini Concessionaires man did have rather a lot of stuff with him. My overnight case had to be kept in the car alongside my feet, my hat had to go on the floor beneath my knees, and I personally had to twist myself a bit in order to get in. Legroom on the passenger's side was okay but headroom was lacking, because the roof starts scraping downwards immediately aft of the windscreen, so only by moving my seat forward so that my knees jack-knifed into the air could I avoid a crick in the neck. This didn't promise well for the next 1000 miles, but there was nothing that could be done about it now. The LC man made himself comfortable in the driving seat – he is about 5ft 10in and could enjoy a perfect driving position – and twisted the starter key.

The exultant whoop of a thoroughbred V12 is like nothing else in motoring. It is immediate, urgent, peremptory. The Lambo idles at about 800rpm, and a gentle blip up to 2000 produced a sort of instant quickening of everybody in the square like a WO calling parade to attention. Mr LC slid the big lever into the gated slot for first gear, I breathed a private prayer that he might not be a nerve-wearing driver and we eased away into the busy morning traffic. The first gearchange showed me that I probably need not worry about my new friend's driving: it was slow, methodical, straight out of the ONE-pause-TWO Army drivers' manual. Before the second gearchange I had time to appreciate that the

low-speed ride over a rather broken, irregular road surface was surprisingly good – firm, but without shake or harshness. After the third gearchange, the last for some time, it dawned on me that the big four-litre Lambo engine was amazingly flexible. It might develop 87.5bhp per litre, but from ridiculously low revs it would pull as smoothly and inexorably as a Silver Ghost. Clearly this was going to be an astonishing motorcar.

Looking about me I could see some astonishing things already. Glue, for example: yes, glue, between the carpeting and the sides of the backbone tunnel that forms part of the chassis and fences off the driver's compartment from the passenger's. Clearly Mr Bertone's bodybuilders are like all other Italian bodybuilders, though maybe not quite so bad (I gather that Englishmen buying Miuras usually take them to somebody like Hooper or Radford for an interior refit). Basically the interior decor is quite pleasing, the whole thing being done in dull black leather, door handles, ashtrays, everything. Mark you, things like ashtrays are basically the regulation issue chromium things that you get on most Italian cars, sprayed with a light coating of black paint that might resist a finger nail but not for long. The facia, the instrument binnacle, the door panels, the outer panels of the seats: all are in well stitched black leather. The central seat panels are knitted from plastics in an open design that encourages ventilation, the window winders are huge perforated metal cranks painted black and turning in recesses that allow them to remain flush with the door trim: considering the length of the crank handle, I found the low gearing ridiculous and the stickiness of the action discouraging. By way of compensation there was some intelligent switch location, notable in the series of toggles mounted centrally at the top of the windscreen to control things like lighting and fans – the latter not only the ventilating kind but also a Kenlowe for the water radiator. Actually there are two of these electric radiator fans, one switching itself automatically on and off by a thermostat: but Mr LC was using the other in traffic as a precaution.

Precautions were the order of the day, really. In the first place the car had to be delivered to England whole and unmarked. In the second place it had to be run-in, which was tiresome but unavoidable. All Lamborghini engines are given 24 hours' running-in on the bench under their own power before installation in the chassis, but thereafter they still have to be nurtured carefully for a while. Our orders were not to exceed 5000rpm and generally to treat the unit gently as one would in normal running-in procedure. The peak of the power curve is at 7000rpm, so we were not too gravely handicapped, but it is rather galling to be limited to a miserly 126mph in a car that looks as if it ought always to be travelling at its easily achieved 176mph. With the 4.09 to one axle ratio that is normal issue the Lambo is so geared that when the engine is doing its 7000rpm the car will be doing 56mph in bottom gear, 83mph in second, 116mph in third, 144mph in fourth and 176mph

in fifth. Lamborghini claim 300 kilometres an hour as the maximum speed, which on this axle ratio would be equivalent to exactly 7450rpm which is not too much for the Miura engine, certain owners being known to have taken it beyond 8000rpm without apparent harm.

After what seemed ages, during which I was reluctant to smoke lest some ash get on the spotlessly clean floor, we left and crawled away at our beggarly 120mph on to the *autostrada*. Everybody seemed to be driving so slowly that morning. Fiats of all sizes, Alfas of all types were passed with such promptness that it seemed as though they were all playing a trick on us, driving around at a snail's pace so as to kid us into thinking that we were going fast whereas in fact we were crawling too. Weren't we? It was so difficult to tell – there was no sensation of speed, no feeling of movement, no wind noise, no tyre noise. No shortage of noise either: the noise level inside the car is quite high, and the navigator should be a Stentor. But the noise level is more or less constant regardless of engine or road speed: a steady, mechanical mezzo-forte made up of all the mumbling, thrashing, whining, whirring, groaning and grumbling metallic *obbligati* that a race-bred engine furnishes to fill the octaves left unoccupied by that exuberant exhaust. It is a lovely noise, an expensive noise, but I suppose when all is said and done, it is a noise.

The *autostrada* was much busier than on the previous day, and although the roadgoing Italians were still well-behaved there was a sprinkling of holiday-making Dutch and Germans who could not or would not use their mirrors. Oh yes, we made progress, and having a speedo calibrated in kilometres makes it seem rather satisfying to cruise at 200. But staying below 5000rpm in the Lambo is a bore, and despite the physical discomfort of being wedged between my luggage and the roof I went to sleep. All right, how many cars have you slept in at 126mph?

So we cruised on, up to, and through Milan, along the lovely

Ivrea *autostrada*, and then up the even lovelier hills towards Aosta. I was awake now and taking interest: dull would he be who did otherwise in this breathtakingly beautiful country, where the foothills of the Alps provide lighting and colour and buildings and people and roads of surpassing interest.

All the same, my relief was tempered by a rising irritation: when the devil was this man going to let me drive? Apparently various business-like reasons made him want to be at the wheel while we negotiated customs barriers and his idea was that I should take over once we had entered Switzerland. My frustration was that this was a stinking rotten trick because I hate driving in Switzerland and because I wanted to fling the Miura up the winding mountain roads towards the Grand St Bernard. However, I remembered that there were roads down the other side of the hills that were just as good, and some approaching the French border that were in fact more difficult: and undoubtedly I could see a lot more of this beautiful bit of Alpine Italy from the passenger seat than I could from the driver's. So Mr LC was forgiven and when we pulled up soon after at an attractive Swiss hostelry only my desire to envelop a good bellyful of red meat and pasta could overcome my urge to get to grips with the Miura. Maybe it was a very substantial bellyful, but for some reason I seemed to

Big dials and bulky centre console characterise the Miura's interior, above, as do the slightly cramped quarters and the not insignificant din of the V12 engine

sink further into the driver's seat than I had into the passenger's. With the seat as far back as it would go, the wheel was at a comfortable distance – perhaps a little high and tilted away too far in the Italian fashion, but manageable for all that. The gearlever was perfectly placed and had a lovely big wooden knob with a finger groove for comfort: but it worked in a very rectilinear gate, and was heavily spring-loaded towards the plane of third and fourth. The clutch pedal was fairly heavy which was to be expected but dear Lord! the accelerator pedal was heavy beyond belief. You may remember that back in the days when the Hispano Suiza was the best car in the world its designers reached the conclusion that 'the brake pedal should require no more effort to make the car slow down at a given rate than was needed on the accelerator pedal to make it accelerate' at a similar rate, wherefore the brake servo was invented. Lamborghini appears to have approached the problem with the same object in mind but from a different direction: it has simply made the accelerator pedal as heavy as the brake, instead of making the brake as light as the accelerator. To make matters worse the linkage to the throttles is terribly digressive. The first half-inch of pedal movement seems to trigger off an explosion in the engine compartment and the next four or five inches serve merely to amplify this somewhat. I know there are 12 throttle butterflies to be controlled, and several accelerator pumps, and that they are all rather a long way from the pedal, but the whole affair is still ridiculously heavy. Oh well, it would help to discourage me from exceeding the rev limit – and I wasn't really comfortable enough to start flinging the car around just yet anyway.

I had to tilt my head forward and to the right to keep it clear of the roof, and in fact was not sitting square in the seat at all. Mark you, there is room to lower the cushion by one inch and the steering column can be adjusted for rake by dint of a few minutes' spanner work, in which case the lofty Setright would fit into the lowly Miura pretty well, I reckon. Such modifications were scarcely possible in mid-Europe however, and it was time we were off, so with a final reminder from LC that the car cost an awful lot of money and had to be delivered intact – we were off!

Not so fast. I stalled it. The pedals are heavy, and the clutch turned out to be as sudden as the engine. A second try with a few more revs took us smoothly away. The change from first to second gear went through quickly and smoothly. If all the others were going to be like that I would have no complaints: there was resistance from the synchromesh, but only just enough. I let the spring-loading of the lever do half the work of finding third for me, and getting fourth was hardly any work at all. Coming down to second was much harder, for that spring is really powerful and it is impossible to cut the corners of the gate.

By this time the Swiss had been alerted to the fact that there were a couple of foreigners seeking to cross their precious country at high speeds without actually spending anything, and they rose up

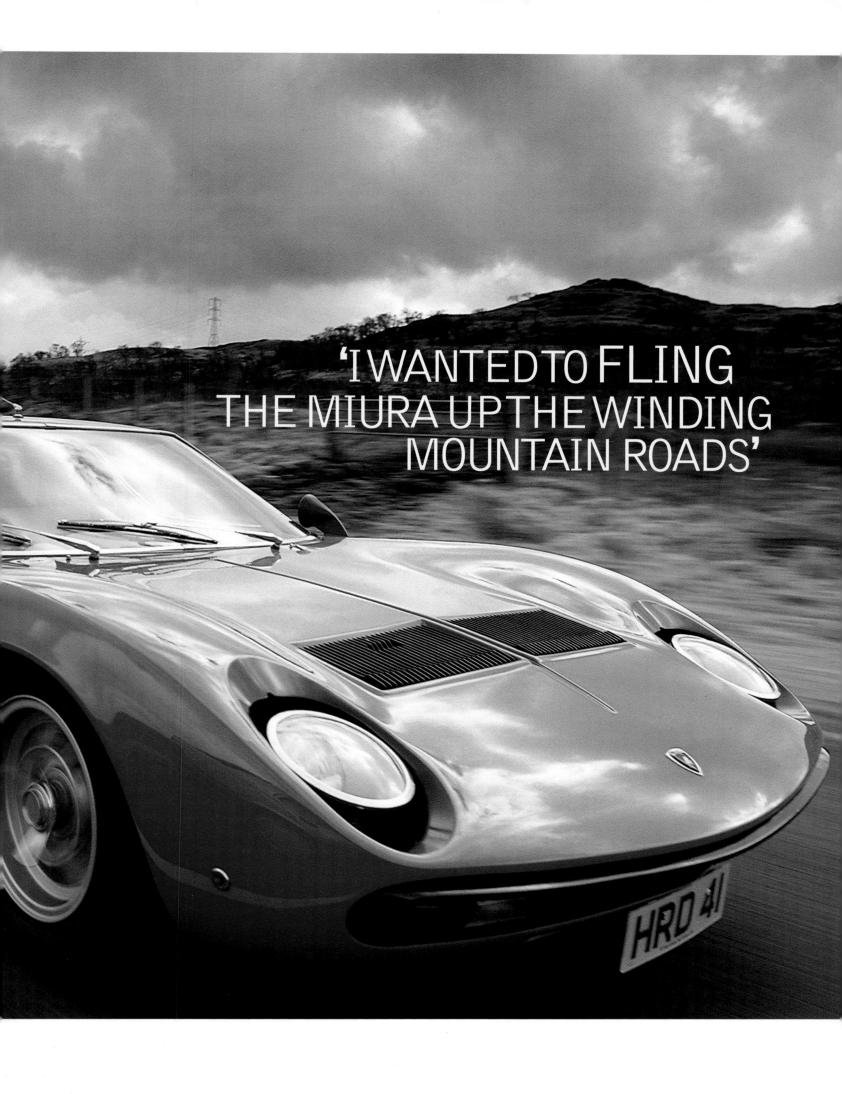

'I WANTED to FLING THE MIURA UP THE WINDING MOUNTAIN ROADS'

in force to prevent this dastardly possibility being accomplished. Mrs Castle would feel at home in Switzerland; so would Fabius Cunctator. The first thing that the Swiss Defence did was to establish a traffic jam around some apparently non-existent roadworks, this delay enabling them to put up a few more speed limit signs. The netted effect was in fact to foil their obvious intentions, for although the hold-ups resulted in our reaching the northern shore of Lake Geneva just as the Montreux-Vevey-Lausanne traffic jam was building up to its evening peak, I had by that time had so much practice in the difficult art of balancing an instant-engagement clutch against an instant-full-noise accelerator that we were more inclined to press on rather than to stop and wait for it all to disappear.

Although those first few dozen miles of snail's-pace driving through Switzerland were miserable, they were not overwhelmingly so. They also proved something about the Miura: that a breathtakingly powerful engine is not so mettlesome that it will not endure prolonged idling or low-speed pulling. Once the clutch is fully home, the big four-cam V12 is completely and utterly tractable and will pull as smoothly and surely as a steam engine from tickover speeds in any of the three bottom gears. It does not overheat, it does not foul its plugs, it does not cough or splutter, it does not vary in the regularity of its idling.

Once away from the lake, gratification in the things that the engine does not do was replaced by delight in the things that it does. The winding roads over the hills to Valorb were full of variety with lengthy straights, fast curves, hairpins, and all. The Miura revelled in it. As I began to use more and more power, the acceleration was beginning to verge on the incredible. Using the permitted 5000rpm in each gear it was seldom necessary to drop below 3500rpm, and gearchanges came fast and free. Upward ones were pleasant enough, but downward changes were sheer delight. This high-revving four-litre has no discernible flywheel effects, changing speed with the sort of immediacy that we used to marvel at a decade ago when listening to the racing Gilera four-cylinder motorcycles. Approaching a 50mph corner from a 100mph straight was sheer bliss, the change from fourth to third going through like lightning punctuated by an immeasurably brief and incomparably crisp zip of revs. The brakes seemed just right for this kind of car and this kind of driving: extremely progressive in their response to the pedal, as sweet as honey if you pressured it gently and like a kick in the chest if you booted them hard.

However, such things are mere preliminaries for a corner and what really counts is the car's behaviour thereafter. What counted even more on this occasion was the feelings of the proprietor for the time being, who was sitting there obviously hoping that I would not do anything rash. This was inhibiting but fair: after all, the agreed object of the exercise had been to make acquaintance with the car and not to wring its neck. In any case there is no

greater sin in driving than to alarm one's passenger, unless it be to alarm him in his car. We Setrights can bite the bullet, so I did not attempt to explore the farthest reaches of the Miura's cornering and handling departments. Even so we did not hang about. At what felt like about seven-tenths for the Miura it simply went where it was steered, with no roll and no sensitivity to the use of throttle and brakes in the corner. There is not much feel in the rack and pinion steering, which is rather low geared and heavily damped, but it lacks nothing in precision and since it seems to have rather little castor action it does not vary much in weight. Even though the fun was circumscribed, it was great fun nevertheless. Yet it could not last, for it was growing dark and the French border was near. Customs formalities for a new car being taken overland to England are inevitably more complex than the ordinary sort of touring transit, and previous experience had indicated to LC, Esq, that the best time to cross this particular border was first thing in the morning. A couple of miles short of the frontier was a pleasant and clean little motel with a huge menu and there we halted. Early next morning, when what sounded like a couple of hundred cowbells stopped ringing so that it must have been milking time, we rose, and as the mists began to clear to reveal a grey and chilly morning, we set off to cross France.

For the same reasons as in northern Italy, LC was driving. I just sat there and froze. It was a cold morning admittedly, but we covered 20 miles before the engine's oil temperature rose enough to allow spirited driving. With every kilometre nearer to England I felt more and more chilled. It was all right for LC – he is one of these Nordic types with glycol in the arteries, who breaks out in a sweat if somebody strikes a match but is apparently frost-proof. Personally I am more inclined to wear full tweeds in mid-Sahara and I could only conclude that the Miura, being a sports car, had no heater. This led me into an evil train of thought about Italian

automobile engineers who never travel further north than Turin and probably winter in Taranto. It made me fume, which is one way of keeping warm: but when I took over the driving after an early lunch in Chaumont I discovered that there in front of me was a heater control. While LC was looking the other way I turned it on and engaged in a spot of rapid estimation and calculation to see how long he would take to slow roast at the usual 40 minutes per pound. I reckoned that we would make Calais before he needed to be turned over and basted, and warmed to my work.

Unpleasant work it was too, but through no fault of Lamborghini. Since mid-morning we had been driving through heavy rain in company with lots of obstructive traffic on slow, narrow roads liberally set about with huge diversions. Every time we got away from one crocodile of cars and lorries we promptly caught up with another. Nobody wanted to let us by, and the limited vision available on the switchback roads made it hazardous to stay in the opposing lanes for long even with the sort of acceleration that the Miura could summon. Our route was to take us through Troyes, Soissons and Bapaume, and as we staggered on I could not help but think sorrowfully of the occasion a month earlier when in equally heavy rain I put 97 miles into the hour northbound from Paris in my own car. On this more easterly route our average was less than half that, and frequently less than a third. Every so often the road would clear ahead for long enough for me to give the car its head, and I was now using occasional bursts of full throttle to hustle it up to maximum speed. When treated to the spur, the Miura fairly rockets forward. There is never any hint of breaking traction, even on those streaming wet and bumpy

4.0-litre V12 sits across engine bay, and gearbox lives in sump, just as it does in a Mini. Front compartment, left, good only for housing spare

French roads: just an unhesitating and almighty shove that suddenly leaves the mirrors empty.

There were times during these intermittent sprints when I wondered whether the chassis was really as fast as the engine. On Italian and Swiss roads 120mph had been plain sailing, but in France the bumps and camber made the car something of a handful at similar speeds. There seemed to be some bump steering from the independent rear suspension whose wheels are set with three degrees of toe-in at static deflection. Quite a lot of work at the wheel was sometimes necessary to maintain course on a straight road at three-figure speeds, and I was jolly glad that the situation was not further complicated by sensitivity to gusting side winds such as we encountered from time to time. Occasionally the car's headlong flight over wavy roads had to be checked as the suspension movement got in phase with the road contour and something bottomed with a nasty screech. The something later turned out to be one of the rear tyres making contact with the inner wall of the wheelarch at full bump.

All this I was prepared to forgive a little later when the Miura redeemed itself beautifully. We had gone rushing over a long hill brow at no little speed only to find beyond the crest that the wicked French wanted us to divert ourselves to the right but had not chosen to tell us in advance. With right foot shifting smartly from accelerator to brake, the Miura was swung gingerly into the fork, and I braked as hard as I dared as we shot down a wet concrete hill to a junction below. With the road still curving to the right, the sheer power of the brakes and the speed of the car at last overcame the grip of those very special Cinturati and all four wheels locked simultaneously. The car slid and wriggled: I backed off the pedal pressure by perhaps a fifth, and all of a sudden the tyres were biting, the car was under control, on course, and to a rapid and most commendable halt as the last bit of road curved away to the left. Inwardly damning the French and blessing certain Italians, I looked up and down the road we were to join, slotted first gear, and shot off into the rain.

It was really a miserable journey made worse by an appalling traffic jam in Bethune where we lost nearly an hour. A telephone call to Calais suggested that we had also lost any chance of a flight home, since we merely had an open ticket, so we trundled on into the murky twilight, hoping that there might be a cancellation even though the number of holidaymakers heading the same way and cluttering up the road made it seem improbable. We could not help recalling the Bradford boy racer who had accosted us shortly after we entered France when we were held up behind him in a queue. Where, he wanted to know, are you heading – Calais or Boulogne? As though there were no other conceivable possibilities. But we thought more cheerfully of him upon arriving at Calais Airport, wondering if by any poetic chance his might have been the cancellation that enabled us to travel on the day's last plane to England.

During the final leg of the journey home from Southend to London, with LC at the wheel, I had time to reflect on what I had

'THERE WERE TIMES
WHEN I WONDERED WHETHER
THE CHASSIS WAS AS FAST
AS THE ENGINE'

learned of this unique car on this unusual trip. Of one thing there could be no doubt: that engine is absolutely superb. In terms of performance the car has little to fear from anything else anywhere. How much of its performance can be used is more debatable: as I have explained it was simply not on to try for cornering conclusions, but the car did feel skitterish on French roads and the steering is perhaps too low geared. At night the lights are only good enough for perhaps 90 or 100mph, giving plenty of spread but seeming to have little range. The pilot lights on the instrument console are angled downwards, forsooth, and cannot be seen in daylight, and there are several other details of interior appointment that could well be revised. There is virtually no stowage for odds and ends for example – just a little shelf ahead of the passenger which would not only not accommodate Mr LC's Rolleiflex but would not even take my Zenith, though it would presumably be spacious enough for a Minox. Still, if you wanted a practical everyday car you would not be spending £4025 per seat. In fact, unless you are a rabid go-it-aloner, you will not buy the Miura as your one and only car.

As part of a stable, however, this dramatically conceived Lamborghini can be employed for what it is – an immensely fast, modern two-seater with the world's finest engine, society's highest cachet, and plenty of scope for further development. It may indeed be that Lamborghini would rather not have been pressurised into selling the Miura so soon. It is in reality still a prototype car, but one which is already undisputed master of the road.

IN RETROSPECT

The Miura, first of a new breed of fantastic road cars, appeared as a rolling chassis in November 1965 and everyone assumed it was some sort of racing car. When the first cars reached customers in 1967, the price was an eye-widening £8050 (an E-type cost less than two grand).

Top speed was said to be 180mph. We'd treat that with more scepticism today, but if its performance was dramatic, its looks were even more so. They have not diminished: it still is more extravagantly proportioned than almost any other road car.

It was not a racing car, nor a gran turismo, but it was more than a sports car. Thirty years ago, though the word was seldom used, it was the first 'supercar'.

SPECIFICATION
LAMBORGHINI MIURA

Years manufactured: 1966 to 1973
Numbers made: 764
Concept: the first mid-engined two-seater V12 supercar, adapting race practice for the road. V12 mounted transversely over gearbox, which lived in the sump, like a Mini's. Unitary chassis is in sheet steel, to which aluminium exterior panels were attached. The Miura revolutionised the mechanical layout, and look, of supercars, and the legacy of its ground-breaking design lives on today.

ENGINE
Layout: V12
Capacity: 3929cc
Max power: P400 350bhp at 7000rpm, P400S 370bhp at 7700rpm, P400SV 385bhp at 7850rpm
Max torque: P400 271lb ft at 5100rpm, P400S 286lb ft at 5500rpm, P400SV 286lb ft at 5000rpm
Power to weight ratio (per ton): P400 271bhp; P400S 281bhp; P400SV 295bhp
Installation: transverse, mid-mounted, rear drive
Construction: alloy heads, alloy block
Valvegear: two valves per cylinder
Compression ratio: P400 9.5:1, P400S 10.2:1, P400SV 10.7:1
Ignition and fuelling: four triple-barrel Weber carburettors

GEARBOX
Type: five-speed manual
Traction control: no
SUSPENSION
Front: double wishbones, coil springs, anti-roll bar
Rear: double wishbones, coil springs, anti-roll bar
BRAKES
Front: 305mm solid discs
Rear: 279mm solid discs
Anti-lock system: no
STEERING
Type: rack and pinion
Assistance: no
TYRES AND WHEELS
Front: P400/P400S 205 HS15, P400SV FR70VR15
Rear: P400/P400S 205 HS15, P400SV FR70VR15
BODY
Construction: sheet steel chassis unit, aluminium exterior panels
Weight (kg): P400 1295; P400S 1320; P400SV 1305
PERFORMANCE
Max speed: P400 163mph, P400S 168mph, P400SV 177mph
0-60mph: P400 6.3sec, P400S 5.5sec, P400SV 4.5sec (0-62mph)

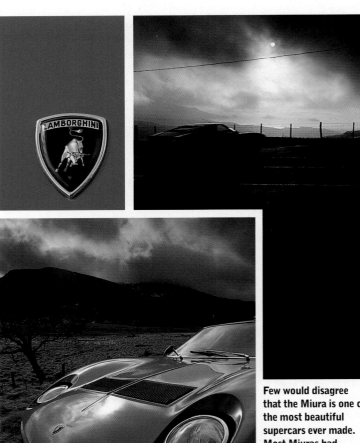

Few would disagree that the Miura is one of the most beautiful supercars ever made. Most Miuras had characterful 'eyelashes' around their headlamps which the final SV series did without

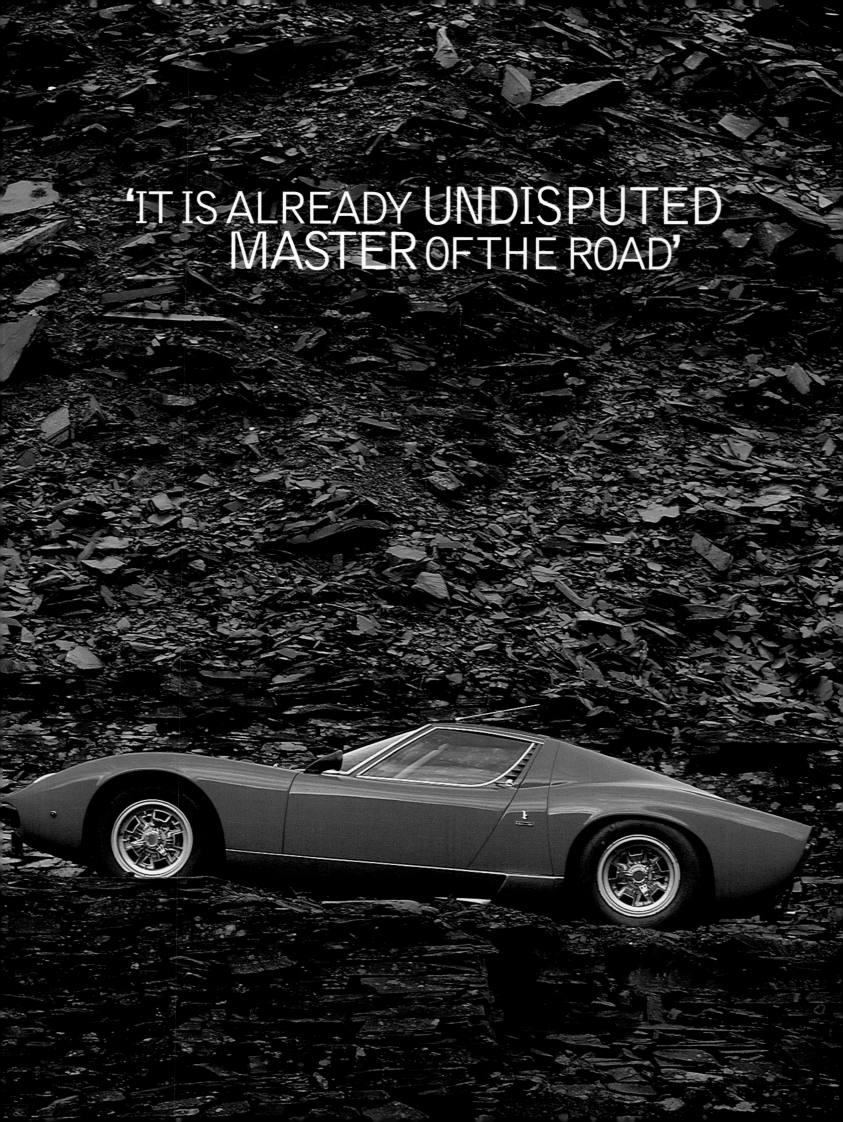

'IT IS ALREADY UNDISPUTED MASTER OF THE ROAD'

MYTH HAS IT THAT MILLIONAIRE TRACTOR MANUFACTURER
FERRUCCIO LAMBORGHINI VOWED TO PRODUCE A BETTER
CAR THAN A FERRARI WHEN HE WAS REFUSED AN
AUDIENCE WITH ENZO TO COMPLAIN ABOUT THE ONE HE

The GT40 was all about racing. After
a poor start, intensive development
made it a four-times Le Mans winner.
A (somewhat flawed) road version,
sampled here, was also built

FORD
GT40

By Nick Brittan

FOR ONE BRIEF, BEAUTIFUL moment I thought I'd found it. A car that would break the speed limit in first gear. But the thought, like the car, was almost too good to be true. As usual, I'd made a cock-up of my sums.

I never was much good at that bit with the tyre radius versus the revs per minute multiplied by the axle ratio over the number of valves per cylinder times the number you first thought of. What it boiled down to was that by the time we'd used up all the revs in first gear we were doing 61mph. And I want you to know that at this speed we still had four more gears left.

Second gear pulled us to 90mph: third gave us 128mph: fourth was going to be 140mph and in fifth, on a good day, you could have 165mph. But 130mph in fourth going into the Robin Hood roundabout on the A11 is enough.

The beast we were riding was a Ford GT40, cousin of the thing that wins Le Mans, half-sister of the Daytona victor, stepbrother of one of the world's finest long-distance racing cars, on paper one of the greatest, most desirable road cars of all time and the very

thing that (according to the adverts) you wouldn't want your daughter to marry the owner of. In the adverts. Anyway this thing can pull you along under acceleration with the sort of g-force that makes you think your brains are being sucked into your boots. Through twisty Essex country lanes not much wider than the car, the speedo hovered around the 70s and 80s – no drama. Just the feeling that you are strapped to the front of a slot racing car with someone else operating the button. Like something out of a maniacal automotive *Gulliver's Travels...*

My GT40, thigh-high to a tall Indian, stuck to the road like porridge to a blanket, drew more stares than a nun with her knickers in her hand and cost more than you and me would pay for a house. It was everything that a masculine car should be: it had class, and muscle. Yet beneath its Le Mans-proved body this £6000 car was a cheap-jack load of junk.

The carpets, for example. They looked as if they'd been tailored to fit another car. All round the phoney leather trim there were great smears of adhesive. Vast expanses of facia had been painted matt black with a loo brush by the look of it. The fixed windows were Perspex with tatty little hinge-out opening sections. The aeroflow nozzles on the facia looked as if they'd come out of a Cortina – which they probably had. All right, so basically it's a road version of a racer. But it was built and released, amid a great brouhaha of publicity, as the ultimate road car. I know the body

GT40 so named because it stood just 40.5 inches tall. It looked muscularly aggressive from every angle, and didn't disappoint, performance-wise, either. Much of its style simply evolved from racing mods, to great effect

shape looks like a million dollars. I know the engine is big and strong and powerful. For six grand I want more than that. I want leather, not matt black paint. If I wanted all that I'd go and build a Mini Marcos and keep the change.

This car, a Mark One, was built in 1965 by John Wyer's operation when it was called Ford Advance Vehicles. It went to the US as a promotional display and then came back and was sold, with three others, to Shell, which used them in a strange test programme. Three of the four wound up owned by Rodney Lyons and Peter Albon of the Epping Motor Company, which specialises in off-beat motors. The asking price was £5750, compared to £6700 new.

I borrowed the car from Mr Lyons. The only condition was that I would not bend it (honoured) and that I wouldn't write horrid things about it, on account of how he had to sell it. Well, I hope it got sold, Rodney, 'cos I think I broke the last promise. Anyway, that's how we came to be doing almost twice the legal limit in Mr Ford's high-powered light truck.

Come to think of it, calling it a truck is unfair since it doesn't boast enough carrying space to stow a packet of fags. If you're thinking about a dirty weekend in it, send all luggage on ahead.

Getting in is fun. Almost as much fun as getting out. It's a game best suited to field athletic specialists – long jumpers, maybe. The gearshift is on the right of the wheel and in order to get your right leg in you must first engage first gear and thread the leg through the available space. Then there's a wide ledge to straddle while you're coping with that. Miniskirted ladies would be well advised to travel by bus rather than accept lifts from GT40 owners. Then there's getting out. Clambering out takes two hands and while the door is unsupported it's likely to swing closed. The force with which it does this is governed by the prevailing wind. In a mild breeze the knife edge of the door top almost sliced through my windpipe. All this for only six grand.

But what about the mundane details? Mechanicals. The 4.7-litre engine runs on a compression of 10.5 to one and breathes through a four-barrel Holley carb and, with the four-in-one Indy-type exhaust, it kicks out around 306bhp. Six-two is as far as it should be revved. The old pushrod drinks a gallon every 12-15 miles depending how much time you spend with your foot buried.

One look through the rear window immediately behind your head, to see the carbs and the throttle linkages at work, will

'THE KNIFE EDGE OF THE DOOR TOP ALMOST SLICED MY WINDPIPE'

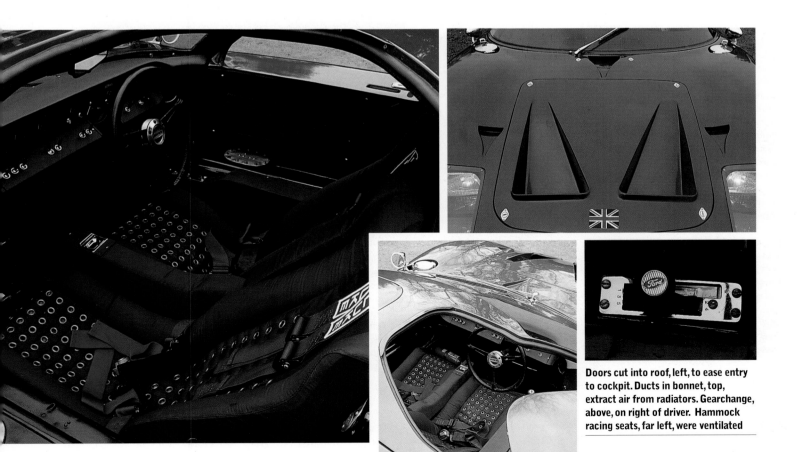

Doors cut into roof, left, to ease entry to cockpit. Ducts in bonnet, top, extract air from radiators. Gearchange, above, on right of driver. Hammock racing seats, far left, were ventilated

remind you that petrol has just gone up in price. Twin tanks with necks you can get a leg into carry 30 gallons. The quick-release fillers live on the front wings just ahead of the screen.

For reasons best known to someone other than Rodney Lyons, the 15in Borrani knock-off wire wheels on our car carried Goodyear racers on the front and Dunlops on the rear. The fronts live on 6.5in rims and the rears on 8in. Clutch pressure is light thanks to a twin-plate affair and a non-racing flywheel. The brakes are something else. Only muscle brings you to a halt. The all-up weight is around 2800lb and it comes as no surprise to discover that she'll get up and go from standstill to 30mph in just 1.6sec.

The racing tyres make the whole thing go hoppity-skippity over anything but smooth surfaces. And when that's happening everything, but everything, is clattering away like it's going to fall off. The seats are the hammock-type, replaced in later models. Tough on anyone who got the replacements: these are great. The seat not only breathes but is ventilated, because works drivers need more money if they're to fry as well as drive. The cockpit gets hot once that engine behind your head has been pounding for an hour.

Handling is hard to fault. The ride is firm and you have the impression of being able to feel the car in the same way you would if someone had nailed two wheels to your ankles and two to your elbows. The ZF gearbox is a delight and you can slice away at it without the clutch. Fifth gear takes you to 165mph, but also toddles at 20mph. The big Fraud is at least tractable.

Would I own it? If someone gave me £6000 to spend with Ford I'd probably buy six Cortina 1600Es: each a different colour, each signwritten with a day of the week. What would I do on Sundays? Stay home trying to convince myself I'd made the right decision.

IN RETROSPECT

Unlike the Miura, which was never intended for racing, the GT40's raison d'etre was the track. That the roadgoing version qualifies as a supercar is unquestionable, though in road trim it was a raw car, even by '60s standards. Four consecutive Le Mans wins mean GT40 values today outrun practically all its contemporaries'. In 1968, you could get one for £6000. It was devastatingly quick on the road, but rather too compromised by its race-car roots to be 'the ultimate road car' that Ford claimed at the time.

SPECIFICATION
FORD GT40 MK3

Years manufactured: 1964 to 1969
Numbers made: 31 road cars, of which seven were Mk 3s
Concept: mid-engined two-seater built as a GT race car, but later emerged as a road car, albeit heavily compromised. Adapted from a Lola design in 1963, the GT40 was announced in 1964 but initially proved an unsuccessful race car until development passed to race outfits such as Shelby American and Holman and Moody. After this, the transformation in its fortunes was rapid and spectacular, the car going on to win the Le Mans 24 hour race four times

ENGINE
Layout: V8
Capacity: 4736cc
Max power: 306bhp at 6000rpm
Max torque: 329lb ft at 4200rpm
Power to weight ratio (per ton): 306bhp
Installation: longitudinal, mid-mounted, rear drive
Construction: iron block, iron heads
Valvegear: overhead, pushrods and rockers, two valves per cylinder
Compression ratio: 10.5:1
Fuel system: single Holley four-barrel carburettor

GEARBOX
Type: five-speed manual
Traction control: no

SUSPENSION
Front: double wishbones, coil springs, telescopic shock absorbers, anti-roll bar
Rear: transverse top links, radius arms, lower wishbones, coil springs, telescopic shock absorbers, anti-roll bar

BRAKES
Front: 292mm solid discs
Rear: 285mm solid discs
Anti-lock system: no

STEERING
Type: rack and pinion
Assistance: no

TYRES AND WHEELS
Front: 205/70VR15
Rear: 205/70VR15

BODY
Construction: sheet steel semi-monocoque, glassfibre exterior panels
Weight (kg): 999

PERFORMANCE
Max speed: 154mph
0-100mph: 11.8sec

Air intake trumpets, top, an elegant clue to GT40's go. Various versions of V8 fitted during its racing life, but most road-going models came with a 4.7-litre unit. Under the rear lid, right, the car looked very much a racer. Proximity of engine to driver's ears very apparent on move

FOUR LE MANS WINS FOR FORD

In 1957 the American car manufacturers agreed 'to exclude speed and racing from automotive advertising and publicity'. But five years later, Henry Ford II had had enough of this, and Ford re-joined the race world with a vengeance. It won shed-loads of trophies, but among its most impressive victories was at Le Mans, which it first carried off in 1966 with a 1-2-3 victory, Bruce McLaren and Chris Amon winning. Dan Gurney and AJ Foyt repeated the win the following year, beating the Ferraris again, after which Ford officially withdrew from prototype racing. The GT40s were privately campaigned in '68, in the famous Gulf livery, Pedro Rodriguez and Lucien Bianchi winning on strategy and reliability rather than outright power. And in 1969, Jacky Ickx scraped a fourth victory against the potent Porsche 908.

WITH A METAPHORICAL WAVE OF THE HAND, HENRY FORD II TRIGGERED THE GT40 PROJECT BY ENDING FORD'S ABSTENTION FROM MOTOR RACING, WHICH HAD BEEN IN FORCE IN THE US SINCE 1957. THE COMPANY EMBARKED ON A 'TOTAL PERFORMANCE' PROGRAMME, INTENDED TO DEMONSTRATE ITS IMAGINATION AND RESOURCES WORLDWIDE. SO BEGAN A DECADE OF COMPETITION EFFORT THAT BROUGHT MUCH SUCCESS, THE PINNACLE OF WHICH MANY CONSIDER TO BE THE GT40'S LE MANS WINS

Ferrari's reputation for building
monstrously fast V12 coupés
arguably reached its zenith with
the fearsome 352bhp 365 GTB4
of 1968. Also known as the
Daytona, it could top 174mph

FERRARI

Daytona

By Mel Nichols

WE CAME OVER THE CREST AND INTO the valley and there ahead of us lay an open, loping stretch of road. It dropped gently, ran flat and diagonally across the valley floor and then started to rise towards the valley's far rim. Before it reached the top there was a bend that flicked it suddenly to the right, so that it then ran square-on up on to the rim.

The Daytona had been in full flight for miles; this was more grist to its mill, and we swooped down into that pretty little valley with the nose lifting and the V12's yowl bellowing out behind us. Second ran out at 86mph, third gave 116mph at the same 7700rpm red line and then we were pushing furiously in fourth.

The bend, the high-speed kink, loomed. We'd be doing around 130mph when we reached it; 6800rpm or so in fourth. Around 340bhp coming from the engine. If I kept my foot flat, there would almost certainly be oversteer. But how much oversteer? How suddenly would it come; how savagely? What does a Daytona do when it lets go at 130mph? What happens if you can't cope with it? How do you ring its owner and tell him you've overcooked it and his Daytona's laying shattered at the far end of a field deep in Dorset? Should I try it or not? My mind raced with apprehension.

But there was something, something discovered in the days and miles between awesome expectation of driving the Daytona and comfortable familiarity with it, that said it would be all right, and I could not resist. The throttle stayed flat, the six Webers wide open, the exhausts thundering and very soon the car was at the turn-in point and there was no longer time for anxiety.

There was an obvious line and the Daytona came on to it with now-familiar but ever-impressive alacrity; you just need a firm mind and hands firm upon the wheel. The inside wheels clipped the apex. The nose began to drive outwards again to the far side of the road. And in the same instant, there it was! The rear tyres let go and slid, and in the very split second that they let go, I knew. The message was delivered to me as clearly as if it had been the seat of my trousers itself that was touching the road. Somehow, even as it happened and spanning so minute a slice of time as it did, I had time to wonder how much the wheels might go on to slide. But then there was the quick flick of the wrists to wrap on a twist of opposite lock at the leather-rimmed wheel – just the one quick, instinctive, parsimonious

Daytona cockpit was very '60s and looked busy, but was logically laid out and major dials could easily be read at speed. Controls were heavy, but seats comfortable, grippy

flick – and the tail came back, as flatly, precisely and positively as it had broken away. In my peripheral vision I'd seen Colin Curwood's right hand snap out to grasp the grab handle, and then withdraw again as he too felt that it was all right. We didn't even need the full width of the road for the exit. The Daytona just swept a couple of feet out from the road's inside edge, lined itself up as the wheel was neutralised, and stormed onwards, heading straight as a die for the crest, with fourth, too, almost running to its 146mph limit before there was call for the brakes.

There were other sublime moments, plenty of them, during my time this winter with Nick Mason's 1972 Ferrari 365 GTB4 Daytona. There was the awesomeness of the ease with which, when the traffic cleared momentarily on the motorway, it whisked me to 165mph and so obviously had more to give had I not been forced to lift off. There was the pure thrill to be had, so many times, of unleashing the sort of power that brings up 60mph in 5.5sec and 100mph in a little over 12sec. There was the satisfaction, after a long, fast drive, of switching it off and remaining in it, listening to the ticking metal cooling down, and recalling the miles. There was the prolonged, adrenaline-filled high of balancing it finely, against the wheel and plenty of second-gear power, through one of the long and open bends we found that looked so good for Colin's pictures. But the climax was that lone left-hand kink. It was there, for me, that the Daytona told its story. There, it despatched the last of the suspicion that had been implanted in my mind by the mythology that has accompanied its passage through the '70s and into immortality. A monster, a great big old brute of a thing that goes like crazy and must be treated, so the myth

seemed to have it, with extreme caution, if not downright trepidation. But the Daytona is not like that.

The model arrived late in 1968 to a mixed, even mildly disparaging, reception. Some acclaimed its styling as a masterpiece from the outset; others criticised the wide glass panel that covered the four headlights as being silly and impractical (later, mostly for legal reasons, the arrangement would be changed to the twin sets of pop-up headlights that were to stay with the Daytona until its demise in 1974). But most of the reaction against the Daytona stemmed from those who had expected Ferrari to follow the little Dino 206 GT and answer the technical novelties. Maranello's path, so often, has been a traditional one pursued to the upper reaches of development, with the wind of change growing irresistibly strong before the course has been altered.

The Daytona critics probably cared not to consider perspectives: that the 4.4-litre 365-series engine had been developed for use in an assortment of front-engined cars, that there was considerable lead time, that Maranello had an engine and chassis design that it obviously liked very much and a body styled by Pininfarina to which it was also, undoubtedly, very attracted. There are many clear, supportable reasons why Ferrari laid down the Daytona the way it did; but when it's all boiled down, the core of the matter is that in the mid '60s, for the big grand touring road cars, Ferrari's belief rested firmly with the front-engined layout, its development and refinement. There would be one more all-out front-engined Ferrari two-seater of the traditional mould. And it would have capability sufficient to deal with the upstart Miura from the other side of Modena, loudly hailed as the

Later Daytonas had pop-up headlamps, as left; early examples' headlights sat behind glassed-in panel

machine that had taken the wind out of Ferrari's sails. A neat 300kmh – 186mph – had been claimed for the mid-engined Miura, but around 172mph was nearer the mark until the SV came along later. Ferrari just said that the Daytona would reach 280kmh – 174mph – and it wasn't long before independent testers proved it.

There is as much purity as individuality in the Daytona's styling. Nothing else conveys the long-bonnet, small-cabin, chopped-tail slingshot look as dramatically – and if the proportioning is uncomfortable to the eye, then walk up close and feast upon the deliciousness of the car's detail, the sultriness of its curves and the way they go together to make the whole. Stand back and consider that this car, weighing 3500lb dry, is sufficiently slippery to permit not only a top speed of 174mph but upper-end acceleration in fourth and fifth that is unequalled in a road car. And consider that, without a trace of a spoiler, the Daytona is impeccably stable.

The Daytona replaced the Ferrari 275 GTB4, and was very much a development of it. Its steel body, by Scaglietti to Pininfarina's design, was bolted on to a similar tubular steel chassis frame, and the wheelbase, at 94.5in, was identical. But the Daytona benefited from wider 56.6in and 56.1in tracks. Its suspension was Italian conventional, a system proved time and again to work exceptionally well: upper and lower wishbones with coil springs, telescopic dampers and an anti-roll bar at each end. To help balance the car as finely as possible, Ferrari mounted the engine a long way back in the chassis – almost all of it behind the front-axle line. It went further: the transmission was despatched to the rear, in unit with the differential, and linked by driveshaft and torque tube to the engine and clutch.

The Daytona's engine is a member of Ferrari's classic road-going V12 family, and descended directly from the 3.3-litre four-cam 12 of the 275 GTB4. The angle between the cylinder banks is 60deg, the capacity 4390cc. The compression ratio is 9.3 to one; there are two camshafts on each cylinder head, six downdraught Weber carburettors, twin coils and distributors, and a dry sump. From this engine, running on 100 octane fuel, comes nothing less than 352bhp at 7500rpm. And from it flows massive torque. It peaks at 318lb ft at 5500rpm but the curve is so flat and hefty that even at 1000rpm there is almost 190lb ft, and everywhere from 2000rpm to 7000rpm something in excess of 260lb ft is available.

The Daytona is long and

Daytona was a heavy car whose considerable power needed respect. But its handling was faithful to those who dared, and entertaining, too

fairly low – 14ft 6in by 49in – and you hook a finger on those strange little catches on its doors and swing them out and drop down into its cabin; into seats like old-fashioned racing buckets, which hug the body cosily and say that they will keep you in place when the car is going hard about its business. The driver is faced with an alloy-spoked and leather-rimmed wheel, with a large metal boss that encircles the vaunted black-on-yellow prancing horse horn button. It is connected to Fiam air horns. The wheel, whose flat spokes are drilled, is somehow very businesslike and yet somehow casual too. Your hands just drop on to its rim comfortably; perfectly. Through it, enclosed within one oval and deeply hooded pod, are the instruments – the vast tachometer and speedo, the four most important minor gauges grouped between them. You see all of them well; best of all, you're never in any doubt about the whereabouts of the tachometer needle.

In the corners of this big binnacle are two final gauges: on the driver's left the fuel gauge and on his right a clock. All the gauges are black-rimmed, standing out from the metal panel that carries them. They reflect a little in some lighting conditions. Overall, they have a certain flair and appeal that does not interfere with their efficiency; and if they are less stylish than some other Ferrari gauges they are also more efficient and more easily read than most. There is a small lever on the steering column for the indicators, behind it a larger one that controls the headlight functions.

On the other side of the column there's a stalk for the two-speed wipers and electric washers. Three of those familiar Italian sliding levers sit in the centre of the dash, outside the main instrument binnacle, to control individually the heat supply to each side of the car and regulate the temperature. Toggles below them switch on the heated rear window and the hazard flashers. On the central console, down near the base of the gearlever, are rocker switches for the electric windows. Like the radio, the cigarette lighter and ashtray are dropped into the tunnel cover; not afterthoughts, but accorded a casualness that indicates their standing in this particular cockpit.

The gearlever is tall and spindly, unbooted, sprouting from one of those marvellous open Ferrari gates. Its height means that the arm need simply extend to it, not drop to it, and that the hand does not have to move far from the wheel's rim to seize it.

When the arms are comfortable at wheel and gear-

'FROM THIS ENGINE
COMES NOTHING LESS THAN
352 BHP. AND
MASSIVE TORQUE'

lever, the legs extend forward with just a little bending to big, manly, businesslike pedals. The clutch does not travel very far, and if it is not light, it is not what you expect. Put the right foot on the brake pedal, and feel with the outer edge of it the tall throttle pedal. The proximity of the toe for toeing and heeling is perfect. There is a closeness about the Daytona's cabin that helps the driver feel in tune with it, part of it, not overwhelmed by it. The roof is small above the head, and the windscreen and side windows curve well in to meet it, so that at the same time they feel as if they curve in around the head; you wear this car. And if the long bonnet appears from the outside as though it will be ungainly and difficult to see and to place, it is not like that from the driver's seat. It is not possible to see all of it but it doesn't matter; it does not take long to sense its extremities and to feel at ease with them. And nor – and this is the marvellous thing about the Daytona – does it take long to know and understand, and feel at ease with, all its extraordinary performance. It is there to work with you (if not exactly for you, for it could never be servile, this car) but it is never there to intimidate.

Pump the throttle a couple of times on a cold morning, then turn the key and the V12 will fire immediately. And from its first beat it runs evenly without snapping or popping or missing. It is ready to be driven away, asking nothing more than due respect by way of warm-up. The gears need to be shifted slowly and deliberately, for the oil stays thick in the isolated transmission for a long time – 10 or even 15 miles. After that the lever will shift quickly and cleanly, and with considerable pleasure for the palm of the hand and the section of the mind that controls it. Such is the precision of the throttle, and the fine, measured response of the engine to it, that even when the roads are very slippery it is easy enough to mete out the power so that the rear tyres do not spin. The Daytona just gets on with it. Push too hard on the throttle and the wheels will spin crazily, somewhere between 45 and 90deg to the direction of travel at a stroke. But such is the Daytona's inherent balance and stability that releasing the power and snapping on a bite of opposite lock will bring it back perfectly into line. Knowledge of that sort of controllability makes it easy to live with whatever the road surface, makes it easy to come to grips with the

SPECIFICATION
FERRARI DAYTONA

Years manufactured: 1968 to 1973

Numbers made: 1284

Concept: front-engined, rear-drive, two-seat V12 supercar, the penultimate in a long line of front-engined, V12 Ferraris. The gearbox was rear-mounted this time to improve handling balance, but at launch the Daytona was nevertheless criticised for being technically backward compared with the mid-engined Lamborghini Miura. Today the Daytona has an awesome reputation – but, strangely, that gathered momentum after production ended in 1973

ENGINE
Layout: V12

Capacity: 4390cc

Max power: 352bhp at 7500rpm

Max torque: 318lb ft at 5500rpm

Power to weight ratio (per ton): 200

Installation: longitudinal, rear drive

Construction: alloy heads, alloy block

Valvegear: two valves per cylinder, twin overhead camshafts per bank

Compression ratio: 9.3:1

Fuel system: Six Weber DCN20 twin-barrel carburettors

GEARBOX
Type: five-speed manual

Traction control: no

SUSPENSION
Front: double wishbones, coil springs, telescopic shock absorbers, anti-roll bar

Rear: double wishbones, coil springs, telescopic shock absorbers, anti-roll bar

BRAKES
Front: 288mm solid discs

Rear: 297mm solid discs

Anti-lock system: no

STEERING
Type: rack and pinion

Assistance: no

TYRES AND WHEELS
Front: 215/70VR15

Rear: 215/70VR15

BODY
Construction: tubular steel spaceframe, steel exterior panels

Weight (kg): 1762

PERFORMANCE
Max speed: 174mph

0-60mph: 5.5sec

DISEGNO di *pininfarina*

Daytona faithful in corners, even if grip isn't top notch. Integration of glass, brightwork, right, underlines coachbuilder Pininfarina's skills

power, and to know that that power can be used.

And with knowledge of the communication that is there in the chassis, coming through the seat of the pants, the palms of the hands and somehow even the soles of the feet, it is possible always to extract the optimum level of performance. You just bring on enough power until you sense, or are told, that there will be loss of traction and, with the toes, you readjust.

On a dry surface, the first unleashing of the full acceleration is electrifying, for it is neck-snapping. But the mind adjusts quickly and thereafter, while always thrilling, even stunning, it is temptingly usable. It is simply part of the Daytona. More than anything, more even than 0-60mph in 5.5sec and 0-100mph in 12.5sec, it is the span of the performance that is enticing. First runs to 59mph at 7700rpm, second to 86mph, third to 116mph, fourth to 146mph and, yes, fifth will go to 174mph at just under 7400rpm. Going up through those gears, there is just one long, sustained thrusting forwards. And all the while the Daytona feels so secure within your hands, never fighting to get away.

It just has too much inner certainty of its own, this car, ever to be

nasty or fussy. It is set up to maintain a very slight touch of understeer, just enough to be detected in the wheel angles in pictures and to be felt at the steering wheel by way of a steady tug in a bend taken hard. It can be neutralised with power; and the best way to corner the Daytona is to come into a bend fractionally below what might be the highest possible entry speed, let it settle momentarily and then steadily squeeze on the power. You will feel the car balance out; you will feel it simply sweep around the bend on the line you have selected. Bring on some more power if you wish to tip the balance the other way when you are going sufficiently fast in a high gear or are in a low gear in a slow bend, and you will feel the tail begin to go a little light and then edge into oversteer. More power and it will let go altogether, and you will have to get it back with the wheel or by lifting off the pedal.

It is a positive, finely-controlled car to drive, but it is not a light car. It requires physical effort, for its steering is not power-assisted and although the brakes are assisted they require a hefty shove to work hard. And the clutch is not for feeble legs. But the efforts match, and you aren't aware of them intruding on your pleasure.

So you feel at one with the Daytona, and you learn to revel in its performance and its possibilities, to use it. And it is perhaps the fact that you can find its limits and take it to them again and again with confidence that makes it so special in a world where the cars that have taken over from it are mid-engined. Their limits, those of the Boxer and the Countach, are higher in terms of pure cornering power, and they are harder to find and even harder to play with. Perhaps that is why, magnificent achievement though the Boxer is, there were tales of Ferrari owners switching back from Boxers to Daytonas in the first years of the BB's life.

Liken the Daytona to a shark, for more than the obvious visual reasons. The shark, biologists will have it, stopped developing 20 million years ago because it couldn't be improved; it had reached a level of perfect efficiency. When the tide turned in favour of the mid-engined supercar, it left the Daytona stranded on a patch of high ground that will never, it now seems, be trodden by another. In the development of the front-engined supercar, the Daytona is the ultimate. And, like the shark, it is transcending time.

IN RETROSPECT

There was a time when the Daytona was seen as obsolete, for having its V12 in front of the driver. After all, the older Miura was mid-engined. Now, with the 550 Maranello, Ferrari has gone back to front-engined supercars, so maybe the Daytona was ahead of its time…

In 1968, the Daytona was viewed as Ferrari's riposte to the Miura; when the two were tested back-to-back, the Daytona accelerated faster and ran to a higher top speed. Today, the Daytona is seen as a practical GT, with more space and better visibility than mid-engined cars. At the peak of the '80s classic car price boom, they changed hands for over £200,000. Now £80,000 buys a good one.

Enzo
FERRARI
■ 1898 - 1988

ENZO FERRARI ONCE RACED ALFA ROMEOS, BEFORE RUNNING THE COMPANY'S RACE TEAM. BUT A FALLING OUT LED HIM TO SET UP ON HIS OWN, AND SO FERRARI WAS BORN. ENZO SAW HIS ROAD CARS MERELY AS A MEANS TO PAY FOR THE RACERS, BUT THIS DIDN'T PREVENT THE EMERGENCE OF SOME GREAT MACHINES, ANY MORE THAN DID FERRARI'S INABILITY TO LISTEN TO HIS ADVISERS. ENZO WAS AN INTRANSIGENT AUTOCRAT, BUT HIS COMPANY SURVIVES AS THE MOST FAMOUS MAKER OF FAST CARS IN THE WORLD

WE LEFT THE 1960S WITH JUST A COUPLE OF MID-ENGINED EXOTICS (MIURA AND DIMINUTIVE DINO) to bring to the road the fantasy of a race car. In this next decade, though, things were to hot up. First off, again, was Lamborghini, whose angular Urraco of 1970 lacked the drama of the Miura despite being styled by the same man (Marcello Gandini), but it still trumped the Dino for power and pace thanks to its 3.0-litre V8 engine (transverse and mid-mounted, like the Miura's). Then Maserati joined in. Long a maker of potent front-engined grand tourers, the Modenese maker took the mid-engined cue and launched the Bora with a 4.7-litre V8 of, this time, longitudinal orientation. Its elegance was typical of a Giugiaro design of the time. Meanwhile, De Tomaso, which would later become another in a sequence of hopeful owners of Maserati, offered its Pantera. This angular, Tom Tjaarda-styled car might have lacked a supercar's mechanical pedigree with its simple but powerful 5.7-litre Ford V8, but it had unofficial Ford US backing, so Alessandro de Tomaso wasn't worried. Maybe there were still GT40 ghosts at Dearborn, for the Pantera's mechanicals were similar.

So, where was Ferrari all this time? Making ready with its own mid-engined, full-Monty supercar in the shape of the 365 GT4 BB, or Berlinetta Boxer. Its design was a little odd, with the engine sitting on top of the gearbox to the detriment of the centre of gravity's lowness. Luckily the engine itself was low, a flat-12 (or 'boxer') like that of contemporary Ferrari F1 cars. At its 1973 launch it had a capacity of 4.4 litres, and arrived in time for the first energy crisis.

The energy crisis. More than anything else, that's what the early '70s meant to car-minded folk. Rocketing fuel prices and unpredictable shortages seemed to spell the end of driving for enjoyment, especially in a conspicuously consumptive car. What would become of Ferrari, Lamborghini, Maserati and the rest now? Even the new-found power of the Middle East's oil barons wouldn't be enough to assure a future supply of supercars if Maranello, Sant'Agata Bolognese and Modena all went under.

Lamborghini, having spent heavily on developing a Urraco that no-one now wanted, very nearly did, and Ferruccio had to sell his share. Maserati's then owner, Citroën (its SM also suffering in this car-hostile climate) came up with an economy Bora in the V6-engined Merak, and Ferrari just held on until the panic was over.

In 1974, it was, and the world hadn't ended after all. Lamborghini celebrated by launching the Miura's replacement, Gandini's outlandish Countach. Meanwhile, the supercar idea took root outside Italy, Porsche contributing its own interpretation in 1975 by tipping the 911 over the potent sports coupé/unreasonably rapid tyre-smoker knife-edge. This was achieved by means of a turbocharger, fat wheels and chunked-up bodywork to cover them. There was nothing delicate about the 911 now. We'd seen turbo cars before, but it was the 911 Turbo that shot the word into every product marketing department's lexicon. Throttle lag, terminal oversteer, only four gears... this could be the scariest supercar of them all, even if it had only six cylinders.

Back in the 12-cylinder zone, Ferrari's Boxer grew into the 4.9-litre Boxer 512 in 1976 to become, probably, the definitive 1970s supercar. Two years earlier the smaller Dino had been reinvented as the V8 308 GT4; the prettier and more Dino-esque 308 GTB followed in 1975.

Taking a different tack in Britain, Aston Martin injected steroids into its soft-living V8 to recreate the Vantage. In 1977, it seemed, there was still a place for a front-engined, brute-force heavyweight. Porsche, too, went big-league front-engined. The 1977 928's claim to supercar status is debatable, but only now is it clear just how ahead of its time it was. No 1970s car has dated less, especially in the detailing. It's ironic, then, that it has been dead two years while the 911 idea has just been reincarnated. Again.

THE
Seventies

Very probably the most dramatic-looking supercar of them all, more startling even than the Miura that it replaced, the Countach had abilities to match, earning it a long career as an ultimate supercar

LAMBORGHINI
Countach

By Doug Blain

IN CASE YOU THINK YOU'VE HEARD it all before, bear in mind that our earlier encounters with Lamborghini's Countach have been as passengers. This time was to be for real, with me in the hot seat.

I must say I didn't get all that much sleep the night before, what with trying to remember what it used to be like driving fast on public roads in Miuras and GT40s and all those wild, way-out wonder cars of the late 1960s and at the same time rehearsing how I was going to put it to our insurers that this £18,000-worth of... well, we can work out in a minute what it really is. As usual, there had been a bit of a build-up, with cables flying back and forth (if flying is the word for an Italian postal service which takes 10 days to get an urgent wire from door to door) and several last-minute changes of plan due to strikes at the factory, missed connections and what have you. In the end, Ian Fraser and I wandered out to Sant'Agata on the appointed day to find the car earmarked for our use whole and in a semi-completed state towards the end of the assembly line, but still with some wiring and plumbing to do and of course no road-testing or last-minute adjustment even in sight.

We are old hands at this game and had expected no better, so we simply got on with our other appointments, armed with a firm promise from boss man Paolo Stanzani that the countdown had begun and that zero hour was to be Saturday morning at 0900...

A proper flow-line batch production system has been established for the Countach, within which six or seven cars at a time take shape, via huge precision jigs and formers, literally from a pile of assorted steel tubes and aluminium sheets. For this is one of the few examples anywhere in the world of production from the ground up under a single roof, not only the complex tubular space-frame but also the bodywork, upholstery, suspension, engine, transmission and a host of minor assemblies all being created within a single, spacious, light and airy building, off the spotlessly clean tiled floor of which one could still, as in the very earliest days of Lamborghini production 10 years ago, cheerfully eat one's midday tortellini.

The whole place reminds one irresistibly of a high-class aircraft factory before the era of standardisation, and as one watches the workers, most of them young and keen and immaculately clad in their pale blue overalls, it is hard to imagine this picture of quiet efficiency being disrupted by strikes or unpleasantness. Yet this is just what is happening, and in a conversation with Stanzani I established that he, like all thinking Italians, is convinced of the need for a return to political and hence industrial stability before the country can get on its feet again. This having been achieved, however, he is equally sure that there is a place for Lamborghini in the future, despite the threats by which he feels surrounded. It is a matter, he points out, of producing the right product for the times. Man cannot suppress for long the peacock instinct which makes him long to strut and show off his plumage any more than he can forget the sensual pleasure he derives from the manipulation of a really fine piece of engineering. As long as cars are needed by the many, superior ones will be wanted by the few, and having heard something of Stanzani's plans for the next 10 years or so, I must say I feel inclined to agree with him. How reassuring to hear a man in authority speak of the need to aim even higher, in

Countach as dramatic to sit in as it is to look at, right. The driver sits very low, unable to see the bonnet, clamped on one side by the door sill, on the other by transmission tunnel

terms of engineering as well as of workmanship, at a time when one is listening to talk of cost-cutting, retrenchment and decline! Boldness in all things – as ever, that is the Lamborghini ingredient.

And now to the Countach, as bold an automotive project as, I think, anyone has yet succeeded in carrying to fruition. I suppose logically I ought to refer you to my recent piece on its rival, the Ferrari 365GT-BB, and then run through the differences, but these things are never altogether logical and the clearest way of putting it is just to say that the Countach is different. Completely different. So different that it is impossible to conceive of there being any choice: you are either a BB man or a Countach man, just as you are a Burgundy man or a Claret man, with the Ferrari as the bland, softly rounded yet subtly refined Romanée Conti and the Lamborghini as the austere, tantalising Château Lafite.

Similarly, there can be no question that the Ferrari would be the choice of the average enthusiast. Not that it looks more exciting: it doesn't. But it offers more of the features you expect in a very expensive sports car including, in addition to immense power and formidable roadholding, super-fine finish and more than a modicum of genuine luxury. It is an impressive vehicle in every way, as well as an effective one. The Lamborghini, by contrast, is much less of a compromise. Even its way-out looks are the result of a concern for efficiency, the unique centralised cooling system being responsible both for the slenderness of the flat, chisel snout and for the dramatic, wing-like effect of the vast duct which spreads either side of the steeply raked glasshouse cockpit. Seen close to, it has the lean, hungry look of a racing car, and the cockpit furnishings are almost as sparse. There is no attempt anywhere at decoration. The only materials visible are painted aluminium, pile carpet and fine leather. The standard of finish is high, but it is not luxury. No stereo or power windows even: and assembly is to the standard of hand craftsmanship, which is to say that when tiny

blemishes occur they are of the sort that no machine could perpetrate – the human failings, if you like, of men who are pre-occupied with something else. That something is, of course, as near as earnest endeavour can approach to perfection in performance and behaviour, not of the refined sort associated with an outing in, for example, one of the better Porsches, but on the higher plane which brings fast driving to the level of squash as an exhilarating and highly exacting but at the same time exhausting activity. The Countach breathes naked aggression from every pore: just to look at it is either to want to climb in and thrash the living daylights out of it, or else to run. To the average millionaire businessman, paunchy, satiated, intent only on upstaging his colleagues while adding to an already impressive list of female conquests, it can only be an instrument of horror, which is why Lamborghini has been at pains not to dress it up as what it cannot be.

Of all these things I was well aware as, on that preliminary visit, I watched a team of fitters putting the finishing touches to the car I was to drive several days later. I had learned from Stanzani that this was number nine of the first series of probably 50 cars, all of them ordered against cash deposits, as are many more besides, by impatient clients all over the world. Walking round it, I noted some of the more obvious changes from the second prototype, in which I had ridden with Bob Wallace in the spring of '73. Outside, these included a rearrangement of the frontal ducting within and below a narrow, buffer-like strip which comprises the point of the chisel, with a couple of spotlamps now built-in for daytime flashing; oh, and a much-needed revision of the rear-end cosmetics, with some neat, purpose-made tail-lamps and an unpretentious, painted Countach logo. The name, incidentally, is an untranslatable piece of Milanese dialect, not obscene, but rather the sort of half-amazed, half-admiring expletive a man in the street might exclaim on first seeing the car: I suppose the Londoner's 'Cor!'

Alien look of this, the most extraordinary Lamborghini ever made, heightened by glassed-in lights, spindly pantograph wiper, left. Slatted air vents in rear wings, above, expel air sucked through V12's twin radiators

must come close. It is pronounced gutturally: C'n-tatch.

Inside, the cockpit has been further simplified, plain leather replacing black suede for everything except the dashboard and scuttle, the sills reduced and the handbrake moved to a more accessible position near the tunnel, the gearchange given a prominent, slotted steel gate complete with racing-style lockout for reverse, the mirror moved inside, thus declaring redundant that funny little window in the roof, and the interim oversize instruments replaced by a neat set of American-made Stewart Warner dials, the first I have seen in a road car that approach the optimum (ie very small) dimensions recommended by those who understand optics. Air-conditioning, rendered essential by the vast and almost horizontal windscreen, is housed in the space reserved on boy-racer cars for one of those meaningless central consoles.

The mechanicals, by contrast, are essentially unaltered. These were the real priority, and were completely rearranged at an early stage, with the original monocoque chassis/body structure and five-litre engine giving way to a tubular spaceframe and four litres, since when they have been proved to provide more or less exactly what the designers had in mind in the first place in the way of roadholding, handling, braking and, of course, performance.

So. Enough of the pudding – what about the proof? Well, Saturday dawned grey but clear, which at least had the effect of keeping some of the holiday hordes off the roads. Fraser and I threaded our way to the factory gate at the appointed hour to find it manned, as usual, but with no other sign of life whatsoever.

Our hearts sank, only to be resuscitated just in time by the unfamiliar bark of an all but unsilenced V12 exhaust echoing from the direction of the refuelling bay. We were waved through and there, standing with both of its pop-up doors open ready to receive us, was Number Nine – complete, warmed-up, hosed-down, pulsing with life and raring to go.

I'm not going to give you all that stuff about shaking fingers and tingling toes and all the other symptoms of nervous anticipation: there would be something wrong with us if we didn't feel them when confronted by something substantially less awe-inspiring than the world's most expensive and reputedly fastest production car. Enough to say simply that the Countach's hunched, purposeful lines and incredible... well, lowness, make it more than usu-

ally daunting and that on first acquaintance with that carefully planned but undeniably cramped cockpit it feels literally undriveable. Why? Well, your nose is on a level with the tops of the pebbles, for a start. There's no bonnet to speak of, and you're surrounded by undulating expanses of glass so that you seem to be lying in the bottom of a light bulb, clutching this black doughnut of a wheel trying to imagine doing the best part of 200mph. Then there's the engine, gulping and roaring, with only a sheet of glass between you, leaping half into shock at every tingling pulse of your big toe on the ultra-sensitive throttle. Alongside is the shrouded mass of the gearbox, upon which you know you must soon play tunes for your very life. Your passenger (in this case a test driver I hadn't met before) seems as far away as he might be in a lorry. He is lying down, too. Your neck hurts because the headrest, experimentally on this car only, you're told, as if that were a comfort, is in the wrong place. The mirror shows heat haze where that terrifying engine is snorting and belching and champing. Someone is beckoning. The clutch is stiffish, but painfully precise.

The tachometer moves in little jerks: yes, one of those. The gearchange feels older and wiser than you. The minor controls are all unlabelled. The responsibility is more painful than anything. 'Give it 3000rpm at least to start with,' says the Unknown, in Italian. Oh, God – and they call this pleasure?

Somehow, I got the thing out of the factory yard without stalling; having been unprepared for the fact that the engine gives virtually no power at all at 2900rpm and a very great deal at 3001rpm. After a bit of trying I got second gear, not because I needed it (the maximum in first is very nearly the same as the British legal limit) but because it made me feel I wasn't going as fast. Fraser and the others were ahead in an equally new Espada. A camera was pointing down at me from the slot beneath the back window, and I could follow the run of the Espada's exhaust system right to the point where it leaves the manifolds. Think about that. Ah, there's third – oops, too slow, as we hiccup a bit and then Bang! the power comes in with a wallop that snaps my gasping jaw shut again.

To drive a car like this for the first time is really to begin all over again. They ought to deliver it with L-plates. Me, I just blunder on, coughing and farting into the suburbs of Bologna, practising gearchanges – the

There's a double-overhead-cam 3.9-litre V12 in there, good for 375bhp at a yelling 8000rpm. This was an LP400; the LP500 QV delivered 455bhp

'ON FIRST ACQUAINTANCE IT FEELS LITERALLY UNDRIVEABLE'

THE INSPIRATION

This astonishing green machine is the Bertone Carabo (it means 'beetle'), a concept car built by the famous Italian coachbuilder in 1968 which had a major influence on the Countach's look.

The Carabo was built on the chassis of the mid-engined V8 Alfa Romeo Tipo 33 racing car, and was striking not only for its lack of height and the angularity of its lines, but for the amazing hinging arrangement of its doors, which were completely novel.

Bertone's Marcello Gandini, who had already created the beautiful Miura for Lamborghini, included all three of these characteristics in the Countach. But he was also influenced by the long-distance endurance racers of the time, particularly the Porsche 917.

The Countach was like no road car yet seen, being the first to take up a wedge profile so completely. This was partly for aerodynamic reasons, the aim being to eliminate the front-end lift that threatened Miuras at high speed. It also featured

Gandini's inspired asymmetric rear wheel-arch, to be found on today's Maserati Quattroporte.

The Countach's name was an inspiration too. Legend has it that on the very night that the prototype was being completed for its debut at the 1971 Geneva Show, someone at Bertone saw it, stepped back, and exclaimed 'Countach!' Piedmontese dialect, it is a difficult word to translate, but is the kind of thing a northern Italian male might utter in appreciation of a very attractive female.

gate is very precise, as it ought to be with the gearbox directly beneath, and the movements are short, but on this brand-new car they felt rather stiff – and learning to place the front wheels with sufficient accuracy to allow for later indulgence. I am growing used to the driving position, finding I have plenty of room after all and pronouncing the visibility pretty good except to the rear, where it is poor despite the addition of those half-hearted quarterlights which in fact allow an excellent view of the radiators.

Directly rearwards, I could see plenty, and the whole car was beginning to shrink around me: an essential preliminary. I had begun to notice noises, and to trace them to their sources. For a start there was the engine, which, apart from the remote bellow of its four exhausts, emits a constant drone from the camshaft drives, fans and accessories. I did not find it obtrusive. Far more so was a loud whine from between the seats which turned out to be from the auxiliary oil pump serving the gearbox, with an accompanying continuo from the transfer gearing where the drive drops down in readiness for its return journey via a short, rigid propshaft concealed within the sump. These were racing car sounds, and being some kind of a nut I rather enjoyed them, but apparently the customers don't and Ing Baraldini (design engineer) and Ing Parenti (development) are working on their elimination. By contrast, I had already noted that there was absolutely no road-generated noise from the tyres, or suspension noise either, though the ride is fairly taut. Entering Bologna for a coffee dictated by Lambo's amiable PR man Dott Tavasani, I observed that even cobbles and tramlines failed to make themselves heard.

In town, the Countach creates as much of a sensation as would a full-blown Can Am Porsche or any other racing car, yet it continues to behave itself. Despite heavy traffic, the coolant temperature never budged from the norm mark, oil-pressure and temperature likewise, and the air-conditioning coped manfully. The engine idled happily at about 800rpm, but still called for careful handling if one was to avoid either stalling it or blasting passers-by into next week on take-off. When the time came to park, I at first cursed the lack of visibility to the rear and then twigged to the obvious solution: open one of the flip-up doors and peer out that-away. There are no bumpers at all, backwards, so it pays to be careful if you want to

Despite undersized tyres, Blain found roadholding, steering, handling and braking of Countach fantastic. Performance? On another plane

avoid squashing the luggage in the surprisingly spacious boot.

The plan was that, coffee over, we should investigate the car's high-speed potential before heading for the hills. Top-speed runs were out of the question because of the mileage which by now stood at rather less than 200 miles, dictating an arbitrary rpm limit of 7000 as against the engine's official maximum of 8000, but there was no reason why I shouldn't do my damnedest within those parameters. Unfortunately there was already a good deal of traffic about as we headed out along one of the motorways, the Espada behind us now, and although the Countach's science-fiction silhouette proved more effective than anything I have yet known at shifting even the more tenacious Topolinos from the fast lane we were at first unable to do anything except blast up to an indicated 200kph or so between applications of the brakes. Meanwhile I was learning more about the gearchange and the power curve, discovering precisely when to pour it on, how far I could trust the brakes (answer: implicitly, as in a competition car, leaving it later and later in the certain knowledge that the car would stop four-square in incredibly short order without smoke, nose-dive or discomfort). The Countach is high-geared with maxima in the intermediates of about 60mph, 95mph, 120mph and 150mph, so that a lot of the time one finds oneself using third to dispose of even a persistent Alfa or Lancia coupé. Fifth feels too tall even at 120mph, and one soon learns to overcome that instinct which in a normal car rules out even the thought of a downshift at over 110mph. In fact one re-learns a great deal, including all one's ideas about speed. It would be true to say that at 140mph the Countach feels like a good conventional sports car might at half that speed. Its stability is uncanny, seeming almost to increase as the needle marches round the dial.

The ride grows more supple, the steering more accurate, even the noise level seems to diminish as this extraordinary car gets into its stride, just when other road-users are running right out of theirs. Instead of tensing, one begins to relax, developing a rhythm as one brakes, changes down, brakes again and piles on the power, lashing the ever-willing V12 to a howling 7000rpm ridiculously quickly before slapping the lever home again.

But what's this? At last, a clear stretch. Hard down in third – no pause now as we snap across against the

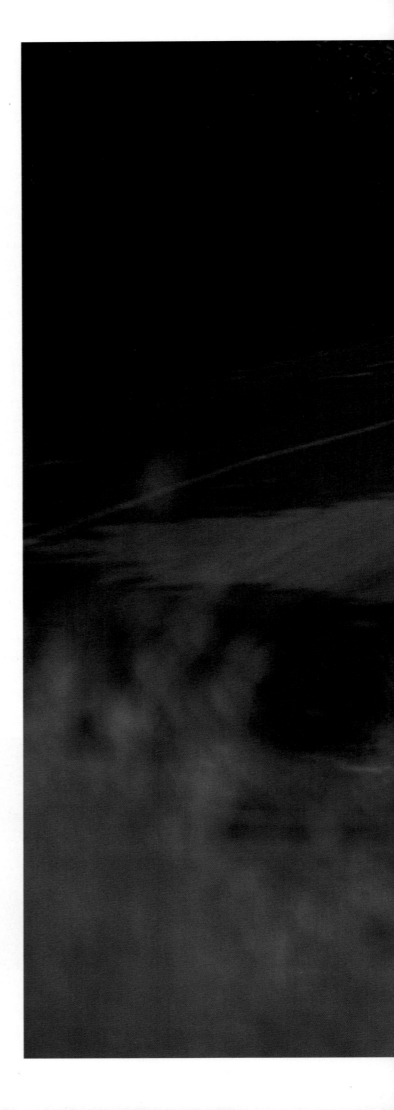

spring-loading, catching the torque curve right at its peak, feeling the car fairly leap towards the horizon. The nose seems to settle, snuggling down against the conveyor-belt of the road surface. No time to enjoy the view though, for with another gear to go we are watching the tach out of the tail of an eye half-dazzled by a flickering procession of roadside impedimenta and at the same time straining half a mile ahead towards the horizon for signs of an encroaching truck: 6000rpm, 6500, 7500... Crisply back into fifth, the wind caressing us still with barely a sound, the engine thrusting eagerly on into the forbidden zone, a dimension hitherto almost unknown among users of automobiles for everyday purposes. The Espada, until now more or less in sight, has disappeared abruptly at 160mph... 165... 170... Surpassing the limit we have set ourselves out of sympathy for a new engine which feels eager for more, still accelerating hard, we lift our hands momentarily from the wheel, glancing at our smiling companion and tapping the tell-tale dial. What a car! If only legislators could be convinced that speed can be this safe, where might technology not lead us?

Meanwhile, there are the familiar restrictions, legal as well as financial. In the present climate it would be madness, even if one could afford it, to buy a car for its top speed alone. But the Countach has other strings to its bow, as I discovered when we peeled off the motorway and onto the road which curls up into the Apennines towards Florence. This is the legendary Passo della Futa, 50 miles or so of steeply climbing corners, everything from wide open sweepers to the tightest of hairpins piled on top of each other in such bewildering succession that it is hard to believe they once formed part of Italy's spinal artery, the Via Emilia. These days the Futa is relatively quiet, though in our case holiday traffic was cluttering it. More disturbing, the weather, which had been lowering all morning, had now broken, and the lower slopes of the hills were being swept by skeins of thin, drenching rain.

Time was when any weather apart from clear sunshine would have constituted an excuse for calling off the session. Time was, too, when I should have been the last to resist, for it only needed one nightmare experience with the old breed of high-speed Pirelli to convince any prudent person of the folly of venturing into a damp corner thus shod. But not any more. Even Pirelli has discovered rain, and in any case this Countach was shod with Michelin tyres because the proper Pirellis, specially developed for it, hadn't arrived in time. The Michelins were several sizes too small as the French company doesn't make anything of the size specified. I was not sorry to have the Michelins, still less to have the rear ones smaller than they ought to have been, for I have learned the value of a marginally undertyred car on a wet road, particularly when it is as powerful and as unfamiliar as this. What it means is that you get your warning sooner, and have more time to do something about it...

To begin with, I wasn't even getting to the warning stage as I

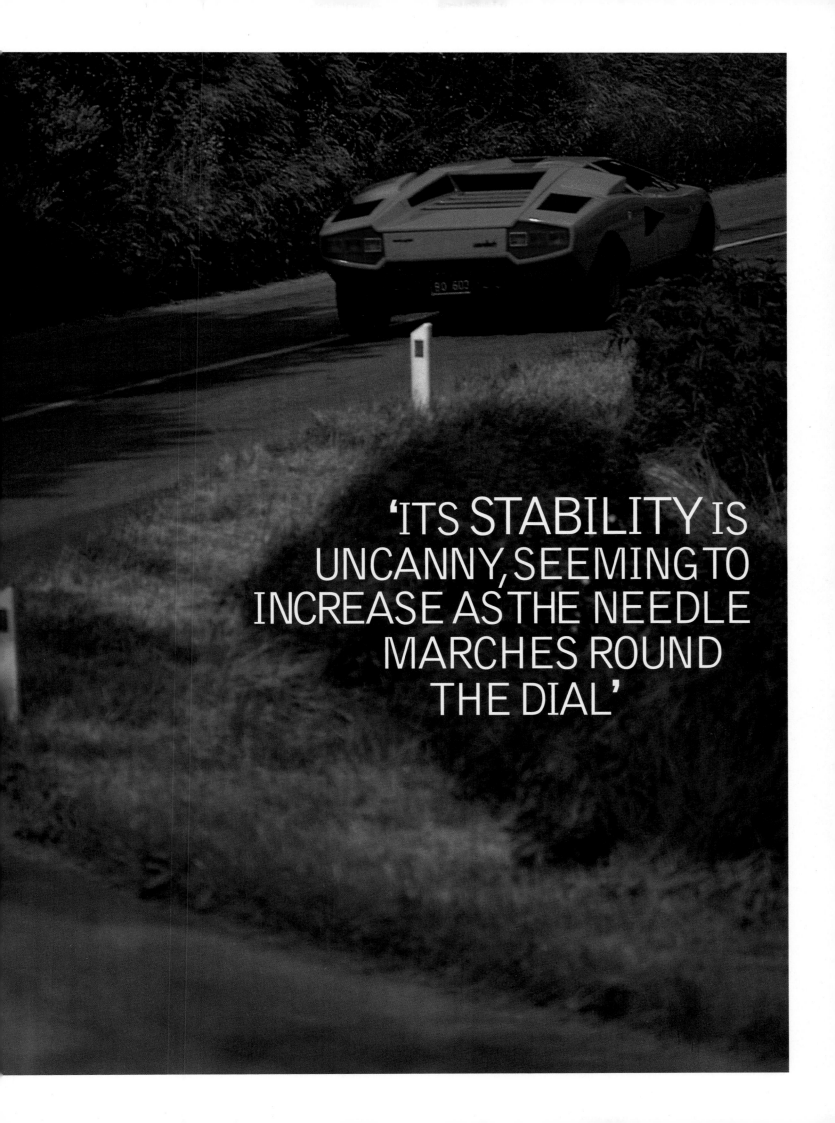

'ITS STABILITY IS UNCANNY, SEEMING TO INCREASE AS THE NEEDLE MARCHES ROUND THE DIAL'

pussyfooted up through the first few hairpins in first gear, gingerly exploring with the throttle to discover how much I could feed in before one end or the other broke loose. The answer turns out to depend on what stage in the corner you choose, for the Countach is set up to understeer with some consistency. This means that until you are moving quite quickly and then only on the exit from a bend, it will tend to break traction at the front if you brake or accelerate too hard. In practice, any kind of breakaway takes some doing, even in heavy rain. There is bags of warning, and correction is child's play, but you don't achieve anything by doing it on purpose, so that the real challenge becomes how to achieve relative smoothness while exploiting at least some of the potential. Really, this Lamborghini could do with a sixth gear, for as with any car in which first is intended as a driving ratio, there are times when it feels too high, as when accelerating out of a slow uphill bend through which one has been forced to follow a crawling truck – common enough in the Italian mountains, God knows. Another way might be to sacrifice a little top-end power for a milder cam,

but that would be a pity. The third alternative is for the driver to practise, balancing clutch against throttle like a grand prix driver does when belting away from the line.

A similar juggling act, using throttle and brake, is of course going on all this time on the approaches to the bends. But it is hard to persuade the Countach to break traction under braking: it stops straight and true, every time, without hot smells and without the firm but not-too-heavy pedal going soft. You can brake right up into the apex if you want, though I thought it best not to do that too often in the streaming wet. Heel and toe downchanges come naturally which isn't always the case in Italian sports cars, and the single, huge, parallelogram wiper succeeds in keeping the centre of the screen clear. I noticed later, though, that it lifts off like all Lambo wipers over about 120mph, and in the mountains one misses the clear view to the upper corners that a smaller arc might provide. Misting up is not a problem with the air-conditioning, and I soon learn to keep the wind-down panes in the side windows shut as they upset the system in this wet, muggy weather.

SPECIFICATION
LAMBORGHINI COUNTACH

Years manufactured: 1974 to 1990
Numbers made: 1742
Concept: mid-engined, V12, two-seat supercar to replace Miura. Abandoned Miura's transverse, gears-in-sump layout for in-line engine, with gearbox ahead. Drive passed to short propshaft, then final drive

ENGINE
Layout: V12
Capacity: LP400 3929cc; LP500s 4754cc; LP500S QV 5167cc
Max power: LP400 375bhp at 8000rpm; LP400S 353bhp at 7000rpm; LP500S 375bhp at 7000rpm; LP500S QV 455bhp at 7000rpm
Max torque: LP400 286lb ft at 5000rpm; LP400S 267lb ft at 5500rpm; LP500S 302lb ft at 4500rpm; LP500S QV 369lb ft at 5200rpm
Power to weight ratio (per ton): LP400 288bhp; LP400S 261bhp; LP500S 253bhp; LP500S QV 306bhp
Installation: longitudinal, rear-drive
Construction: alloy heads, alloy block
Valvegear: two valves per cylinder, dohc per bank; QV four valves per cylinder
Compression ratio: LP400, LP400S 10.5:1; LP500S 9.2:1; LP500S QV 9.5:1
Fuel system: LP400, LP400S, LP500S: six Weber 45 DCOE carburettors; LP500S six Weber 44DCNF carburettors

GEARBOX
Type: five-speed manual
Traction control: no
SUSPENSION
Front: double wishbones, coil springs, telescopic shock absorbers, anti-roll bar
Rear: upper lateral links, lower reversed wishbones, upper and lower trailing arms, twin coil spring, telescopic shock absorbers
BRAKES
Front: ventilated discs; LP400 267mm; LP400S, LP500S, LP500S QV 300mm
Rear: ventilated discs; LP400 267mm; LP400S, LP500S, LP500S QV 282mm
Anti-lock system: no
STEERING
Type: rack and pinion
Assistance: no
TYRES AND WHEELS
Front: LP400 205/70VR14; LP400S 205/50VR15; LP500S, LP500SQV 225/50VR15
Rear: LP400 215/70VR14; LP400S, LP500S, LP500S QV 345/35VR15
BODY
Construction: tubular steel spaceframe, aluminium skin panels
Weight (kg): LP400 1301; LP400S 1351; LP500S 1480; LP500S QV 1488
PERFORMANCE
Max speed: LP400, LP400S 174mph; LP500S 180mph; LP500S QV 190mph
0-60mph: LP400 5.6sec; LP400S 5.9sec; LP500S 4.8sec; LP500S QV 4.2sec

Countach was a challenging drive; Lamborghini planned that buyers should 'qualify' to buy it. But that changed

There is a kind of unspoken challenge in driving a car like this that keeps you on your toes. Further up, the clouds begin to lighten and we find the odd clear patch between corners. This is the signal to pile on power, peering anxiously ahead so as to leave space to shed a couple of gears and get set up in case the next corner turns out to be damp halfway. The noises are marvellous. Up through the first three gears and down again, the transfer-set singing away, those blatant exhausts barking exultantly (one reason I'd had the window open!), the front end snaking snugly under braking like something out of the Targa Florio...

How does it feel to take corners like that on a public road? Bloody uncomfortable, that's how, although the discomfort is nothing to do with the car: it's all in the mind, or rather in the head, which feels as if its insides are slopping right over the rim of the bucket. Even at the absolute limit, this extraordinary car feels safe. The steering tells you precisely what is happening to the front wheels, and the grip at the back is so good you can rely on it (even in this undertyred state) to stay in hand unless you provoke it.

The Countach is the only vehicle of its type, by which I mean with this sort of performance potential, that can boast of handling to match its roadholding right up to and beyond the limit. It is an easy, forgiving car to drive really hard. On the other hand it is considerably less 'easy to drive', in the accepted sense, than the others at anything less than eight or nine tenths of its own and its driver's capacity – less smooth, more inclined to magnify clumsiness or lack of familiarity in the use of the controls. It is not the kind of car, either, in which to indulge in those super-refinements of technique so beloved of certain Advanced Motorists: you know, the

arm-crossing, the double-declutching, the constant keeping of the hands at 10 to two. If you drive a Countach like that you're driving it about half as quickly as it wants to go. To be effective, you must get in there and boss the thing, using muscle but not force, urging it deeper and deeper into the corner with little twitches of the wheel, banging gears home, stamping on brake and clutch till you ache. But my, aren't you rewarded! The bends in any given stretch of road feel as if they've been compressed. Imperfections in the surface become imprinted in your mind as you feel the tyres react eagerly, yet ever so slightly, under violent acceleration or braking. The door sills and tunnel become imprinted in your thighs. Your neck hurts from being slammed back into the headrest and your right hand feels raw from the perfectly smooth knob of the gearlever. These are the symptoms of enjoyment. These things mean you have been driving so much faster than you could in almost any other car as to justify an outlay of this magnitude. You have been driving a Porsche Carrera multiplied by two, or a Ferrari 512M tamed for the road, only you have been doing something more meaningful, because the Countach is purpose-built, a balanced entity with manners and a soul.

IN RETROSPECT

Being born at a time when fuel-rationing was on the cards only made the Countach seem more outrageous. It should have died at birth, but lived 'til 1990. When launched for £16,314 in '73, an MG Midget cost a little over £1000. Early 190mph claims were tosh, though the later 5.2-litre QV made 190mph. If you believe horsepower, outlandish looks and zero practicality make a supercar, then the Countach remains the definitive article.

FASTER AS IT GOT OLDER, BUT UGLIER TOO

As it evolved, the Countach gained more power, outputs rising from 375bhp to 455bhp. At the same time its body swelled, sprouting fussy wheel-arch extensions to house ever-fatter rubber, and optionally, a rear wing much favoured by the poseurs who, sadly, became the car's most common customer

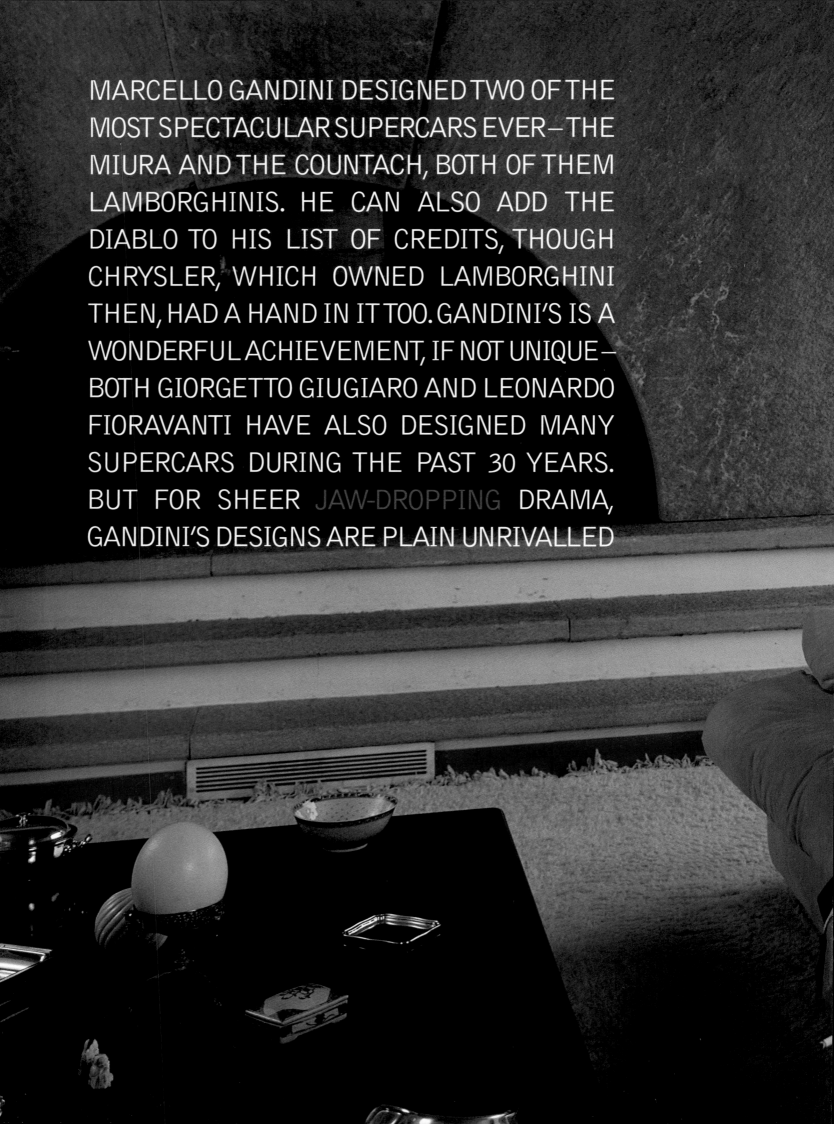

MARCELLO GANDINI DESIGNED TWO OF THE MOST SPECTACULAR SUPERCARS EVER—THE MIURA AND THE COUNTACH, BOTH OF THEM LAMBORGHINIS. HE CAN ALSO ADD THE DIABLO TO HIS LIST OF CREDITS, THOUGH CHRYSLER, WHICH OWNED LAMBORGHINI THEN, HAD A HAND IN IT TOO. GANDINI'S IS A WONDERFUL ACHIEVEMENT, IF NOT UNIQUE— BOTH GIORGETTO GIUGIARO AND LEONARDO FIORAVANTI HAVE ALSO DESIGNED MANY SUPERCARS DURING THE PAST 30 YEARS. BUT FOR SHEER JAW-DROPPING DRAMA, GANDINI'S DESIGNS ARE PLAIN UNRIVALLED

Marcello
GANDINI
■ 1939 -

Conceived in 1968 and
part-inspired by the Miura,
Maserati's first mid-
engined supercar emerged
in 1971. It wasn't great at
first, but the Bora was to
improve dramatically

MASERATI
Bora

By Doug Blain

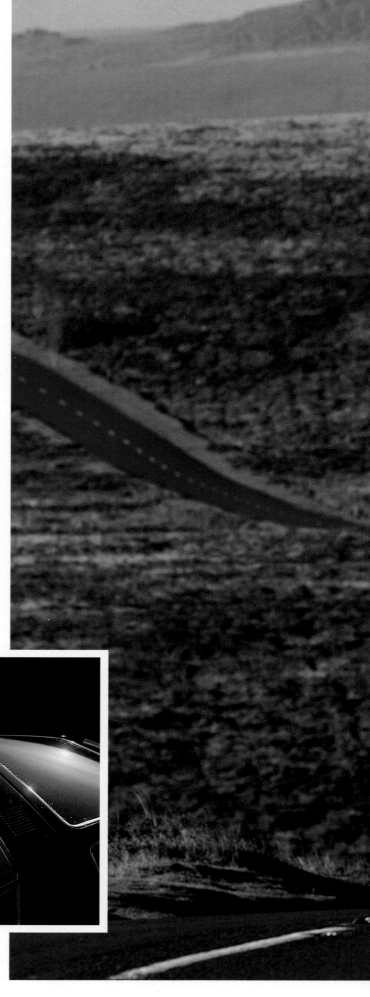

LOOKING BACK AT WHAT I wrote about the Bora in January, I can hardly believe that the car I drove on my latest visit to Italy was from the same stable.

Not that I want to retract any of my more profound impressions. I still rate the model 'a restful, practical, long-legged and very fast high-mileage two-seater'. My abiding memory is still of 'a taut, responsive and yet undeniably luxurious' car with an uncanny appetite for distances, as well as for expensive Italian petrol. The difference is simply that almost none of my original detail criticisms of the prototype apply to the production version, and I want to take this opportunity of making it quite clear that the Bora is one of the finest fast cars ever built.

The galling thing is that I only found this out by accident. Your editor and I were in Italy for a week after the Targa Florio, doing the rounds as usual, and we had set aside a day in expectation of being allowed to drive Maserati's forthcoming 'mini-Bora', which a little bird had told us might be ready about that time. It wasn't, but our good friend Dr Tarusio had arranged for us to have the company's demonstration Bora for the afternoon instead.

We arrived in good time, only to stumble over a comprehensively crunched example parked conspicuously outside the front door. And when you have known the Italian supercar factories for as long as I have you are left in no doubt what that means.

Dr T was one step ahead, however. Bursting into the waiting

'I WANT TO MAKE IT CLEAR THAT THIS IS ONE OF THE **FINEST** FAST CARS EVER'

room with his hands spread in a gesture of despair, he blurted out wildly: 'Meester Blain, I am so sorry...' and then fell about laughing. True the car outside was the demonstrator. True we were supposed to have had it. True the works driver had crunched it on the way up from Salerno the day before (twice for good measure, would you believe). But the genial Dr had bypassed the system and found us no fewer than three other cars to choose from, according to colour. As the choice was black, grey or purple we settled for the last even though it was the same as last time, sought out our favourite factory tester to sit in the passenger seat (keeps the insurers quiet, and he enjoys it) and headed for the hills.

Among my lesser gripes after last winter's encounter, I see, was one about the change-speed mechanism for the five-speed ZF box located behind the engine and final drive. Now this is the same box that De Tomaso uses for the Pantera, and it has been used in other mid-engined machinery including the daunting Monteverdi Hai. My experience of it had more or less convinced me that there was no way in which it could be made more than barely acceptable, and I knew full well that if the systems engineers failed to get their sums more or less dead right the result could be very nasty and even dangerous. But the latest Bora has a redesigned shift linkage, and the result is a revelation – smooth, precise movements between ratios, and no more effort required than one might expect in a front-engined car of this potency. Other designers who have despaired of translating the leverage of a man's hand via a system of rods, levers and bell-cranks into a series of sliding and meshing movements in a hot, foam-filled container which is itself oscillating independently under torque reaction nearly six feet further rearward may take heart from Ing Alfieri's achievement.

Then there was the problem of the steering. A rack and pinion set-up by ZF, it felt fine in the prototype at lowish speeds and on winding roads, but on the straight, and particularly on bumpy surfaces, it allowed too much wander. This I found hard to explain, although for some reason I remember feeling sure it was a steering problem – perhaps a geometrical one – rather than a question of instability arising through aerodynamic or other imbalance. Anyway, whatever it was it was shortlived, for once again the production car showed no sign of it. In fact no sooner had I got clear of Modena than I changed my mind about making off into the mountains and turned instead onto the Autostrada del Sole, thinking I might discover whether my early impression of a tremendous improvement in the feel of the car held good at really high speed.

Bora was another successful car from ItalDesign, above. Maserati's brief to designer Giorgetto Giugiaro was for a mid-engined, V8 sports car with good ride, roadholding and aerodynamic looks. The car debuted in 1971

It was lunchtime, and the usual heavy traffic on the main north-south highway had dropped off a good deal. This augured well for conditions on the spur motorway from Bologna towards Ferrara, which is newer and much less frequented, and sure enough when we turned off the Bologna *cintura* the wide, straight road ahead of us was clear for miles. I turned to my impassive companion and asked doubtfully whether I ought to extend the big 4.7 litre four-cam V8 all the way to the red line, admittedly conservatively positioned at a mere 5800rpm; I was very conscious that this was a brand-new car with only a few hours of bench-testing at the very most to its credit (the distance recorder said less than 200km!). But the mechanic wouldn't hear of anything less than the full treatment. 'Take it to 6250rpm,' he said, with a laconic wave of the hand.

'They usually seem to hang together at that.'

I planted my foot, noting the change points as I went at roughly 50mph from first to second, 80mph from second to third, 120mph from third to fourth (two more ratios to go and 120mph on the clock) and a whisker short of 150mph as I pulled the lever smartly back into fifth, staring out into the shimmering heat haze on the horizon for signs of other traffic.

The needles in the two big instruments ahead of me continued to march steadily towards the ends of their scales, and within seconds, it seemed, the tachometer was edging towards the red band. I glanced across towards my passenger, who only grinned broadly, mouthing the words, 'Forza, forza' with appropriate gestures. I pressed on until finally I had to back off for fear of bursting the

'THE MECHANIC WOULDN'T HEAR OF ANYTHING LESS THAN THE FULL TREATMENT. "TAKE IT TO 6250RPM"'

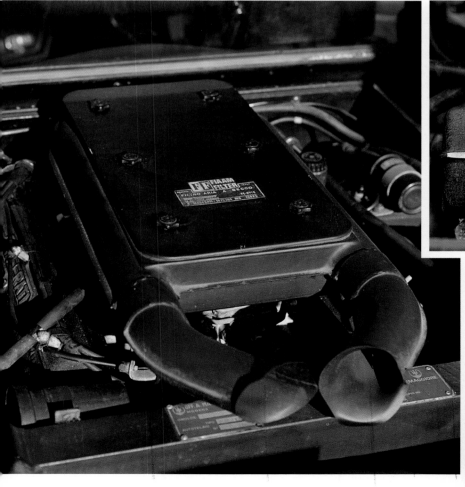

Bora used a detuned 4.7 litre V8 from the Ghibli, producing 310bhp. This rose to 320bhp when it grew to 4.9 litres 1976, but neither version was quite up to the Bora's excessive weight

whole plot at an indicated 6200rpm, by which time the presumably less truthful speedometer was showing almost 300kmh. Sober calculation afterwards against a fifth gear km per 1000rpm figure of 45.1 gave no less than 172.98mph, so even allowing for tyre expansion and a small margin for instrument error we must have been nudging 170 during those few magic moments in the red.

And they were magic, for the mighty Maser felt uncannily stable and quiet – a stark contrast in these respects to the competition machinery and semi-racers (and Miuras!) in which I had attained such unnatural velocities before. On a trailing throttle, particularly, it held its speed so well with so little mechanical fuss that I quite forgot how quickly we were moving so that I felt positively grateful when the Maserati man touched me on the shoulder and pointed about half a mile ahead to a truck which was about to pull out and overtake the inevitable Fiat 500. I had seen it, of course; and had planned to slow down in time to tuck gracefully in behind, but in fact it took us all of the available space to haul off so much speed without either setting the disc pads on fire or locking a wheel.

The latter phenomenon, I know, was one of my original grumbles, and I am still no fan of high-pressure hydraulics such as the Bora uses. My fear is not that the system will fail altogether (if it does, a dashboard warning light is supposed to give the alarm while the huge reservoir on the central bulkhead is claimed to hold enough reserve energy for more than 40 stops) as that the short travel and hypersensitivity of the pedal action will cause me to over-brake. Several hair-raising experiences in Citroëns have convinced me that this is inclined to happen when one is least expecting it. I must say, however, that even in this I noticed a big improvement in the production Bora over the prototype, and it is only fair to record that in exchange for some anxiety one gets actual braking power of an enormously high order.

I managed to put in a good hour of hard charging up and down the unfrequented mountainsides of the Apennines before stopping for lunch in our usual haunt, the idyllically situated castle restaurant at Guilia. Not that I would advise anybody, even now, to get too carried away in the Bora. It is an extremely solid and heavy hunk of machinery, much of whose weight sits over the

SPECIFICATION
MASERATI BORA

Years manufactured: 1971 to 1979
Numbers made: 571
Concept: mid-engined two-seat supercar, Maserati's first. Styling by Giorgetto Giugiaro at ItalDesign. A softer, more comfortable supercar than Ferrari's equivalent 308 GTB, and as a consequence overshadowed, especially with its high weight denting the 4.7 litre V8's potential. Nevertheless, superb to drive, and good for over 170mph.

ENGINE
Layout: V8
Capacity: 4719cc, US version 4930cc from '72; all models 4.9 from '76
Max power: 310bhp at 6000rpm, US version 300bhp at 6000rpm, 4.9 320bhp at 5500rpm
Max torque: 325lb ft at 4200rpm, US version 310lb ft at 3500rpm. 4.9 335lb ft at 4000rpm
Power to weight ratio (per ton): 204bhp, US version 194bhp, 4.9 203bhp
Installation: longitudinal, driving rear wheels
Construction: alloy heads, alloy block
Valvegear: two valves per cylinder, twin overhead camshafts per bank
Compression ratio: 8.5:1, US version 8.75:1, 4.9 8.75:1
Fuel system: four Weber 42 DCNF carbs

GEARBOX
Type: five-speed manual
Traction control: no
SUSPENSION
Front: double wishbones, coil springs, telescopic shock absorbers, anti-roll bar
Rear: double wishbones, coil springs, telescopic shock absorbers, anti-roll bar
BRAKES
Front: 280mm (240mm pre '71, 248mm '72-'73) ventilated discs
Rear: 280mm (240mm pre '71, 248mm '72-'73) ventilated discs
Anti-lock system: no
STEERING
Type: rack and pinion
Assistance: no
TYRES AND WHEELS
Front: Michelin XVR 185/70 15; post '74 Michelin XWX 215/70 VR15
Rear: Michelin XVR 185/70 15; post '74 Michelin XWX 215/70 VR15
BODY
Construction: steel monocoque
Weight (kg): 1520, US version 1545, 4.9 1580
PERFORMANCE
Max speed: 174mph, 4.9 165mph
0-60mph: 6.5sec, 4.9 7.2sec

The Bora was good for over 160mph, although forays to the limit were tempered by its huge thirst - single figures were possible, 12mpg typical. Interior was lavish, with dials and buttons galore, leather trim, hydraulically adjusted pedals and air conditioning

rear wheels. It is powerful and responsive, and in common with many of its ilk it is fitted with a self-locking differential.

To the experienced this will suggest a measure of unpredictability in extremis, and it is so: hang the tail out, poke an exploratory toe into the last segment of the throttle pedal's generous and well regulated travel, feel the locking device suddenly clench and unclench and – wham! You have the daddy and mummy of almighty slides on your hands, and you will have to move fast to prevent the formidable weight in the tail from taking over. How do I know? I tried it once, and after I had sorted myself out, leaving great black marks all over the nice clean tarmac, my friend the mechanic smiled and murmured, 'Autobloccante...'

In this respect the Bora falls into a category of its own, between the ultra-sporting supercars such as the Miura, the Ferrari Dino and the De Tomaso Pantera and the impeccably mannered front-engined grand tourers, most notably the Daytona and the Lamborghini Jarama. Its roadholding is very nearly as good as the best of the mid-engined cars, and at the same time it can boast at least as much performance and refinement as the finest of the conventional breed. Above all it is an enjoyable and rewarding car to drive just short of the limit. In view of which, and faced also with a high standard of finish together with a profusion of luxury amenities, what can I say but that the Bora now takes over as the most desirable car in the world in which to tackle a high-speed continental journey of 1000 miles or more?

IN RETROSPECT

No-one knew it, but in the mid '70s Maserati was reaching the end of a golden age. In 1975, it was on a par with Ferrari and Lamborghini. Only now, after almost 20 years in the wilderness, is the company re-emerging as a force. So the Bora is perceived as the last great Maserati, and as the marque's stock rises again, so a good one could be a shrewd investment.

First seen in 1971, it was a rung below the Countach and Boxer. It was also a more subtle car, more sophisticated and significantly cheaper too, at £11,473 in 1975. It was never shockingly quick – road tests spoke of 165mph and 0-60 in about 6.5 seconds – but it certainly looked and felt like a supercar.

Silver roof, left, is stainless steel. This was the last time the evocative badge, above, graced a Maserati supercar, the firm turning to less adventurous designs in the '80s

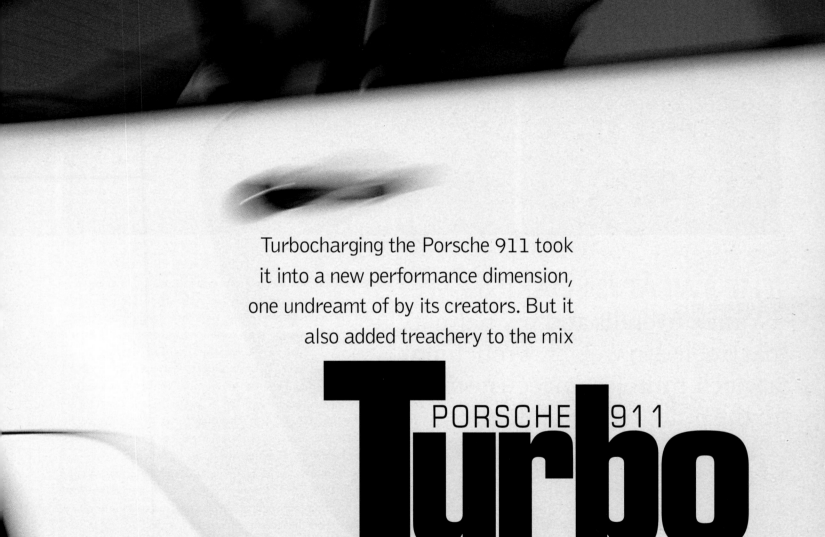

Turbocharging the Porsche 911 took
it into a new performance dimension,
one undreamt of by its creators. But it
also added treachery to the mix

PORSCHE 911
Turbo

By Roger Bell

THE SWEAT IS SOAKING MY Nomex overalls and my helmet has trebled in weight, wrenching at neck muscles unaccustomed to the pull of such *g*-forces.

Zakspeed's Group Five Turbo Ford Capri is teasing my senses with intoxicating vigour. Ahead, Ford's arch rival, the Kremer Porsche 935, is out testing. I do not know its driver but he cannot be anywhere near the limit because I'm able to keep in touch, following his rump round the short Nürburgring circuit. We loop the long 270degree righthander onto the back straight in tandem, four lengths apart. The live-axled Capri feels secure, stable, balanced, evidently with grip to spare, though caution – call it plain fear, if you like – prevents me from using it. Suddenly, the Porsche, travelling no faster than I, is enveloped in rubber smoke. I am no longer chasing its tail but veering away from its flank, and now it's orange nose as it pirouettes into the Armco.

That fleeting (and happily harmless) incident sprang vividly to mind as I read Mel Nichols' most recent column. 'The 911 still worries me', said Mel. 'I don't like cars you can't trust.' Whether such a wayward and unexpected spin by the Kremer 935, the ultimate racing version of the 911 Turbo, was the sort of misgiving Mel har-

boured about the handling of so potent a car with its engine in the wrong place, I can't say. At the time I was concerned with too many other things, like the 550bhp under my right foot, to ponder the matter. But the point he makes is not one that any prudent driver fortunate enough to be tossed the keys of a 3.3-litre 911 Turbo, as has happened to me, will cast aside with alacrity. Any car that's not totally predictable in its behaviour, least of all one with a 300bhp sting in the tail, should be viewed with caution. Yet for all that, Porsche's £28,000 armchair dragster is still to me crown prince of the supercars, even though it can bite when abused and punish when wronged. If that makes me a masochist, so be it.

The 911 Turbo was conceived in 1974 to succeed the normally aspirated Carrera RSR racer as a homologation special. Dr Ernst Fuhrmann, then chairman of Porsche, decreed that the 400 cars needed to satisfy the rules would not be stripped-down boy racers but swanked-up exotics that would enhance Porsche's reputation as builders of quality road expresses. Porsche were then at the forefront of turbo technology: the blown 917/30, still the most powerful circuit racer ever, had been so dominant that the rules were changed to ban it. The lesser Turbo Carrera followed as a blown version of the RSR, paving the way for the road cars Porsche needed to homologate their new generation of racers.

The 3.0-litre Turbo, first seen in 1974, used essentially the same flat-six, all-alloy engine as the 3.0-litre Carrera, but with a lowered compression ratio of 6.5 to one. Boost pressure of the Kuhle, Kopp and Kausch (KKK) compressor was limited to 0.8bar by the usual wastegate, while an exhaust by-pass system, effective when the

911 Turbo interior, far left, is ergonomically flawed but comfortable. Turbo searingly fast when on boost, the rear-engine layout providing superb traction

throttles of the Bosch K-Jetronic fuel injection were closed, cut rev-reducing back pressure on the turbine to minimise throttle lag. A new four-speed gearbox was also needed, to cope not only with the road car's greater torque but also the 750bhp of the 935/78 racers, too. The first Turbo prototype, fitted with standard Carrera suspension, oversteered strongly, a problem relieved if never totally remedied by changing the pick-up points for the semi-trailing rear suspension, and making adjustments to the rates of the torsion-bar springs and anti-roll bars. Wider wheels and tyres also necessitated the use of larger bearings, but the cross-drilled, all-disc brakes developed for the car were temporarily shelved because they cracked during severe testing. Body rigidity was increased, too – and a Targa killed for the lack of it.

I vividly recall my first drive in the 3.0-litre Turbo, when I wrote: 'It's the combination of peace and power that makes this incredible machine unique...'. The 7.0-litre Cobra and GT40 with which I compared it 'were brutal, frenzied, writhing machines that bombarded all your senses with their aggressiveness and noise. What makes the Turbo so different is that it hurls you forward with similar ferocity but in an uncannily effortless way'. I remember it well.

But that was six years ago and turbo tearaways, albeit of lesser standing and pedigree, are now relatively common. No longer is the fluent potency of an engine force-fed by an exhaust-driven air pump confined to thoroughbreds like the Porsche. So what of the 3.3 now? It supplanted the original blown 3.0-litre in 1977 when the 911 was already 12 years old, yet it's still Porsche's fiscal flagship despite formidable in-house competition from more modern

front-engined cars that are configuratively superior and equally well built and engineered. Yet persistent rumours of the 911's demise were recently scotched by chairman Schutz.

The 3.3 differed from the lesser car it replaced significantly. The addition of an intercooler lowered the temperature of turbo-compressed air, allowing an increase in compression ratio from 6.5 to 7.0 to one. This gave an improvement in output disproportionate to the 10percent capacity increase, which grew to 3299cc. Power went up by 15percent, from 260 to 300bhp at 5500rpm, and torque by 20percent, from 254 to 304lb ft at 4000rpm. Larger main and conrod bearings were fitted, and the cooling fan speed increased to 1.8 times that of the crankshaft to cope with the terrific thermal loads imposed on the gasket-less cylinder heads.

Yet more performance meant even better brakes, those cross-drilled four-caliper ventilated discs perfected now and servo assisted to boot, to the horror of traditionalists. A stronger and thicker clutch meant moving the engine still further rearwards, dictating compensatory suspension tuning and even higher (42psi) rear tyre pressures, which did little for the choppy ride.

Despite its strikingly muscular build, the 3.3 Turbo is quite a small car and not lavishly furnished. There's no cowhide trim, no hand-polished timber. Can Porsche be serious? £28,000 for this? Ah, but feel the quality. Smooth your hand over the body. The touch becomes a sensuous caress and no more is said about the car's finish, flawless to the last plastic clip. Not that the spiel ends there, for there are other shortcomings to explain, if not excuse, before the Turbo can show its true mettle.

The engine fires explosively first time, and idles instantly with a deep, even drone. There's no need to warm up – in fact, the handbook advises against it. The clutch is heavy, the rigid gearlever – too far forward if you're sitting well back – is reluctant to engage first. Another stab and it slots into place like an oiled switch, as it usually does once the gearbox is warm. Clutch bite is firm, its sharpness exacerbated by an awkward over-centre action. There's a hint of shudder, too, when moving off. Accelerate gently and the deep drone behind persists monotonously, mixing now with an underlying whoosh as the cooling fan churns air over alloy heads.

Playing yourself in gently, prudently, it is the Turbo's tractable docility that first impresses, not its fearsome punch. There's no snatch, plug fouling, not even when trickling in traffic at 25mph in top. Torque is sufficiently strong, as well it should be from 3.3-litres, to give energetic lugging before the turbo's doing any real work, though sizzle from the transaxle discourages the use of full throttle below 1500rpm. Pick up, never less than brisk, progresses to the brutal in a fluid, exhilarating surge as boost pressure rises at around 2000rpm, when the tacho needle suddenly snaps round the dial. The torque curve, although it peaks at 4000rpm, is virtually flat between 3000 and 5000rpm, when the turbo's on full boost at 12psi, and it's at these revs that the 3.3 is at its thrilling best.

There may be quicker cars to 100mph from rest, but the ferocity of the Porsche's acceleration at full bore, emphasised perhaps by the relatively modest shove when the engine's off boost, is sufficiently fierce to alarm, even frighten unsuspecting passengers. From rest to 60mph takes just over 5.0sec, to 100mph under 12. But these somewhat academic yardsticks, impressive though they are, do less than justice to the mid-speed acceleration figures. You can count on one thumbless hand the number of genuine production cars that will rocket from 80 to 100mph in third in 4.0sec, around 6.0sec in top. All out, the Turbo will exceed 160mph and lope along unfussed at 130mph with so much in reserve that there's little incentive to show a clean wing to anything clawing its way by at 135mph. Big Mercs are easy, Ferraris sterner stuff.

Provided the revs are kept above 2500rpm, there's virtually no throttle lag, no frustrating pause after brief lift-off or changing gear. Such is the potency of the surge when the turbo's on song, fluid though it is, that you need to keep a wary eye on the road surface ahead. In the dry, there's no real problem: it's possible to floor the throttle in second exiting a roundabout sure in the knowledge that the huge 225/50 Pirelli P7 rear boots will dig in and hold. In the wet, it's different: the tail can whiplash into power oversteer through injudicious use of the massive torque, though it will normally snap back into line as soon as you lift off. Just as well, too. Beyond quite modest angles of drift, swift and precise application of opposite lock is required to prevent a spin, sharp and accurate subsequent realignment to avoid fish-tailing. Even on the straight, it's possible to snake the tail with wheelspin at 70mph in second gear.

The tacho's red line at 6800rpm allows maxima in the intermediate gears of 52, 90 and 134mph, though in practice there's no need to exceed 6000rpm (46, 80 and 118mph). The engine, though hardly breathless at the top end, has given its best at 5500rpm, after which power tails off sharply. Little is lost by restricting the revs to 5000rpm, and much gained in reducing noise, as the flat-six's frenzied wail at high revs is far from quiet. Exciting though.

Fluid acceleration depends as much on a sweet gearchange technique as on the turbo's progressive response. Throttle feathering, a decisive hand on the long-throw lever, and precision clutch work are skills that are rewarded by super-smooth changes when mastered – if they're not, your passenger is in for a jerky ride. The distant position of the gearlever, and offset pedals set too high, are evidence of imperfect ergonomics. Despite these and other shortfalls, though, you sense that the car's been tailored for your frame, so well does it fit, so in command do you feel behind the low-set steering wheel in firm, supportive seats, heavily bolstered around your hips and thighs. Beanpole drivers can stretch out to a point where the muddled switches (that for the heating and ventilation needs handbook explanation) are virtually beyond reach.

Modestly laden front wheels make the sharp, unassisted steering quite light (except when parking) but it is the feedback that gives it such extraordinary telegraphic properties. The wheel bucks and writhes in your hands, excessively so on bumpy roads perhaps, imparting terrific feel from the front tyres, smaller than the rears to help achieve the right grip and handling balance from a car that is inordinately unbalanced in its weight distribution. Not that the car feels tail heavy, even when driven briskly. On dry roads, you just aim and squirt, picking your line with pinpoint accuracy, cor-

Rear wing, now such a trademark of the Porsche Turbo, was needed to improve high-speed stability, as were the fat rear tyres, which necessitated a widening of the bodywork. It worked, too

'ACCELERATION IS SUFFICIENTLY FIERCE TO FRIGHTEN UNSUSPECTING PASSENGERS'

recting it with minor steering inputs or, if you're really hammering on, feathering the throttle to pull the nose into the apex. You need a firm hold on the wheel to counter strong self-centring, but not a stiff-armed one to fight it. Turn-in is sharp, body roll minimal, the grip (on dry roads) sensational. So what's the catch?

For a start, driving hard on twisty roads, especially indifferently surfaced ones, you have to work quite hard, physically and mentally, to get the best from the car, to keep it in check, make it do what you want. Unlike, say, the Audi Quattro, the Porsche is not a car to flatter bad drivers. But get it right, and the rewards will raise goosepimples. What else? Well, you can't discount the car's readiness to unleash its tail under provocation on wet or greasy surfaces: even P7s have a limit. But that's predictable, avoidable and, to a large extent, controllable if you know what you're doing. No,

SPECIFICATION
PORSCHE 911 TURBO

Years manufactured: 1974 to date
Numbers made: 34,074 to October 1997
Concept: rear-engined two-plus-two sports car turned supercar, thanks to hugely powerful 3.3-litre turbo engine. Rear-mounted, air-cooled flat-six has grown bigger and more powerful over the years; current generation car tamed with four-wheel drive

ENGINE
Layout: flat-six
Capacity: '75 3.0 Turbo 2994cc; '78 3.3 Turbo 3299cc; '92 3600c; '95 3600cc
Max power: '75 3.0 Turbo 260bhp at 5500rpm; '78 3.3 300bhp at 5500rpm; '89 300bhp at 5500rpm; '91 320bhp at 5750rpm; '93 360bhp at 5500rpm; '95 408bhp at 5750rpm
Max torque: 3.0 253lb ft at 4500rpm; '78 3.3 304lb ft at 4500rpm; '83 318 lb ft at 4000rpm; '89 317lb ft at 4000rpm; '91 331lb ft at 4500rpm; '93 384lb ft at 4200rpm; '95 398lb ft at 4500rpm
Power to weight ratio (per ton): '75 228bhp; '76 218bhp; '78 231bhp; '86 225bhp; '91 218bhp; '93 245bhp; '95 272bhp
Installation: longitudinal, rear-mounted, rear-drive
Construction: alloy heads, alloy block
Valvegear: two valves per cylinder, single overhead camshaft per bank
Compression ratio: 3.0 6.5:1; 3.3 7.0:1; '89 7.1:1; '93 3.6 7.5:1; '95 8.1:1
Fuel system: Bosch K-Jetronic, KKK turbo; '93 Bosch KE-Jetronic, KKK turbo; '95 Bosch Motronic DME, twin turbos

GEARBOX
Type: four-speed manual; from '93 five

speed manual; from '95 six-speed manual
Traction control: no; from '95 four-wheel drive, traction control

SUSPENSION
Front: MacPherson struts, lower wishbones, torsion bars, telescopic shock absorbers, anti-roll bar
Rear: semi-trailing arms, torsion bars, telescopic shock absorbers, anti-roll bar

BRAKES
Front: '75 282mm ventilated discs; '78 304mm, cross-drilled; '91 322mm; '95 304mm
Rear: '75 290mm ventilated discs; '78 309mm, cross-drilled; '91 299mm
Anti-lock system: from '91

STEERING
Type: rack and pinion
Assistance: from '91

TYRES AND WHEELS
Front: '75 Dunlop 185/70VR15; '76 Pirelli P7 205/55VR15; '77 P7 205/55VR16; '87 205/55VR16; '91 205/50ZR17; '93 225/40ZR18; '95 225/40ZR18
Rear: '75 Dunlop 215/60VR15; '76 Pirelli P7 225/50VR15; '77 P7 225/50VR16; '87 245/45VR16; '91 255/45ZR17; '93 265/35/ZR18; '95 285/35ZR18

BODY
Construction: steel monocoque
Weight (kg): '75 3.0 1140; '76 1195; '78 1300; '86 1335; '91 1470; '95 1500

PERFORMANCE
Max speed: '75 3.0 155mph; '78 3.3 162mph; '91 3.3 168mph; '93 3.6 175mph; '95 3.6 180mph
0-60mph: '75 3.0 6.0sec; '78 3.3 5.1sec; '91 3.3 5.0sec; '93 3.6 4.8sec; '95 3.6 4.5sec 0-62mph

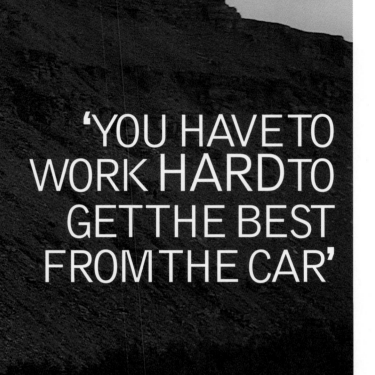

'YOU HAVE TO WORK HARD TO GET THE BEST FROM THE CAR'

Just the kind of road the 911 was made for, far left, the Turbo able to shorten roads like no other. 130mph an ambling cruise, above, when 180mph is a possibility

I don't think it's that that worries Mel Nichols, who is as skilled at the wheel as any motoring scribe I know. It is the 911's occasional unexpected behaviour that is the cause of his mistrust. Porsche has done a fine job in largely eliminating the inherent handling flaws of a car with a drivetrain behind the back wheels rather than ahead of them. But not even Porsche has totally mastered the shortcomings of so unbalanced a layout. That said, four days in the Turbo, sometimes going very hard indeed, failed to reveal any unnerving traits, though I've experienced them, as Mel evidently has, in other 911s – the capricious understeer driving into an unexpectedly sharp bend, the sudden tail-flick mid-corner when backing off sharply. Front wheel lock-up, which can induce alarming straight-on plough, occurred only once, and I put that down to an over-ambitious manoeuvre, not a shortcoming of the car's. To me, the noise of the tyres, particularly their harsh thumping over ridges, is more disturbing than their occasional sudden loss of grip under provocation. Poor noise suppression, the penalty you pay for taut suspension pick-ups and high tyre pressures, certainly mars refinement, even drowning the engine's wail except when it's extended. Yet the Turbo rides pretty well, more smoothly than it sounds, even allowing for the jiggling on indifferent roads. Front seat occupants might express disquiet at the firmness of the cushions, but they're likely to praise their comfort later. As ever, the heating and ventilation system is not only hard to fathom but inconsistent, calling for constant adjustment. There's little wrong with the instruments, though, and the car is well-equipped. I averaged 18mpg over 600 miles, giving a range of over 300 miles. High-speed stability? Cross-wind weave was once a 911 flaw, but the combination of fat tyres and rear wing has largely checked it. No, the remaining flaws are far outweighed by the car's terrific dynamism, its comfort, practicality, build quality and durability. Even with questionable handling predictability, the 911 Turbo has no betters in the supercar kingdom.

IN RETROSPECT

Always the most fearsome – and fear-inducing – road-going 911, the Turbo has become part of 911 legend. It has always been fast, and always carried question marks over the degree to which a keen driver can trust it. With each 911 generation the question marks have shrunk and the performance increased, keeping the Turbo in touch with its bigger and more flamboyant challengers from Italy. But for the really keen driver, the Turbo has never quite had the draw of the assorted 911 RSs there've been over the years, nor even some of the standard models, because it has never handled as well. Quicker but trickier to drive, the 911 Turbo remains an enigma.

Butzi
PORSCHE
■1936·

THE PORSCHE 911 IS FAMED FOR MANY THINGS, BUT MOST OF ALL, PERHAPS, FOR THE SIMPLICITY, BEAUTY AND LONGEVITY OF ITS SHAPE. YET THE MAN WHO DREW IT IS BARELY KNOWN AT ALL. CHRISTENED FERDINAND ALEXANDER PORSCHE III, BUTZI IS THE GRANDCHILD OF FERDINAND PORSCHE, CREATOR OF THE BEETLE. ALWAYS UNDER PRESSURE TO RUN PORSCHE, BUTZI PREFERRED TO CREATE, EVENTUALLY RESIGNING TO SET UP PORSCHE DESIGN. FURNITURE, PIPES AND SUNGLASSES WERE AMONG HIS MANY DESIGNS, BUT POSTERITY IS LIKELY TO RECORD THAT HIS GREATEST WAS THE 911

FERRARI BERLINETTA
Boxer

By Steve Cropley

The Boxer, so-called because of
its horizontally opposed flat-12,
was Ferrari's belated answer to
Lamborghini's Miura, as it finally
embraced the mid-engined layout
for its most potent supercar

I CAN REMEMBER QUITE WELL driving my first Boxer. It was in Australia about eight years ago, it was a 4.4-litre 365 version – the first in the country – and we were punting it hard on the flat, open, mostly smooth-bitumened roads to the north-west of Melbourne.

Two of us had been taking turns to drive the Ferrari and a big-hearted Peugeot 504 we'd brought along as chase car. It was new to the market itself, the Pug, and it did a remarkable job that day. Whereas the Ferrari rushed from one open corner to the next at speeds up to 170mph (we were proud of that), the 504 merely ran gamely at its 94mph maximum everywhere. It was never more than a few minutes behind.

After a couple of hours we drew up on a flat space at the side of a particularly long straight to inspect and photograph the red car. As we peered into the engine bay, eyes smarting from the heat, we heard, above the ticking of contracting metal, the sound of a rough diesel engine, distant but approaching. Vaguely I remembered a man on a Chamberlain tractor we'd passed a couple of miles

back, one of us at 94mph, the other at 150mph.

The noise grew louder and stopped. A tall, middle-aged man with a face like a beetroot jumped down and strode towards us. We presumed, somewhat guiltily, that we'd offended him; not many people can have travelled through his neighbourhood at upwards of two miles a minute. But as he came close, his face split into a grin. 'Crikey,' he said. 'I've been waiting a long time for this. Mind if I take a Captain Cook at your Puggy wagon?'

Since then there have been two more versions of the BB (if you leave out the numerous running changes that Ferrari has introduced). In 1976 the Boxer became the BB512, its flat-12's engine capacity increased by a little boring and rather more stroking to 4942cc. The engine was given a dry sump. The torque output was increased at lower revs and the maximum power, rather than being raised or lowered, was honestly quoted for the first time as being 340bhp at 6200rpm. Some people said the car didn't have the appeal of the 4.4-litre Boxer (with its 7500rpm red line) but it was indisputably more refined, easier to drive and just as fast.

There was confusion about a 188mph top speed quoted for an early prototype 4.4, and the production cars were supposed to have achieved it. But none of them ever did in standard tune, just as none of the 512s did.

Now there's another Boxer. Following the swing to fuel injection

This Boxer, right, is from the third and last generation, with fuel injection and improved suspension. Never quite as fast as it looked – 170mph was a struggle – the Boxer was nevertheless an entertaining and challenging drive. It also sounded magnificent, the animal bellow of its flat-12 an absolute spine-tingler

for Ferrari engines, the magnificent alloy flat-12 has been equipped with a Bosch K-Jetronic system with the twin advantages of making it run a lot cleaner, and saving fuel. Again there are detail changes to the car's tune – the camshaft timing has been radically overhauled – but the upshot is an engine whose power and torque outputs – 340bhp and 333lb ft – are unaltered. The maximum power is derived 200rpm lower now at 6000rpm, and the max torque comes 400rpm lower at 4200rpm. Ferrari's story is that a considerably greater percentage of that maximum torque is available below 4000rpm than it was before.

When you open the engine bay and view the flat engine – mounted high and therefore close to you (its crankshaft is 24 inches off the ground, yet the whole car's only 44 inches tall) because the gearbox and differential plus driveshafts are mounted underneath – the familiar pancake air filter housings have gone, replaced by two elegant alloy castings from which a dozen induction pipes sprout. Two black, crackle-finished filter boxes clean the air the car will breathe. Nobody ever complained about the appearance of the carburettor flat-12's engine bay; this injected version shows how it could have been improved.

The other crucial change is the fitment of Michelin TRX tyres – 240/55 VR415s on this car, though the 512i handbook indicates that smaller TRXs are possible on the front in the unlikely event that an owner requires it. Perhaps they lighten the steering.

As experience with the 308GTBi and its TRX tyres shows, this rubber change implies much more than an altered tread pattern. For a start, the wheels must change to suit Michelin's metric sizes.

The tyres have entirely different diameters from the Michelin XWXs fitted as standard to the carburettor 512. The effective final-drive ratio (there is no single final drive; the ratio is a combination of the diff ratio and that of the transfer gears which take drive from the engine to the gearbox below) is now 2.866 to one, which, with the smaller-diameter TRXs, gives the car a top gearing of 26.6mph per 1000rpm, not 27.25mph per 1000rpm as previously. The kerb weight of the Boxer is reduced by the fitment of fuel injection; it goes down 27lb to a still-considerable 3484lb.

The other way that the car is affected by its tyre change is in its suspension specification. One does not merely fit tyres of the TRX/P7/NCT variety and expect them to make the car go better. The system must be tuned to take them. As with the changes on the 308 GTBi, Ferrari is saying little. It merely quotes a modest track increase front and rear, attributable to the TRX's extra width. But it becomes certain once you drive the car that extensive testing has taken place, that bush specifications have been altered and that adjustments have been made to the ride height, and probably the spring/damper rates, to cope with the change. Thus, the Boxer is a considerably different car – different engine tune, different gearing, tyres and suspension settings.

A lot has not changed, of course. The chassis is the traditional semi-monocoque: a unitary design around the cabin with a structure of square tubing running forward and rearward to bulkheads that support the suspension. Smaller tube frames support the car's unstressed panels. It's steel for the cabin's outer panels, alloy for nose and engine covers and glassfibre for the lower panels.

Typical Ferrari interior, left, looked glamorous but was quite spare with appointments for a car so pricey. Seats trimmed in Connolly leather. Switches on centre console, above, control heating, air-conditioning and electric windows. Gearlever is shifted in the traditional Ferrari metal gate

The Boxer's super shape, which so happily shares a family resemblance with the 308 GTBi, still shows no sign of ageing in spite of the fact that it's been 10 years in production. The men from Ferrari have made no attempt to change the car to match its latest under-skin modifications; they haven't felt the need. The sole differences are a pair of (rather vulnerable) parking lights not mounted in the bumper, a grille that protrudes more than it used to and a pair of ungainly looking side mirrors in place of the teardrop-shaped single one our previous 512 test car wore. The tyres make a difference: they leave more space in the wheel-arches but make no difference to the car's considerable beauty.

The Boxer keeps its dart-like profile, especially when viewed squarely from side on, and painted all one colour, not a darker one below the waistline as some buyers prefer. The nose, with its large overhang and low spoiler, is rather blocky and heavy; you aren't surprised when you learn that the claimed Cd is 0.38 (rather worse than next year's Sierra will boast).

All that is reduced to minimum importance when you start the engine. Who cares about a little untoward body weight when there are 340 barely broken horses to push it around? And who cares if it must disturb rather a lot of air?

We decided to take this Boxer to the Teesdale district. Not only are they magnificent driver's roads here – smooth, little-trafficked, winding but capable of supporting an 80mph average if you're in a car which can touch 120mph on the short straights – but they're testing. The suspension must withstand considerable vertical displacement of the body when it is being driven hard, testing the ground clearance, and the bends are open enough for the driver to take the car closer to its cornering limits, in safety, than he can normally do on the Queen's Highway.

But first we aimed the car towards a private road we use as a handling course, where the surface is perfect and where there is no traffic at all. It showed us, in short order, what it would have taken 100 miles of 'white knuckling' to know on the open road. On its TRX tyres, the Boxer tends to oversteer as it nears the limit. It's not a conventional tail-slide oversteer though; the attitude never seems to be as total as the word 'slide' implies. It's not breakaway at all, really; it's a kind of 'give' which tightens the car's line. Of course, as you'd expect of a car with a fairly iron-willed limited-slip differential, the Boxer can threaten initially to go straight on if you tug it suddenly into a corner while accelerating too early.

But it turns in beautifully, and at high speed, on neutral or trailing throttle, and it can absorb a stunning amount of its 340bhp afterward. In fact, it takes a trot in one like this to show just why cars with lots of power are faster through corners than those with the same ultimate stickability but not much urge.

With the Boxer you turn in fast, feed power to the point where the TRX treads are beginning to creep outward. As the car turns and you widen the curve to exit, the tyres can absorb more power. Horsepower allows you to hold a good chassis at the limit of its roadholding for a greater proportion of the corner's length; it thrusts you down the straights like a cannonball.

The Boxer is a back-off oversteerer with fast reflexes. It's one of those cars which feels as if it has infinite grip when cornering under power but needs care if throttling off is contemplated when you're near the limit. It can slide at the rear for a fairly long way before your hastily applied correction has full effect – but you shouldn't need to contemplate massive use of engine braking in mid-corner if you're driving well. What is nice about the characteristic is that it is instant and quite exaggerated. You don't back right off; you need only ease the pedal to tighten the nose.

There's another reason why the Boxer needs high-order throttle control. The engine has very little flywheel effect, so you cannot rely on inertia to keep the engine revs as high as you want them when changing up or down. As you change up at, say, 5000rpm in third, you must use your right foot to see that the engine is turning at 4100-4200rpm in the next ratio, otherwise the gearchange will not be smooth. The skill is needed even more in the lower gears, most of all first-to-second.

This need for a delicate foot shows up when you're running performance figures. That first-to-second change, through a dog-leg and needing unusually good throttle management, is all-important to the Boxer's 0-60mph time. Using a precise but near-new

Berlinetta Boxer was styled by Pininfarina and was first shown in 1971, to much acclaim. But it would take Ferrari two years to get this complex car into production

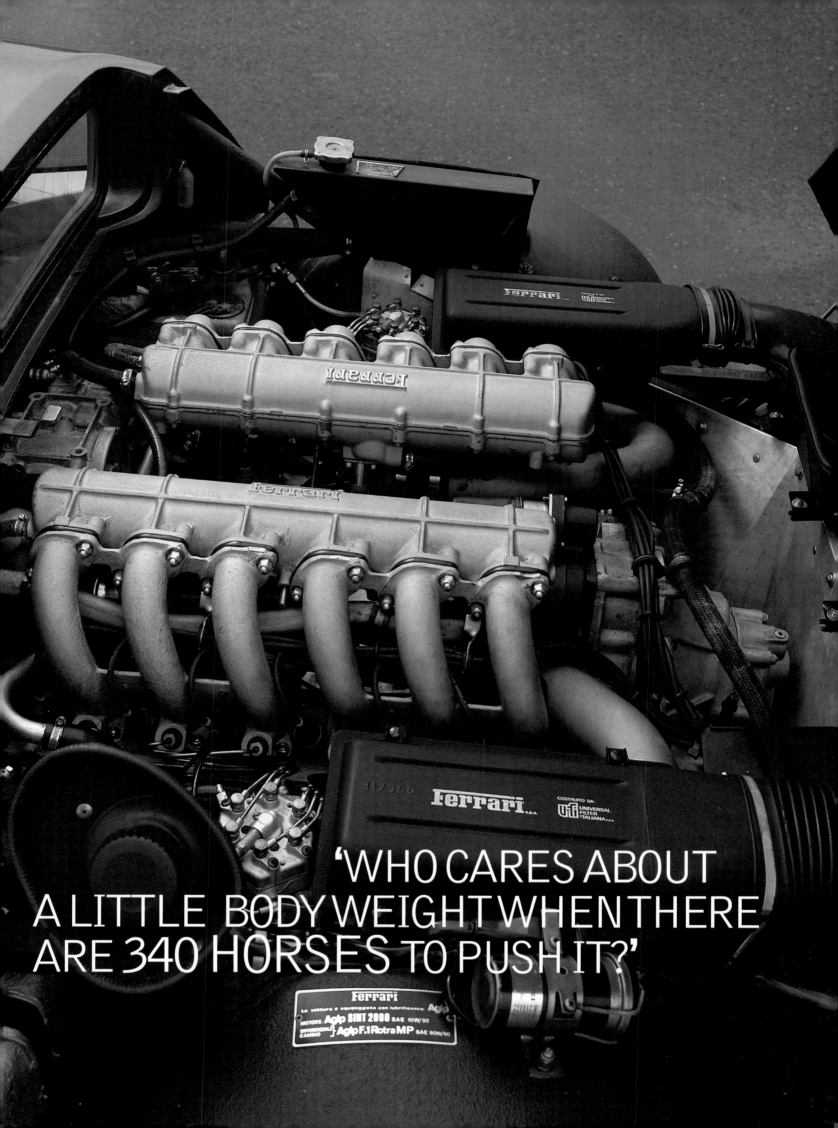

'WHO CARES ABOUT A LITTLE BODY WEIGHT WHEN THERE ARE 340 HORSES TO PUSH IT?'

(2000 miles old) gearshift, we were able to record consistent 5.8sec times, with a freakish best of 5.5sec, the same time as we've recorded for a Lotus Turbo Esprit and a whisker slower than a recent Aston Martin Vantage. At 100mph in 13.3sec, it is slower than the Vantage by 0.7sec but within a whisker of the times of both a carburettor 512 and a 4.0-litre Lamborghini Countach S several years ago. The result is that Ferrari's claim that the injected Boxer loses little to the carburettor machine is borne out.

Perhaps only top speed suffers, because of the designers' greater concentration these days on low-end power. Whereas our carburettor 512 ran to 170mph after a lengthy wind-up, we could not get the latest car past 160mph true – in fact we'd have to say that these days, Boxers are 'sluggish beyond 160mph'. That might constitute a demerit in some people's books, but it isn't in ours; the engine is far smoother than it used to be below 2000rpm; though it was always powerful down there, it was never exactly refined.

If you can handle the heavy, very precise clutch and the stiff gearchange (which needs a deft hand), you can drive this car in town. It has low-end power, it never overheats – three radiator fans see to that – and it only misfires a little and for a short time on a hard run after an hour in traffic. The noise, that rasp that becomes a howl, then a wail, then a scream, is enough to make your scalp prickle, whether you hear it from inside or out. I can't remember whether the 4.4 sounded nicer with its 1000rpm-higher rev limit, but this 5.0-litre at 6500rpm is quite the finest exhaust note I know. We listened to it a lot as we ran the car against stopwatches.

Three legs of our trip stand out. One was on a section between London and Yorkshire, when we weren't game to cruise beyond 80-85mph. The car gave an amazing 17.4mpg. Once in the Teesdale district we began to use it harder – full-out at times – and, over 220 miles, the Boxer returned 13.9mpg. In the old car we would have been in the 10s. On a run which included a burst to 160mph (on private roads) and some consistent cruising beyond 120, it gave 14mpg, which is excellent. With more than 26 gallons from two tanks, the Boxer now even has a decent range...

We spent most of one day devouring those roads of Teesdale, most often the B6277. The Boxer, frankly, astonished us. We'd expected ground-clearance problems in such a squat car; there were none. In more than 100 miles, the valance touched lightly once on a particularly cavernous dip in the road. What is more, the suspension travel was fully used yet the car bottomed not once. We gave up worrying about the effect of uneven roads, going where one might have had to watch such soft-but-sophisticated cars as a Mercedes S-class or Jaguar V12.

For the tyres, and the job Ferrari has done matching its car to them, we developed bound-

'THAT RASP, WHICH
BECOMES A HOWL, THEN A WAIL,
THEN A SCREAM, MAKES
YOUR SCALP PRICKLE'

less respect. The 512i is miles quieter than the XWX-shod cars were, and it's surprising how much that matters over big mileages. The grip on dry roads is excellent, but the TRX's two specialities – grip under braking and in the wet – were borne out by our experience. On one particularly treacherous bend, where melting snow caused a flow of water across the bumpy apex, the Boxer arrived at real speed and the driver's heart heaved, but the tyres' line was as faithful as if it had been dry.

In its dynamics, then, the Boxer is a car of greater stature with fuel injection and TRX tyres. It is more versatile, yet as good where it always excelled and just as beautiful. There seem to be no unhappy aspects of its gradual development, save for the fact that its tachometer red line is more 'normal' than it used to be. As far as finish goes, the car is getting better all the time. The panel gaps are now even smaller than they were at the beginning of '81, and more accurate. Our test car had not one rattle after 900 miles. Its solitary fault was that one of the three engine cover catches wouldn't. It merely needed adjustment. Look wherever you like under one of today's Boxers and you'll see underseal rustproofing.

On the comfort side nothing has changed. The car's surprisingly simple cockpit is trimmed in good materials which don't advertise themselves particularly well. The Connolly-hide seats remain as they were – nice-looking, comfortable for a time, but lacking lumbar and side-support when the car is generating the near-1.0g lateral acceleration it's capable of. There's been a price-hike, of course: it now costs £39,991, the price of a slightly faster-accelerating, slightly slower-cornering Aston Vantage. You decide...

IN RETROSPECT

Ferrari seemed to have dragged its heels when its first mid-engined supercar, the 365 GT4BB (Berlinetta Boxer), didn't appear until 1973, seven years after the Miura. However its fabulous 4.4-litre flat-12 and gorgeous lines left people suitably awestruck, even if the handling was seriously flawed by having an engine mounted so high. Ferrari's new flagship was slower than the 'outmoded' Daytona, too, but 170mph or so was clearly enough to compete with the Countach, and that was what mattered. The 5.0-litre BB 512 came in 1976, and was replaced in 1984 by the Testarossa. Today, the BB is rightfully re-emerging from the shadow of the Daytona.

SPECIFICATION
FERRARI BERLINETTA BOXER

Years manufactured: 1973 to 1984
Numbers made: 2323
Concept: mid-engined two-seat supercar, Ferrari's first in the 'ultimate' class. Originally known as the 365 GT4BB, later the BB 512, finally the 512i. Powered by a flat-12, initially of 4.4 litres and 360bhp, later 5.0 litres.

ENGINE
Layout: flat-12
Capacity: 365 4390cc; BB 512/ BB 512i, 4942cc
Max power: 365 360bhp at 7500rpm; BB 512 340bhp at 6200rpm; BB 512i 340bhp at 6000
Max torque: 365 311lb ft at 4500rpm; BB 512 331lb ft at 4600rpm; BB 512i 333lb ft at 4200rpm
Power to weight ratio (per ton): 365 232bhp; BB 512 207bhp; BB 512i 215bhp
Installation: longitudinal, rear-drive
Construction: alloy heads, alloy block
Valvegear: two valves per cylinder, twin overhead camshafts per bank
Compression ratio: 365 8.8:1; BB 512 9.2:1; BB 512i 9.2:1
Fuel system: 365/ BB 512 four triple barrel Weber 40IF3C carburettors; BB 512i Bosch K-Jetronic fuel injection

GEARBOX
Type: five-speed manual
Traction control: no
SUSPENSION
Front: double wishbones, coil springs, telescopic shock absorbers, anti-roll bar
Rear: double wishbones, twin coil springs/ telescopic shock absorbers, anti-roll bar
BRAKES
Front: 288mm ventilated discs
Rear: 297mm ventilated discs
Anti-lock system: no
STEERING
Type: rack and pinion
Assistance: no
TYRES AND WHEELS
Front: 365 Michelin XWX 215/70VR15; BB 512 XWX 215/70VR15; BB 512i Michelin TRX 240/55VR415
Rear: 365 Michelin XWX 215/70VR15; BB 512 XWX 225/70VR15; BB 512i, Michelin TRX 240/55VR415
BODY
Construction: steel tube, steel central monocoque, glassfibre front and rear
Weight (kg): 365, 1555; BB 512, 1643; BB 512i, 1584
PERFORMANCE
Max speed: 365 171mph; BB 512 163mph; BB 512i 176mph
0-60mph: 365 6.5sec; BB 512 6.2sec; BB 512i 5.7sec

Boxer still looks terrific a quarter of a century after it was conceived. Special Michelin TRX wheels and tyres, above, transformed Boxer's road behaviour

An unexpected supercar maker,
BMW, but in the mid-'70s it wanted
the ultimate sports car to race: the
M1, developed by Lamborghini, was it

BMW M1

By Roger Bell

IT IS AT SPEEDS ABOVE TWO miles a minute that the M1 assumes the transcendental quality that's possessed by only a handful of very special cars.

Supercars of rare breeding. It's always there, this sense of the paranormal, but it's keenest at really high speed. At 120mph, the car seems to skim the ground like a low-flying jet. Capsule-cocooned, you feel immensely safe, relaxed, loose-knuckled, fingers caressing the live rim of the firm steering. Directional control is more by telepathy than physical effort. The hedgerows are a blur; far-off objects approach unnaturally fast. Yet the car feels uncannily steady, rock solid, arrow true. The quicker it goes, the more stable it seems, the more remote the crescendo of sound from behind. At 150mph, the noise is receding. You're escaping into a dimension beyond the reach of ordinary fast cars, beyond reality it seems, as if the scene unfurling is that of a movie on a panoramic screen.

A distant hazard looms. You back off, stroke the brakes, blip down to fourth, third... Now you are merely motoring, along with other mortals, aware of the mundane that only the rarest and best of exotics can totally transcend.

Like many great high-performance road cars, the BMW M1 was sired by international motorsport regulations. Remember Group Five? This was the silhouette formula intended to revive the flagging fortunes of world championship sports car racing in the mid-'70s, when the old 3.0-litre Group Six formula was dying, discredited for want of worthy participants. Under the new formula, 400 outwardly similar cars had to be built over a two-year period to qualify the racers. Engine location and basic design had to remain the same. If the passport car had a mid-mounted straight-six, that's what the track lookalike had to have as well.

The new series kicked off in 1976, running alongside Group Six, with a terrific tussle between Porsche's competition 911, the 935, and BMW's front-engine, rear-drive 3.5-litre CSL. Surprisingly, Porsche had to work much harder than it expected to win that series. Thereafter, the rear-engined cars totally dominated it, giving subsequent victories the hollow ring of no-contest affairs. BMW had a winning engine – it always had been hot on engines – in its 3.5-litre twin-cam straight-six, good for over 800bhp with twin turbochargers. Who could forget Ronnie Peterson's tyre-burning, floorpan-glowing CSL turbo at its only Silverstone appearance, in May 1976? What BMW lacked was a decent purpose-built chassis, one with a mid-sited engine, which would outrank Porsche's outmoded, tail-heavy affair.

Enter, with awful birth pains, the M1, first all-out racer of BMW's Motorsport division headed by Jochen Neerpasch. Conceptually, the M1 was inspired by an earlier gullwing show car. Technically it broke no new ground, though in detail design it was state-of-the-art. The chassis was fabricated from square steel tubing that cradled the powertrain behind a cage-protected two-seater cabin. Dry-sump lubrication allowed the tall, 3.5-litre straight-six engine to sit upright, well down in the chassis, keeping the centre of gravity low. It also relieved cooling problems with BMW's normal canted layout. Drive to the back wheels was through a twin-plate Fichtel & Sachs clutch and five-speed ZF transaxle incorporating a 40percent limited-slip diff. Huge ventilated discs handled the braking. The coil-and-wishbone suspension, damped by gas-filled Bilsteins, was engineered around Pirelli P7 rubber, 225/50 at the back, 205/55 at the front, on Campagnolo alloys.

To avoid disrupting Munich's design and production facilities, BMW drew on Italian expertise to create the road-going M1. The GRP body – so crisp-edged and ripple-free that it looked like a steel one – was styled by Giugiaro's ItalDesign, incorporating downforce and stabilising aids as well as air intakes for the mighty engine and brakes. Transformazioni Italiene Resine produced the glassfibre skin, Marchesi of Modena the spaceframe chassis.

Lamborghini, working closely with BMW's Motorsport division, was responsible for much of the M1's design, as well as construction of the first six prototypes. The Sant 'Agata specialist was originally contracted to assemble all 400 road cars, alongside the Countach. But when Lamborghini foundered, deep in financial trouble, the M1 project came perilously close to ignominious failure. Ultimately, Ital took on the job of completing the bodies, bonding and riveting the glassfibre skins to the 195kg spaceframes. Baur in Stuttgart did the final assembly work, BMW itself the testing and quality control.

BMW had hoped to race prototype M1s in 1977 but production problems seriously delayed Group Five homologation. Meantime, what kept the M1 in the limelight was the exciting one-make Procar series that provided a strong supporting show for many Grands Prix in 1979. With big-name drivers slugging it out in identical 190mph M1s built to Group Four spec, it was a great show and a coup for the canny Neerpasch, who fought a rearguard battle to keep the M1 project afloat when it looked like sinking.

The Procar racers, tuned to give some 470bhp, were said to reach 100kph (62mph) from rest in 4.2sec. The road cars were powered by a tamer variant of the same M88 engine, yielding 277bhp. The iron block was essentially that of a 635CSi, with 93.4mm bore and 84mm stroke giving a capacity of 3453cc. Special internals included a forged-alloy crankshaft and longer connecting rods. The telling difference, though, was in the competition-bred light-alloy cylinder head, which had two chain-driven overhead

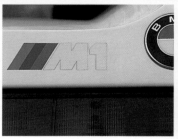

The M1 was a well-sorted car and handled extremely well, even on snow. It should have done, however, for its chassis was built to handle as much as 800bhp

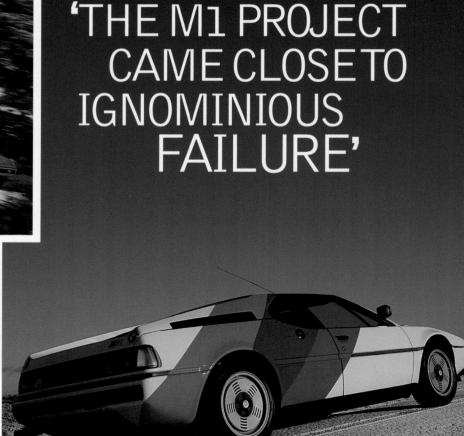

'THE M1 PROJECT CAME CLOSE TO IGNOMINIOUS FAILURE'

camshafts operating four valves per cylinder. Induction was by Kugelfischer-Bosch injection, ignition contactless Marelli. With a compression ratio of 9.0 to one, and a six-branch exhaust, power was 277bhp at 6500rpm, maximum torque 239lb ft at 5000rpm.

Out of 457 M1s built in the 1978-80 period, only six are thought to reside in Britain. It was in one of these rare cars, a 60,000-miler owned by BMW (GB) Ltd, that we headed west for Dartmoor's deserted roads. An M1 is conspicuous enough in monotone livery. Carrying the garish red, purple and blue Motorsport stripes slashed diagonally across the white body, we were to enjoy, or suffer, two days of unrelenting public attention.

Over 14ft long, 6ft across and scaling nearly 26cwt, the M1 is no sylph-like midget. For a two-seater, it feels a big car from the left-handed driver's seat. The invisible corners seem a long way off, the offside flank a lane-width away. On top of that, the rear view is obliterated by buttresses and in-filling slats. Manoeuvring is tricky, and not helped by the large turning circle.

Although ample girth gives the cabin a feeling of spaciousness, the seat has to be hard against the engine bulkhead to accommodate my 6ft frame. Taller drivers would be short on legroom; headroom, too, though seat-sink creates an extra inch or so after a few minutes at the wheel. With no more room to rake the backrest, the driving position initially seems too upright, lateral support inadequate. Some 500 miles later, I change my mind on

both counts. The pedals, pushed inwards by wheel arch intrusion, are nicely aligned, the steering wheel – a thick-rimmed three-spoker carrying elusive horn buttons – is adjustable for reach.

What does impress and surprise as soon as you get in is the high-class finish of the cloth and leather-trimmed cabin, not to mention unexpected equipment like air conditioning and electric windows and mirrors. Sumptuous it is not: black predominates, making the interior sombre if not claustrophobic. The six-dial instrument cluster, orange-lit at night, is set into a simple, crackle-finish dash panel. The speedo and tacho, redlined at 6800rpm, are totally unobscured by hands and wheel rim, though.

The big engine fires instantly, automatic enrichment avoiding cold-start tantrums. Warm-up is ragged, idling hesitant for a minute or two. At normal working temperature, though, tickover is unfaltering. Nor do long periods of idling foul the works. Despite its racing pedigree, the M1's six is soft and docile low down. You don't need to rev it. Mid-range torque belies the 5000rpm peak: in reality, there's oodles of lusty twisting effort from 2000rpm, witness the ability to slog from 20 to 40mph in fourth in the same six seconds it takes to rush from 80 to 100mph.

Punchy rather than hefty inputs are needed to throw the ZF's beefy gearlever through its unfashionable gate, with first gear – not fifth – out on a limb. Quick gearchanging is necessary, too, as the ratios are deliciously close, the engine's flywheel effect small.

BMW's Motorsport division developed the car and the engine, above, a 24-valve straight-six tuned to deliver 277bhp and plenty of torque. It didn't look it but the bodywork, left, was made entirely from glassfibre, to an exceptional standard. The chassis was of steel tube

Off the power, the revs drop smartly. The natural rhythm of shifting is so snappy you have to get back on the throttle quickly, prematurely, to avoid jerking. The hefty, twin-plate clutch needs to be dabbed decisively. Despite its sharp bite, its action is mushy, calling for precise footwork. Gearing could hardly be better, with intermediate maxima of 46mph, 69mph, 98mph and 131mph at 6500rpm, leaving a bit to come before the 6900rpm cut-out.

Five years ago, an independent two-way test verified the M1's claimed top speed of just over 160mph (the '161 BMW' registration of the UK car marks this). Even by mid-'80s yardsticks, the car still feels strong and fast. The BMW engine's great strength is the way it spreads its colossal delivery across a wide rev range; the way it lugs as cleanly and willingly as it screams, with a hard-edged wail of goose-pimple quality. Never is it less than silken. On top of that, it is surprisingly frugal. Reined in to a ludicrous 70mph, the M1 is capable of running from Dover to Nice, nearly 800 miles, on one 25.5gal tankful. That's express touring in the grandest of manners.

Grand is the word. Remember, the chassis was designed to handle over 800bhp: it's just toying with 277. Steering is a bit stodgy at low speeds, if never unduly heavy. It livens up, and lightens, too, the faster you go, wriggling and kicking gently as a communicative rack-and-pinion set-up should, bumps and camber changes nudging the big P7s into life but seldom causing them seriously to deviate. Turn-in bite is true and decisive, cornering power exceptional by normal yardsticks, if not supercar ones.

In performance terms, the M1 is not quite in the same league as the most rampant Ferraris and Lamborghinis. Nor, on its comparatively narrow tyres, is it as fast round corners, given the confines of a closed track on which to explore the limits. Handling, though, is in the super class, up with the very best. The M1's modest boots – and soft, progressive power delivery – make it supremely manageable when pushed to the limit. Roll-free poise you expect; faithful predictability, too. What makes the car such a delight to hustle along twisty roads is its marvellous fluency, its even-keeled stance, the accuracy of its steering and its impeccable balance. Dartmoor, gripped by a freeze that laced the roads with ice, provided ample opportunity to check that out, to toss the car around on opposite lock with near abandon. On

The M1's interior, right, was trimmed to a high quality, but was dark and rather austere, especially for the car's price. The instruments and controls, bottom, were well-designed, the driving position excellent

grippier roads, and at higher speeds, you take no such liberties. It's all down to the chassis then: the driver's role is simply to sit back and aim, occasionally adjusting the line by stroking the throttle. Even on the limit, overrun tuck-in is never aggressively sharp.

You would expect nothing less than immensely powerful, fade-free brakes, perfect in their weighting and response under hard application at speed. The brakes are not flawless, though. On wet roads, especially on mud-splattered ones, the front wheels tend to lock and skid with unnervingly little pedal pressure. We treated the narrow, high-hedged lanes of Dartmoor with circumspection.

For a raw-performance driving machine, the M1 is unexpectedly civilised and comfortable. This is what makes it such a magnificent road car, one you could live with for everyday motoring, no matter what your journey. For a start, it is not unduly noisy. Under hard acceleration, the snarling engine's hard-edged decibels enthral rather than intrude. True, the tyres thump over cats' eyes with a ra-ta-tat thumping that not even a Porsche could surpass. But chassis refinement is remarkably good, road roar and wind noise very well suppressed. Then there's the ride, soft and

impeccably controlled even over pocked secondaries. If anything lets the car down it's a ventilation system we could never quite regulate to relieve cabin stuffiness (the air conditioning helped).

On the track, the M1's promise was never really fulfilled, not as BMW envisaged, anyway. But as a road car it was – and remains – sensationally good, a rare meld of docility and dynamism, manners and malevolence, comfort and charisma. For all-round refinement, it would be hard to find a better supercar.

IN RETROSPECT

The M1 is now almost forgotten, but had BMW stayed in the supercar business it would have been a fair start, combining the glamour, style and handling of Italian supercars with German attention to detail. But as a motorsport venture it was a dud, failing to capture imaginations in the Procar series, and failing to beat Porsche in Group Five. The story was no better commercially – it was too expensive, and lost BMW a lot of money. Curiously, BMW hasn't stayed away from supercars completely, for it designed and built the engines for the McLaren F1, and later extended its involvement in the project when McLaren went racing.

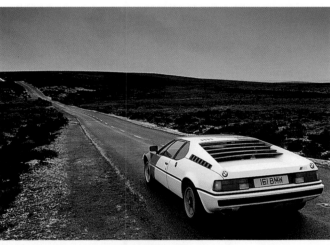

The M1 was a big car, long and exceptionally wide, making it a bit of a handful on narrow roads. Visual drama of this example is heightened by bold BMW Motorsport livery

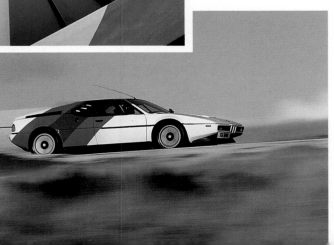

SPECIFICATION
BMW M1

Years manufactured: 1978 to 1980
Numbers made: 457
Concept: mid-engined two-seat supercar, intended to contest the Group Five sports car racing series for BMW. The rules stipulated that 400 must be homologated for road use, and a number of these were used in Procar races that supported Grands Prix. BMW contracted Lamborghini to develop and produce the M1 around its straight-six, 24-valve Motorsport engine. Acute financial trouble at Lamborghini meant that it only developed the car, ItalDesign, which styled it, getting the GRP bodies built and Stuttgart's Baur assembling the cars in Germany

ENGINE
Layout: straight-six
Capacity: 3453cc
Max power: 277bhp at 6500rpm
Max torque: 239lb ft at 5000rpm
Power to weight ratio (per ton): 213bhp
Installation: longitudinal, rear-drive
Construction: alloy head, iron block
Valvegear: four valves per cylinder, twin overhead camshafts
Compression ratio: 9.0:1
Fuel system: Kugelfischer-Bosch injection

GEARBOX
Type: five-speed manual
Traction control: no
SUSPENSION
Front: double wishbones, coil springs, telescopic shock absorbers, anti-roll bar
Rear: double wishbones, coil springs, telescopic shock absorbers, anti-roll bar
BRAKES
Front: 300mm ventilated discs
Rear: 297mm ventilated discs
Anti-lock system: no
STEERING
Type: rack and pinion
Assistance: yes
TYRES AND WHEELS
Front: Pirelli P7 205/55VR16
Rear: Pirelli P7 225/50VR16
BODY
Construction: square-section steel tube spaceframe, glassfibre bodywork
Weight (kg): 1300
PERFORMANCE
Max speed: 161mph
0-60mph: 5.8sec

TWO HUNDRED MPH IN A ROAD CAR? IT HAPPENED IN THIS DECADE, a decade in which there was seemingly money to burn and a rich supply of supercars to burn it in. Ferrari F40 versus Porsche 959, race-rawness versus silicon-chip sophistication; Lamborghini's Diablo, madder even than the Countach; Jaguar's XJ220, which shrank in the gestation: all tapped on the door of the double-ton.

This was the decade in which supercars became a clear genre, not least because there were so many of them. They permeated right through car culture, and CAR culture; where once you'd expect next month's cover to show an arresting image and pose an awkward, industry-baiting question, now the chances were that there'd be a crisp, clean picture of a bright red supercar.

To begin with, the cars were evolutions of the previous decade's offerings, one of the more dramatic being the Lotus Esprit Turbo. There was, and still is, debate as to whether this was a true supercar, given an engine of just 2.2 litres and four cylinders (we say no), but it had the looks and certainly had the pace. It fell to Ferrari, however, to ignite supercar mania with the Testarossa in 1984. Mechanically it derived from the 512 BB, but its monster body, all side striations and skeletal rear-view mirrors, became the most familiar supercar symbol of all. You could even buy a Testarossa telephone: you talked into the sump and awaited a reply from the front suspension.

You couldn't do 200mph in the Testarossa, though, nor in the turbocharged 288 GTO, which resembled a 328 but was a heck of a lot faster. This GTO, like its front-engined namesake of the early 1960s, was designed with racing in mind – something by no means normal for supercars, despite their racer-derived shapes. All the odder, then, that the car that effectively replaced the 288 GTO, and which could just about do 200mph, was designed as even more of a racer but was never intended for serious competition. Subsequently, though, the F40 has competed with some success. It helps that there are more around than Ferrari had planned. They get used, too, which wasn't the case when the F40 was new (1987) and values were going galactic in the hothouse economy of the time.

Porsche's 959 also had a competition career – a rather unlikely one as a jacked-up rally car. This twin-turbo, four-wheel-drive laboratory on wheels remains the ultimate conceptual stretch of the 911 idea, though today's 911 Turbo does most of what the 959 can do and with less complexity. Also German and with six cylinders, albeit arranged longitudinally ahead of the rear wheels rather than opposed horizon-tally in the tail, was the Giugiaro-styled, Lamborghini-assembled BMW M1.

This decade of excess ended with the arrival of the Lamborghini Diablo (it rivalled the Testarossa for extravagant use of road space) and the not-quite-arrival of a car which looked embarrassingly similar, the short-lived Cizeta-Moroder V16. Marcello Gandini styled them both, possibly on the same day. We also saw Ferrari's 348 replace the 328, and two new flings at front-engined firepower: the Aston Martin Virage, and the Chevrolet Corvette ZR-1, with a Lotus V8.

And the XJ220? It came in 1988 as a long-bodied, V12-engined prototype, gained a useful bank of orders, then disappeared, only to re-emerge as a very different car. Some customers were not amused – but that's a 1990s story. So is the Honda NSX, a 1989 illustration of what happens when Japan attempts a Ferrari. Japan succeeded rather well. The first Japanese supercar? Arguably, yes.

THE Eighties

ASTON MARTIN
Vantage

By Steve Cropley

The Vantage does not fit the modern idea of a supercar, but this traditional Brit has presence, power and performance by the bucketful. And ability too

BRD 532T

ON YOUR FIRST SERIOUS trip to the top of the Vantage's performance curve, you will make the last gearchange at 138mph. It will not occur to you until a lot later that this is as fast as a Lotus Esprit or a Porsche 944 will go, however long the road.

Instead, you will be preoccupied with pulling the gearlever cleanly back to fifth, tucking it into your thigh as the engine bellows at 6250rpm – its short-periods-only rev limit. The speedo needle, quicker with numbers than a bookmaker's clerk, will flicker somewhere the other side of 150mph.

When the power goes on in top, the nose will rise again. The car will accelerate so that twin green lines of trees either side of the road, reflected on the looming bonnet bulge, are an unbroken, flashing expanse of colour. The push will go on until you reach a true 160mph, when it will taper off. Probably, if you have only the roads available to us for this test, you will not reach either the 168mph top speed Aston Martin claims or the 165mph at which others claim to have electronically timed the car. But that will not prevent you from believing either is possible.

When your car is gathering 80 yards of road a second, concern about braking distances grows. Besides, it is surprising how little 168mph matters when you have 160mph at your disposal. It is better to take advantage of a generous space to slow down, but you know as you do so that only two or three other cars can accelerate so strongly beyond 140mph – and none can carry four people.

As you stop on a verge and get out of the car, cubic yards of exhaust beat billowing around your legs from the tree-trunk exhaust pipes below, two things will occur to you. One is that even the shortest high-speed run seems to add 30 or 40 miles to the odometer; the other that your attitude to Astons has changed.

If, like me, your familiarity with Astons grew up in the middle '70s when the company was in the hands of men more concerned with the value of the assets than with Aston's heritage, you will remember that the V8 model went unrefined and under-developed for years. They weren't very good cars then. Later, under new management, the cars were improved and the striking Lagonda saloon – after five years still remarkable for the sophistication of its chassis – was produced. Yet somehow, Astons always seemed cars whose high performance had been included not so much to be used and enjoyed to the full, but so that middle-aged-to-elderly owners would not have to work for a lack of it. Astons seemed to have a 'soft' kind of high performance that mostly suited cars driven at a fifth of their potential, inside the stockbroker belt. Right or wrong, that's how they appeared.

The Vantage has no time for this old man's stuff. It is a heavily-muscled, hard-charging extrovert, built with a surplus of horsepower and the tautest of chassis to explore the limits of speed and cornering power. Its deep nose spoiler, huge tyres, blanked-off grille and the thunder of its exhausts tell you that much.

The Vantage is a much faster version of the 'standard' V8 which Aston insists on calling a saloon. This Saloon is, of course, a coupé except when its badges say Volante. Then it's a drophead coupé. The name Saloon is doubtless to remind us that this car can carry four and is thus different from every mid-engined Italian that can crack a mere 150mph. They make Aston V8s, one a week, using techniques that amount to hand building. A bonnet, all in aluminium, is welded up from four pieces. The air extractor vent in the side of a front wing is positioned, cut and finished by one craftsman. All panel fitting is done lovingly by artisans who have been doing it for years – or by young men whose apprenticeships have been spent at Newport Pagnell.

Like all Astons, the car has its aluminium panels riveted over a steel chassis frame and superstructure. The suspension is by unequal-length wishbones, coil springs and an anti-roll bar at the front, a de Dion layout with coils and parallel longitudinal locating arms and a Watt linkage at the rear.

The front suspension has a relationship with that of the cars made as far back as the DB4 of 1959 (though there are no common parts) but the de Dion layout came with the DBS in 1967. The present cars use power-assisted rack and pinion steering (giving an unimpressive turning circle of 38ft) and their brakes are huge ventilated discs with power assistance and separate circuits front and rear. An Aston Martin V8 Saloon is distinguished as a Vantage relatively early in its three-month, 1200-manhour journey through the Newport Pagnell production process. For one thing the front suspension pick-up points are different from the ordinary car's, to provide more suitable camber compensation for the tauter suspension. Thus, the front spring – and front and rear damper – rates are stiffer. It isn't the front coils that are stiffened but the rubber bump-stops, which endow the front suspension with a rising rate. There is also a stiff anti-roll bar at the front of the car.

In the engine, the differences are few. The four twin-throat Webers are substantially bigger in choke size, the camshafts are distinctly 'hotter' than standard. The exhaust is also modified to cope with a greater gas flow – at the cost of slightly more noise. We can't imagine a Vantage owner caring about that.

The whole produces around 15 to 20 percent more power than a standard V8. Aston Martin has for years had the irritating policy of refusing to quote power figures. The habit came late in the '60s when the management felt they couldn't compete with the grossly-inflated figures claimed for torquey-but-weak US engines.

Now, when power figures must be honest, there is much less

Despite its bulk and weight, the Aston is a surprisingly agile car that rolls little, steers with precision and stops well. Its handbuilt V8 engine, right, is good for 390bhp and delivers dramatic performance, including 168mph

excuse for avoiding the issue, and one is forced to conclude that the policy has become a marketing ploy; the sellers believe that those who guess will invariably guess high. There's evidence, of course, that it has been a successful policy. In recent years, people have given that engine 'paper power' of 450 to 475bhp. In fact, 390bhp at 5800rpm has had to be stated for the German market although ludicrously, in Britain the figures are still 'not disclosed'. However, the 390bhp should be reliable enough, and informed estimates put the torque at 370 to 390lb ft at a little under 4000rpm. It's enough.

In the Newport Pagnell works, each engine is handbuilt by one of four specialist assemblers. One man does the whole job – from the stage where the alloy block arrives bare, apart from its shrunk-in cylinder liners. Everything that moves is balanced – even the water pump pulley – and at the end of the job, after an engine has been run for three hours on the bench and been dynamometer-tested for power, it is allowed to wear a small brass plaque on one of the cam covers bearing the name of the assembler.

Frank Matthews, a stocky middle-aged man and a veteran Aston employee, built the engine that usually takes the Aston Martin executive chairman, Victor Gauntlett, down the road. We know: we watched Mr Matthews at work and borrowed Mr Gauntlett's Vantage, bearing the Matthews name, for this test.

It's a typical Vantage, we were told, apart from the fact that it wears monstrous Pirelli P7R tyres of 275/55 section on each of its 7.0in alloy rims. The specification sheets say they should be 255/60 CN12s. Mr Gauntlett, along with most of Aston's staff, calls the car the 'two-ton brick'. It's a vivid, metallic blue car, squat and monstrous, but the two tons part is an exaggeration. Vantages weigh

only 38cwt. They occupy quite some road area, though.

This Aston's power, and torque, is transmitted to the rear axle through that old familiar ZF five-speed, which seems to go on forever. Even its lever knob is a link with the past. Aston Martin has been using a ZF five-speeder since the middle '60s when it decided to stop making its own four-speeder. This box is all you can get with a Vantage; there's no automatic option. In league with a 3.54-to-one final-drive ratio (inside its Salisbury limited-slip differential) the Vantage's overdriven top gear gives 26.3mph/1000rpm; the direct fourth is good for 22.2mph at the same crank speed.

The performance, as reported, is astounding. At the same time, Victor Gauntlett certainly finds it usable judging from the shredded state of his Pirelli P7s. Even with all that power, the slippery diff and the huge rear footprints make it a tough assignment to spin the rear wheels in the dry. You can do it, all right, by taking the engine to the 4000rpm torque peak and dumping the clutch, but doing it is to experience the abuse of fine machinery.

With 2500rpm and a tiny amount of slip, the car chirps off the line and arrows down the road, its engine bellowing towards the rev limit as quickly as you can think about it. Past 30mph in less than three seconds, past 40mph to the first gearchange just short of 50mph. It's a devilish, dog-leg movement and slow with it. You don't want to make mistakes with your management of this car's leviathan torque; it has the potential to bring about some monumental clunks through that transmission. Past 50mph in a mere 4.5sec (despite the difficult change) and on past 60mph a second later. You pull the lever back to third (long-throw action just a little sloppy and vintage in feel) just this side of 80mph, passed in around 8.5sec. The ton is just a number, 12.5sec from the start, and

This Vantage belonged to Aston Martin executive chairman Victor Gauntlett, who had it fitted with wider rubber than standard, making it still harder to break traction on a dry road. But power slides are possible, and at high speeds

'EVEN WITH ALL THAT POWER, IT'S A TOUGH ASSIGNMENT TO SPIN THE REAR WHEELS'

the change to fourth (neater dog-leg than the one-two change, but still slow) comes at 115mph, where the speedo reads over 120. Then it's nose high again, right up towards 140mph, where there's a gear to go and still more hard acceleration on tap. As we said, there's 160mph available on any medium-long straight; the last eight to 10mph needs a driver of icy temperament doing the investigating.

Aston says this car will run a 13.5sec standing quarter mile, and though we didn't try one, the claim falls into line with our other figures. In short, the Aston's as fast as a Ferrari Boxer, which weighs 600lb less and has 50bhp and two seats fewer. The best tuned Ferrari can add 10mph to the Aston's practical top speed of 160mph, but it ought to: it doesn't have the Aston's bluff 'pre-aerodynamics' front end. Perhaps Lamborghini's Countach S is faster, but you won't find anything else. Come to that, you won't find *any* car as fast which will carry three passengers and a set of luggage. If more than two must be carried, the Aston is a commanding winner. Scratch the Ferrari 400i. It just isn't fast enough.

Your performance need not be confined to straight lines; the handling and brakes are impeccable. When you approach a

Vantage (taking in the no-nonsense appearance of its blanked grille and deep nose spoiler) it's still hard not to be struck by its old-fashioned, upright stance. Can this big old thing compete?

It can. The chassis has all that late '70s development, the dampers and springs (and front bump-stops) match one another magnificently, and on P7 rubber the car has a limpet's grip. Two things are overwhelmingly impressive in such a monster. The first is the way it unfailingly turns in, with more dependable front-end grip than any front-engined car we can remember. The second is the way the tautness of the suspension makes rapid, reflex changes of direction effortless. A car of this weight has no right to be so agile.

This is not to confuse agility with lightness of controls or ease of driving. The Vantage needs your best efforts. Its power steering, superb right down to the shape of the wheel's cross-section, will be considered heavy by many. The ZF gearbox always needs concentration. It's not so heavy, but the driver's hand must move precisely if the correct ratio is unerringly to be chosen. The foot controls are hefty, but that merely makes them more progressive since a greater range of efforts may be applied to them. At first, the

SPECIFICATION
ASTON MARTIN VANTAGE

Years manufactured: 1977 to 1989
Numbers made: 310
Concept: big, traditional, front-engined, rear-drive supercar coupé. Less exotic-looking than Italian supercars, the Vantage could perform on a par thanks to its hulking V8 and well-sorted chassis. Always regarded as dated – the basic design ran for 20 years – the Vantage performed, and handled, better than expected, but was always overshadowed by Ferraris, Porsches and Lamborghinis

ENGINE
Layout: V8
Capacity: 5340cc
Max power: 380bhp at 6000rpm; S2 390bhp at 6000rpm; S3 400bhp at 6000rpm; 432bhp option
Max torque: 380lb ft at 6000rpm; S2 390lb ft at 6000rpm; S3 390lb ft at 5000rpm
Power to weight ratio (per ton): 207bhp; S2 219bhp; S3 220bhp
Installation: longitudinal, rear drive
Construction: alloy heads, alloy block
Valve gear: two valves per cylinder
Compression ratio: 9.5:1, S2 9.3:1, S3 10.2:1
Fuel system: quadruple Weber carburettors

GEARBOX
Type: five-speed manual
Traction control: no
SUSPENSION
Front: double wishbones, coil springs, anti-roll bar
Rear: de Dion axle, parallel trailing arms, Watts linkage, coil springs
BRAKES
Front: 273mm ventilated discs
Rear: 266mm ventilated discs
STEERING
Type: rack and pinion
Assistance: yes
TYRES AND WHEELS
Front: 255/60VR15
Rear: 255/60VR15
BODY
Tubular steel chassis and superstructure, aluminium skin panels
Weight (kg): S1 1832, S2 1783, S3 1818
PERFORMANCE
Max speed: 170mph, S2 168mph, S3 170mph
0-60mph: 5.4sec, S2 5.2sec, S3 5.2sec

brakes (fade-free) seem to lack initial bite, but when they're warm, they are progressive in a way few systems are. The car is extremely reluctant to lock its wheels, what with that massive weight and the big rubber. Yet an anti-lock brake system would sit well in the Aston. It is a happy asset for a car with 40bhp, let alone 400bhp.

That leaves the throttle. Its travel feels a foot long, in fact the first couple of Vantage miles may lead a driver to believe the car has far less power on tap than it does. Opening all those throttles takes a long, firm, deliberate movement which is as it should be if all hell is not to break loose as a consequence.

That throttle plays a huge part in the handling, of course. You can break the tail with power in practically any bend you choose below 80mph, and it's an inspiring thing to do, even if it coats the road with vast amounts of rubber dust. The quick, sensitive steering can be wielded promptly enough to hold powerslides at exaggerated angles, while the tightly reined body shows no sign of lurches or disturbing movements. The people at Aston must have driven this Vantage ferociously hard and with the utmost accuracy for many, many days during its development. It shows.

There is a price to pay for all this performance. The first is in fuel consumed. Expect no more than 10mpg when you're really using the car, and you won't be disappointed. Cruising, you'll get 14mpg.

That means with the 23-gallon fuel tank, you'll be stopping every 280 miles to put at least £30 in the coffers of the oil industry and the government. It is fashionable for timid testers to talk of the anti-social nature of this kind of consumption (and there's no doubting that fossil fuels are to be conserved) but another school of thought says that a man whose car price includes £2700 in car tax and £5000 in VAT has earned his little indulgence...

A further price is paid in noise level and the brusque nature of the engine. This is no Jaguar. There is road-patter through the floor (Mr Gauntlett's car had some experimental lead sheet and rubber sound-deadening mats in the boot) and the snuffles and roars and rumbles and whines of the engine are always heard. Even at idle, the car makes the most 'massive' sound of any in Britain. And the engine is a little unruly for a V8, too. There is no choke on the Webers; you pump them three or four times before a cold start and the running is rough for a time thereafter.

Compared with a Detroit V8 this four-cam Aston is a little intractable, too. Detroit iron usually pulls hard from 1000rpm or 1200rpm; this Aston needs 2000rpm at least and it's happier with 2500 if you're expecting it to accept wide throttle openings in high gears. For that reason, the Vantage isn't happy pulling hard in fifth or even fourth under 50mph. Nevertheless, it will rumble along in top at 30mph, as long as the throttle load is light. Of course, 5.0-litre Detroit engines are mostly ready to throw in the power towel at 4000rpm whereas the Vantage has 2250rpm left at that speed.

May the whole car be preserved. It allows Britain to lead the world in providing high-speed motoring for four. This Vantage, so venerable yet so beautifully developed, has performance to see off Porsche Turbos and 928Ss, Jaguar coupés and Ferrari 400s. It has the accommodation and space to render Boxers and Countachs all but impractical. But most of all it still provides, when other members of a rare, raw breed have passed on, agility with massive, progressive controls, and an old-fashioned, thundering power to its mile-eating. A lot of us love that kind of thing.

IN RETROSPECT

The Vantage appeared in 1977, and for the first time Britain had its own premier-league supercar. It may have looked largely like the regular Aston V8, albeit with blanked-off grille and hunkier rubber (that's still part of the charm), but underneath it was the real thing. 'Adequate' power meant as much as 390bhp, and when in 1984 CAR ran one of its celebrated Giant Tests, pitting Vantage against Boxer, 911 Turbo and Countach, from 0-100mph and over the standing quarter the Aston beat the lot of them.
It cost a few bob, mind. In early 1982, a Vantage would set you back the best part of £40,000, compared with the Ferrari Boxer's £36,700. A BMW 316 was less than six grand.

FERRARI 288
GTO

By Gavin Green

When new, the limited-edition 288
GTO was noted for being pretty fast,
pretty advanced, and pretty expensive.
Now, it's mainly remembered for being
pretty. But it was also a great drive

THE TINY VILLAGE OF GRAZZANO Visconti in northern Italy will never be quite the same again. The red Ferrari GTO, on its first day out of the Maranello factory, drove slowly into town, its exhaust burble reverberating down the narrow streets and echoing through the houses and shops.

Shutters were opened, and heads popped out. People ran out onto the streets. We pulled up in the main piazza, gave the engine a final blip, and then turned the key to extinguish the muscle of the most powerful road Ferrari of all. If Ronald Biggs rode down Fleet Street on Shergar, the look of surprise would not be any greater.

But then the amazement turned into mirth. 'G-T-O, G-T-O,' shouted a few of the locals. 'Ferrari, Ferrari,' other voices yelled, accenting the 'Rs' heavily, and rolling the vowels through their mouths with the same vigour they were using to wave their arms. We – new owner Ron Stratton and I – got out of the car and were greeted like a couple of racing drivers stepping from the winning car at Le Mans. Then we lost the Ferrari in a sea of enthusiastic youngsters, slightly more circumspect parents, curious old folk undaunted by the frenzy of the children and even three nuns –

whose sombre black and white contrasted with the colour of the crowd.

The owner of the restaurant that bordered the piazza offered us wine, 'or perhaps some other aperitif – with my compliments', while some parents ran to get their cameras to photograph their children with the Ferrari. Instamatics were clicking while parents entreated their children, standing bright-eyed in front of whatever corner of the car was free, to straighten their shirts and tidy their hair. Grazzano Visconti's other tourist attractions – and it is a very pretty village, owned in its entirety by the late Italian film director Luchino Visconti – were ignored. Nothing could have usurped that Ferrari GTO that day. The new scarlet paintwork shone brightly, and set off to perfection the lines of the most beautiful supercar of all.

The car even halted a wedding procession. Just as the happy couple were being chauffeur-driven through the piazza, the crowd caused the driver to stop his white Mercedes. So Mr and Mrs Newly-Weds got out of the bridal Benz and proceeded to pose in front of the GTO for their official photographer. The restaurant owner approached me again, as the bride and groom smiled radiantly in front of the car. 'Now I know what you are doing here,' he said, eyes beaming and hands waving. 'I have just heard. So this car is a present from the Visconti family to the happy couple!'

Eventually we had lunch in the village, before we took our

Colourful interior, above, a little confined but quite comfortable and quiet too, if the GTO wasn't closing on 180mph. Instruments, right, included a turbo boost gauge, though the driver didn't need that to verify that the 400bhp V8 was on boost

Prancing Horse and directed it north on the next stage of our run back to London. The population of Grazzano Visconti – all 280 of them, or so it seemed – lined the road out of town and waved.

About the only place on our 1000-mile drive back to London where the new GTO was not greeted with awe and incredulity was inside the Ferrari factory itself, where such sights are clearly quite common. Ron Stratton and I arrived at the hallowed gates of the Maranello factory at 2pm. Although Stratton – who runs Ferrari dealer Strattons of Wilmslow – is a Maranello veteran, it was my first visit to the most emotive name in motoring. We parked our rental car and went into the reception, where some hefty Rocky Marciano lookalikes questioned us from behind a glass security screen. When it became clear we had more love for Red Sports Cars than the Red Brigade, they greeted us with big smiles and asked us to wait a few moments.

As anyone who deals regularly with Italian companies knows, 'a few moments' can mean anything from a couple of minutes to some time next year, but in this case Ferrari was to show Daimler-Benz-like efficiency. Stratton, complete with personal banker's draft for £59,690 ('that includes air-conditioning and power windows, which are £250 extra') was quickly relieved of his money and quickly escorted through a large showroom – complete with the ex-René Arnoux Formula One racer and another GTO – to a garage behind. And there, parked behind a Testarossa, was the car.

It did look magnificent. A mechanic was adjusting the tyre pressures of the huge Goodyear NCT rubber – 225/50VR16s at the front, 255/50VR16s at the rear – while the Ferrari man gave Stratton a quick run-down on the car. One thing soon became obvious: the selection of tapes Stratton had brought with him from London would be useless, for an unsightly rectangle of plastic occupied the space where Ron had expected to find a radio. 'A radio-cassette player is an option', explained the Ferrari man, 'although we do fit the speakers and the wiring as standard.' 'What do you expect for your 60 grand?' replied Stratton, half serious.

But the man was genuinely excited and pleased, and who could blame him as he clambered down into the low seating position for the first time and felt that lovely three-spoke Momo steering wheel and savoured the comprehensive cluster of instruments. From the outside, the car is even more impressive – its vast wheel-arch flares, those huge tyres, the scoops and slats lending it extra drama compared to the 308GTB, but without losing the delicacy of the lesser car. Not that you'd get the two confused. The GTO, which has totally different panels from the GTB apart from its aluminium doors, looks far more muscular. As we drove across Europe, few people mistook the GTO for a lesser Ferrari. The size of Stratton's cheque was further testimony to their differences.

Ferrari has made only 200 customer GTOs. Built ostensibly as a Group B racing sports car – 200 is the minimum number needed for homologation – but bought more commonly as a road machine or investment, the GTO is probably the fastest road car Ferrari has ever built. Far more practical than any racing Ferrari sports car of the past – it has a fairly luxurious interior, and is a very easy car to drive in traffic – the GTO is already regarded as an all-time classic Ferrari. Thanks partly to its limited volume, it's one of the most valuable, too. Stratton's machine probably doubled in value before he even saw it.

288 GTO was loosely based around the standard 328 GTB of the day, but the use of composite body panels, then a great novelty, enabled it to be 250lb lighter and a lot more powerful. It was also better looking

Not only is the car one of Ferrari's most valuable, it is one of its most technically interesting. It is the first Ferrari road car to make extensive use of plastic composites, and the first road Ferrari to use turbocharging. The body is made of glassfibre composite with the exception of the doors. The tail and rear bulkhead are made of a Kevlar composite. Despite being longer and wider than the GTB, and despite having heavier mechanicals, the GTO is 250lb lighter. The lightweight plastics technology is the work, mainly, of British engineer Doctor Harvey Postlethwaite.

The engine is based on the 3.0-litre quattrovalvole V8 used in the 308 GTB and Mondial, but much modified. In order to make the GTO qualify for Group B racing, the capacity is reduced to 2855cc (when you multiply the engine capacity by the constant of 1.4, which is applicable to turbo engines, you can see that the GTO just sneaks in below the 4.0-litre class limit). The engine is also turned 90deg compared with the GTB unit, so that it is placed longitudinally. The five-speed gearbox is in-line behind the engine, in the best racing-car fashion. As a result, there is no rear boot in the GTO. Stratton warned me to pack lightly for the trip.

The all-alloy V8 is placed well forward in the engine bay, the front four cylinders hidden under the rear scuttle. At the back of the bay are the twin Japanese-made IHI turbochargers – one for each bank of four cylinders – which boost the GTO's power output to 400bhp and a massive 366lb ft of torque.

After our introduction to Ron's new rocket, we were asked to go back in the showroom, 'while we fit the numberplates to the car'. Ten minutes later, the Ferrari executive returned to tell us, 'Your car is ready'. It was out of the garage now, parked only 10ft from the electric gate of the Maranello factory. Rain was falling. Stratton was handed the keys, given a Prancing Horse key ring 'with our compliments' and was told about the box of spares in the front boot. He shook hands with the Ferrari man and climbed down through the narrow door opening to the thin driving seat. I climbed into the passenger side and bumped the rear-view mirror with my head. Stratton gripped the thick leather rim of the Momo. 'Where's the electric door mirror adjuster?' he asked, eyeing the big exterior mirrors poking from the doors like the heads of oversized golf clubs. There wasn't one. The electric windows were lowered and rain spat on the upholstery. Fingers were applied to mirrors until Stratton, clearly apprehensive, was happy. Time to go.

The ignition key is just to the right of the Momo wheel. Turn it and some red lights jump into action. Then Stratton pushed the little black starter button by the ignition key, there was a brief whirr from the starter motor and 400bhp of V8 muscle burst into action just behind the driver's right shoulder. One quick stab of the right pedal and the engine snarled like a caged wildcat poked with a stick. Not that the engine note is particularly obtrusive: you can certainly hear those four camshafts, those 32 valves and those cogged belts play their tune inside that engine-bay auditorium.

'THE ENGINE SNARLED LIKE A CAGED WILDCAT POKED WITH A STICK'

But the engine, though it rests just behind a carpeted bulkhead only inches from your shoulder, is never uncomfortably loud. The tall plastic-topped gearlever stands amid the six-fingered metal gate. Stratton grabbed the knob firmly. It went into first – which is back, and to the left – with a clunk. First gear would prove stiff throughout our *mille miglia* from Maranello to London.

The factory gate opened and, outside, the Maranello-Modena road beckoned. With only 193 kilometres on the Veglia odometer, Stratton's Ferrari was about to begin life in the outside world. The stiff twinplate clutch was engaged with a slightly uncomfortable jerk – both Stratton and I took time to master it – and the Ferrari left its home, bound for ours.

The rain got heavier as we drove out of Maranello, and out of our first conglomeration of waving fans. Even in Maranello, where Ferraris must be as common as Fords in Dagenham, they looked hard at the GTO. We travelled through the flattest part of Italy, where the sun-parched buildings rise above the verdant landscape like wooden blocks on a snooker table, to the equally flat and featureless city of Modena where Italy's supercar industry is based. The traffic was bad. Eventually we got to the Fini Hotel, after stopping three times to ask directions. Stratton, who'd been driving, looked relieved. Gingerly, with the gruff bark of the V8 bouncing through the car park, Stratton took his car into the bowels of the Fini and parked by a 308 GTB. After he left, a thick grille descended over the exit. The Ferrari man had insisted that the car should be in a lock-up garage that night. In Italy, they don't only revere Ferraris, they steal them. Stratton had heard that two GTOs had already been stolen. So we left the car and ate well and drank well and, for some reason, slept badly. The next day was fine, only a thin shroud of mist hindering the burn of the spring sun.

Speedline alloy wheels, above, added to visual drama, as did periscope-like door mirrors, right. Slats on rear deck lid, far right, needed to cool twin IHI turbochargers

It was my turn on that Saturday. The driving position is good, even though your legs are offset noticeably to the right to clear the left front wheel-arch (all GTOs are left-hookers). The pedals are well placed, with a generously sized left footrest to brace yourself when the *g*-forces get high. The little black steering wheel is set more horizontally than in most sports cars – in the typical Italian fashion, so that you can rest the heels of your hands against the lower part of the rim – and is not adjustable.

Although the GTO is 2.4in longer than the GTB, and almost 8.0in wider, it still feels wieldy and manoeuvrable when you get behind the wheel. The cockpit feels narrow, the steering wheel is small, and you feel cosy and contained in your half of the cabin. Not that it is a light car to drive; quite the contrary. The steering, with 10in of low-profile Goodyear NCTs to muscle around, is very heavy at low speed, and rather lower geared than you might imagine. You really need a strong hand to guide the gearlever into first, and then a positive hand to guide it through the other four cogs, all arranged in an H-pattern. The clutch, too, is firm, with a sharp take-up. Practice is needed to master it.

The frenzy of Grazzano Visconti and the flat plains of Emilia and Lombardy were behind us, as we headed north towards the French border. We were still in part one of our running-in routine – 4500rpm maximum for the first 1000km – but already the power of the Red Horse was obvious. Below 3000rpm, the power is not exceptional. The car accelerates, sure enough, and has excellent tractability right down to 1000rpm, even if you're in fifth gear. But there's not the low-down, torque-laden kick in the small of

the back which the Ferrari Boxer and the Testarossa can deliver. At around 2000rpm, when accelerating, the little turbo gauge – black, with orange markings like the rest of the instruments – moves off its stop, and there's a noticeable helping hand from the twin puffers, already whistling quite audibly. Strong momentum is being gained, but there's still no power explosion. Wait until 3000rpm for that. Sure enough, as the thick orange needle continues its swift sweep of the rev-counter and passes the 3000rpm mark, the turbo gauge jumps to 0.8 bar – maximum boost – and the previous distant whistle of the blowers and grumble of the engine is replaced by a blood-curdling howl. The helping hand turns into a full-blooded right jab, and the GTO bolts forward with more ferocity and fire than any roadgoing supercar in my experience. The effect, as the blowers come in, can most accurately be likened to that of a Porsche 911 Turbo when the boost becomes strong. But the power jump is more savage. It's as though you're in a glider in tow behind a propeller plane, when the tow rope is suddenly intercepted by a low-flying F-111. And so quickly does the crankshaft accelerate when it is aided by full boost from those twin IHI blowers that, if you want to maintain full acceleration, you need to swap cogs very quickly to avoid over-revving.

And it takes practice to swap cogs swiftly and cleanly enough to allow the car to surge on in one uninterrupted blast. The 1-2 change is the one most likely to cause trouble, particularly in a stiff new car. The other lever movements are more fluid. With practice, and without running-in restrictions, Ferrari says the GTO can accelerate from 0-60mph in under 4.9sec, can cover the standing quarter-mile in 12.7sec and won't stop accelerating until 189.5mph. Drive the car, and you believe the figures.

Not quite as impressive as the car's open-road performance, but somewhat more surprising, is the GTO's ability in town. The sheer tractability of the machine – particularly for a turbo racer – is amazing. In Modena, and then in London two days later, the car was capable of trundling around town, dicing with Fiat 500s and Minis without changing out of third gear. Vision out of the car is not bad for a mid-engined racer either.

Our view out of the windscreen, however, became far more scenic as we left the last of the Italian *autostrada* and headed north onto the roof of Europe. Ahead, hiding in a sheet of mist, lay the outline of the most spectacular mountains Europe has to offer. We kept climbing, as we drove through Aosta, heading towards the Mont Blanc tunnel. The mountains became clearer, sharper, and the drops in the valleys became greater. Snow covered the tops of the mountains like pointed white hoods, and trees clung tenaciously to the sides of the hills, temporarily free of the heavy snow with which they had been encumbered only a month earlier. The road wound higher and higher. We passed a few lorries, labouring like old men up a steep flight of stairs, breathing heavily with the exertion. The Italian border guards were playing cards

GTO quite easy to drive apart from sharp clutch and stiff gearchange, and handled superbly. Turbochargers fling car forward, below, once there's 3000rpm on the rev counter

and paid us no attention. So were the French. So we passed through the Mont Blanc tunnel and heard the Ferrari's melodious engine note change as it reverberated around the tunnel walls. If the fumes hadn't been so bad, we would have wound down the windows to savour the Ferrari V8.

We drove through Chamonix and other names better associated with white slopes than red cars, and kept well clear of the spring snow which still clung a foot deep to the roadside. We crossed briefly into Switzerland before reaching the tranquil shores of Lake Geneva, encircled by tall mountains like broad white-haired giants standing around a pond. Millionaires' homes, impressive but inconsequential compared with the rest of the scenery, fought for space on the lake's shore. In Evian, just over the French border, the Hotel de la Verniaz, with its panoramic view of Lake Geneva, fed us as only good French eating houses can.

It was raining again on Sunday. Clouds hid the peaks of the mountains and raindrops pricked the surface of the lake. By this stage we had got packing down to a fine art: Stratton's leather bag could be insinuated in the front boot, while mine – and our odd-

ments – lived on the passenger's floor, against the seat cushion. We were comfortable, if a little cramped.

We crossed back into Switzerland, drove around the east side of the lake to Montreux, and then joined the autoroute, bypassing Lausanne, before heading north-west on back-roads to the French border. Just outside Lausanne we passed the 1000km mark; we could now use 5500rpm. To celebrate we gave the car a quick burst up to 140mph, about our rev limit in fifth. The GTO was still incredibly stable and, although the engine growled, conversation between driver and passenger was still possible. Later, with more miles behind us, we tempted the GTO even higher up its performance tree: to 155mph. It was still so simple and so easy to drive, that to laud that velocity as a driving feat would be totally to underestimate the excellence of the machine. Vigilance was necessary, but not skill. Mostly, though, we cruised at between 90 and 110mph. At 110mph the Ferrari is mechanically quiet, only some wind gush and occasional tyre roar spoiling the tranquillity.

Back in Dover, after an excellent overnight stay in Le Château de Ligny, near Lille, the special nature of our steed was immediately

SPECIFICATION
FERRARI 288 GTO

Years manufactured: 1984 to 1986

Numbers made: 272

Concept: mid-engined two-seat supercar designed to meet Group B regulations in 1985. Loosely based around the Ferrari 308 of the time, the 288 used an entirely new turbocharged V8, a unique transmission and redesigned suspension. It was also novel in making extensive use of composite technologies for its body

ENGINE
Layout: V8

Capacity: 2855cc

Max power: 400bhp at 7000rpm

Max torque: 366lb ft at 3800rpm

Power to weight ratio (per ton): 350bhp

Installation: longitudinal, rear-drive

Construction: alloy heads, alloy block

Valvegear: four valves per cylinder, twin overhead camshafts per bank

Compression ratio: 8.5:1

Fuel system: Weber fuel injection, twin IHI turbochargers

GEARBOX
Type: five-speed manual

Traction control: no

SUSPENSION
Front: double wishbones, coaxial coil springs and telescopic shock absorbers, anti-roll bar

Rear: double wishbones, coaxial coil springs and telescopic shock absorbers, anti-roll bar

BRAKES
Front: 309mm ventilated discs

Rear: 310mm ventilated discs

Anti-lock system: no

STEERING
Type: rack and pinion

Assistance: yes

TYRES AND WHEELS
Front: Goodyear NCT 225/50VR16

Rear: Goodyear NCT 255/50VR16

BODY
Construction: square-section tubular steel spaceframe, composite skin panels

Weight (kg): 1160

PERFORMANCE
Max speed: 190mph

0-60mph: 4.9sec

Turbocharged engine, top, produced crushing 400bhp from 2.8 litres. Intercoolers flank sides of engine bay. Rear of GTO exposes gearbox, much of rear suspension: a fine sight

recognised by the surprisingly friendly man from Customs and Excise. 'This one of the 200, is it?' he asked Stratton, just before he asked him for a cheque for £14,668.45 – which took the total cost of the GTO to £74,358.45. Stratton handed over the cheque with more glee than I have ever seen in any man handing money over to the government. 'I just wanted to get it over with quickly.'

Now, of course, the Ferrari GTO has gone – it lives a couple of hundred miles away from me, in Stratton's showroom in the main street of Wilmslow, and I am left with memories and a notepad full of scrawl. But the car is still so clear, and so fresh in my mind. I can still feel that surge of acceleration over 3000, and the excellent cruising performance. I remember taking a series of bends in France at well over 110mph – bends that most cars would be struggling to conquer at 60. I remember my surprise at working out the car's fuel economy – a worst of 19.8mpg, a best of 21.9, both excellent. I remember the very firm ride which, on some French D-roads, made the car jerk and bob as the stiff suspension fought to conquer bumps. On a concrete section of motorway the tyre noise and the regular thump over joints prompted Stratton to

liken his Ferrari to the Manchester-to-London train.

I remember the wheel wriggling and writhing as the front tyres climbed over bumps and into holes. I remember the growl of the engine on full throttle, the cramped cockpit and the poor ventilation that made the optional air-conditioning a must.

I remember my last sight of the GTO, when Stratton dropped me off in north London on a wet and miserable Monday. It growled off down the High Street, a prince among all the pawns.

IN RETROSPECT
The fact that the GTO was conceived as a Group B racer, and that the initial run of 200 road cars (272 were eventually built) was to satisfy homologation, is now all but forgotten. So is the fact that the GTO broke the mould by extensive use of plastic composites. And the performance, although ferocious, has long been overshadowed by that of the F40.

No, the GTO is celebrated for being the most achingly beautiful of all supercars. Combine that with 190mph performance and exclusivity. What other car could have worn the GTO badge and not suffered by comparison with the '60s icon?

FERRARI
Yellow

By Ian Fraser

What's it like to be driven faster than you know is wise by a man whose job it is to do just that? Ian Fraser, the self-confessed 'world's worst passenger', on being terrified by a Ferrari tester

FASTA! FASTA! FA

PIETRO CAME HIGHLY RECOMMENDED.

He also came in a red Ferrari Mondial Quattrovalvole into which he beckoned me for a couple of laps of the Fiorano test track a few miles up the road from the Maranello factory. Pietro, the public relations man told me, spoke no English but was widely respected in the research and development department for his skill and expertise at the wheel. I would be in good hands, he reassured me as he closed the Ferrari's door and slapped the roof twice in time-honoured manner to signal Pietro, who I could now see had flashing, demonic eyes and molars that looked like Dracula fangs, to drop the clutch and GO! My yellow streak, I knew, was beginning to show luminescent through the back of my shirt.

I had just decided that I did not want to ride with this man, least of all in a red Ferrari, and was groping for the door handle to evacuate the car when it erupted forward, pinning me hard into the seat with accelerative g-forces. The buildings and the other cars and the pedestrians were suddenly a blur. I hastily decided to grope for the seat-belt instead. The new, deep-breathing V8 in the back was roaring like an Indian elephant given Madras curry powder instead of peanuts. Up through the gears – first, second, third. Sliding around the blurring corners blowing the horn; terminal panic, knee joints turned to rubber, sweat forced its way out from under my fingernails and was moistening the yellow streak too. Odd, that: lots of sweat but a very dry mouth.

When we stopped, at the factory gate, to be officially released onto an unsuspecting world, my fumbling hands could not get the belt buckle undone. My plan was to leap from the projectile while Pietro was distracted by the gatekeeper. Too late. Into gear again, more mechanical howling and we were doing 100mph in and out of the scooters, bikes, Fiat 500s and trucks. Drained of 100 octane panic, I resorted to anger. Anger at myself, the World Champion Worst Passenger and the Great Yellow Streaker, for being gullible enough to get into this position again: a passenger in anything, let alone a Ferrari with a demon driving. Cowering, cringing, croaking; my whole life was flashing before my eyes. This was it. This was the last stupid, dumb, crazy mistake because I was going to be killed by some demented Italian at the wheel of a 150mph car.

Through the gate and onto the test track in a cloud of rubber dust stripped from the tyres. The worst was yet to come and I knew it. Pietro, oblivious of my almost total lack of Italian, was chattering away and waving an arm around when it had some spare time between changing into ever-faster gears. He was clearly about to get on with the business of really demonstrating the Mondial's superiority over every other car and, the way things were going, over him as well. I tried to faint but it didn't work.

The track, purpose-built for testing road and race cars, incorporates the cruellest, most difficult corners from racing circuits around the world; exact replicas of the ones you see on TV news

A! FASTA! PASTA! PASTA FASTA!

where the famous racing driver meets his maker (or a surgeon who is good at jigsaw puzzles).

Our direction of travel was no longer forwards. The snaking bitumen was passing under the passenger's door against which I was pinned, the nose of the car pointing into the grass. Pietro The Recommended was twirling the steering wheel every which way but straight-ahead, changing gear here and there, tormenting 240 horses with the accelerator. Twitch and the world approached through the driver's door window. Twitch again and we were pointing straight down a ribbon of tarmac which the Ferrari was consuming at a terrifying rate, the speedo needle surging past 135mph, still accelerating like Argentinian inflation. Suddenly, my earlier, urgent request for Divine intervention was answered.

I trawled from the recesses of my numbed brain the word 'basta'. It means 'enough', though I have previously used it only to stop Italian waiters ladling more food onto my plate. A sort of token word spoken by the greedy to pretend they are not. 'Basta! Basta!' I proclaimed, my tongue as dry as a camel's hoof. But Pietro had at last caught up with the fact that I did not speak Italian and was about to air his English: 'Fasta! Fasta!' he joyously repeated. 'Si, si'.

The strain was too much. I turned as limp as a fiver in a washing machine. Obviously the end was near: we were doing maybe 145mph and the sharp corner was already upon us. What a way to die! The accelerator must have stuck open and the fool conducting me to eternity didn't know what to do. This would be a very

important accident. They'd talk about it around here for years to come, after taking at least a week to find all the bits.

Pietro suddenly woke up and pressed very hard on the brake pedal and slammed the gearlever around a bit. We didn't slow down in the usual way: we just abruptly arrived at a much lower speed, then went sideways around the corner with the tyres and engine rehearsing for a role at La Scala. To avoid further implied encouragement I averted my eyes from Pietro The Recommended but he needed none. 'Buono, eh?' I opted for agreement and he seemed awfully pleased. No slowing down, though, just a relentless piling-on of stark, blood-curdled terror.

Then it was all over. Just like that. Pietro, during one of his flashy gearchanges, glimpsed his watch and was overcome with panic. Flat out along the track, out through the exit, in among the cycles, the scooters, the Fiat 500s and the camions, which had regrouped since we routed them earlier, scattering chickens and pedestrians like a version of Toad of Toad Hall. In the factory gate and back to my colleagues waiting apprehensively, slithering to a stop just long enough for me to scramble clear. With an anxious wave, Pietro The Recommended and his Ferrari were converted to a red haze in the distance. 'Good grief, weren't you terrified?' asked Mr Editor Cropley. 'At first, yes, but on the way back he was great. There's no safer passenger seat than one next to an Italian driver who's discovered he's late for lunch. He'll always be terribly fast and determined, but he won't risk an accident that will delay him more.'

Reds

By Steve Cropley

The two greatest supercars of the mid-'80s were the Lamborghini Countach and the Ferrari Testarossa. This comparison took them to Wales, and then on to the Castle Combe track

WE DROVE OUT OF LONDON IN the gathering gloom, nose to tail between the snow banks that edged every road. Paradoxically, it seemed right for the purposes of a fair comparison that neither Green nor I had driven a Ferrari Testarossa before.

It was clear that the Lamborghini Countach, which we knew and admired, was going to be the underdog. If the old champion was about to head for the high jump, as we believed it was, given that every respectable car commentator had been saying so in individual tests of the Maranello car, then we wanted the bold new pretender to have to prove its supremacy every step of the way.

As we weaved among the peak-hour traffic, there seemed to be quite a good chance that neither car would get a chance to show its real abilities. Light snow was falling and though the weather forecaster on the radio spoke of dry periods in the west over the next couple of days, you could tell he didn't really mean it.

We were on the M4 by about 6pm (more than two hours after our planned departure time), resigned to the fact that any enjoyment of power and speed and agility was at least 100 miles away. Green in the Lambo was rediscovering that the car's complete absence of rear three-quarter visibility made every lane-change a gamble. And that his headlights were largely ornamental.

Leading in the Testarossa, I was having trouble with a sticking throttle. I'd squeeze the power on to pass somebody (it's all you have to do in these cars if you're determined to stay under 100) and find that the horses were continuing to strain when I'd asked them to stop. I had to hook my foot behind the pedal to check the acceleration and so lessen the intermittent danger of ramming the occasional rep in an Austin Montego.

But things improved after we stopped at the first service area. Green discovered that some extra craning of the neck to see around the huge induction hump in the engine cover gave a modicum of rear visibility. I found that the weight of my foot on the clutch footrest had been jamming a rod which runs from a right-hand-drive Testarossa's throttle pedal across to the car's centre tunnel. As soon as I learned to rest my clutch foot with greater delicacy, the problem vanished. But I couldn't help thinking that someone less fortunate might never reach my point of discovery, but would bury themselves into the Armco instead.

Our plan was to peel off the M4 just above Cardiff, taking the fondly remembered A470 up through Brecon and Rhayader to its junction with the A44, which would carry us westward to Aberystwyth on the coast. Our art direction and photography types would already have established themselves in the Hotel Grand Belle Vue, on the seafront, having left much earlier in the day by Ford Granada. From there, the following morning, we would curl upwards for a time, then cruise back to the south-east, to the Severn Bridge and to Castle Combe racing circuit where we planned to show the cars some real speed and load.

It was the middle of the evening when we reached the better parts of the A470, beyond the well trafficked dual carriageways where policemen in BMWs were prowling. Despite the fact that we had stopped for an evening meal of molten fat-with-sausages-and-beans, standard British motorway nourishment, we felt wide awake and very good about the fact that we had shaken off the soot of the city so thoroughly.

That was when we finally began to enjoy the cars – their effortless grip and pin-sharp steering, and the surprising traction of their huge rear tyres on roads kept damp in freezing conditions by the salt. Dominating everything was the towering 12-cylinder power of both cars, carried on a pair of the most blood-curdling exhaust notes production cars ever had. At a twitch of the toe you could be carried forward at a far greater rate than your own body's muscles could ever manage, even for a fraction of a second.

Gradually honing our somewhat rusty technique and getting used to such bulky and powerful cars again, we pressed along through the curves of the A44, getting faster all the time as we began to press the cars on turn-in, then boot them to the threshold of rear-end breakaway with the power. It all felt tremendously safe, comfortable even, because we travelled line astern and tacitly grasped each other's muted excitement. The exhaust notes, rising further now, began to bounce back at us from the sides of frost-covered cuttings, to join the buzzes and whines and sizzles that are the dominating cockpit sounds of such cars.

By the time we reached the hotel, the cars had largely communicated their separate characters. Earlier, what we'd noticed were the similarities – the high levels of road rumble and the engine noises that dominated everything, the surprising wind noise, the enormous torque and flexibility of the engines and the eye-pulling power of both as they rumbled through towns that clearly hadn't seen an example of either for many a moon. Tomorrow, we'd try to get to grips with the issues that were emerging.

What, for instance, was the source and extent of the Testarossa's disconcerting tendency to tramline on longitudinal ridges, especially under braking? Did either car have a decent interior or was our initial disappointment with both justified? Did the Countach's heavy controls constitute a big problem in long term

'TOWERING POWER IS CARRIED ON THE MOST BLOOD-CURDLING EXHAUST NOTES ROAD CARS EVER HAD'

B842 MPB

or long-distance use? Had the obvious effort Ferrari had put into simplifying their car's controls damaged its character? Did the Lambo's poor driving position interfere with one's enjoyment of it? And which of the pair was quickest in tough conditions like Castle Combe's? We had two days to find out.

A warm reception awaited us in sub-zero Aberystwyth, both at the hotel and in the street. An enthusiastic group of local car appreciators had spotted our uncertain and rumbling progress through town. They gathered around as we pulled up at the hotel. Inside, our colleagues had prepared things well. As we went into the warm, we noted in passing that not every one of Aberystwyth's car enthusiasts was male. Next morning there was confirmation. Written in a light and neat hand in the Ferrari's salt-sprayed sides was: 'Please marry me.'

The comparison between these cars is uncomplicated by the intrusion of other pretenders. The two Italians are unassailable. The Porsche 911 Turbo and Aston Martin Vantage, which used to come close, are limited because their engines are in the wrong places. The same applies to hot Corvettes or superheated German saloons or all manner of whizzbang one-offs. No other production cars have the blend of handling balance and roadholding, acceleration and top speed, style and eye appeal.

The Lamborghini is entirely the product of a few remarkable individuals. Designed in the first place by Marcello Gandini, it was painstakingly developed over years by the remarkable racing mechanic-turned-engineer, Bob Wallace, who gave up in frustration when he could not find tyres good enough for his cars. The Countach's suspension was redesigned in the middle '70s by Giampaolo Dallara for the Pirelli P7 which finally emerged (and which the car still wears). Those new low-profile boots were

accompanied in the LP500S by a 5.0-litre version of the V12 (expanded from the original production car's 4.0-litre). Then, under threat from the Testarossa, Lamborghini's new chief engineer, the brilliant Giulio Alfieri, redesigned the engine block for greater strength, replaced the sidedraught Webers with more efficient downdraughts, designed a four-valves-per-cylinder head and procured for the car a hefty power boost.

As it stands in 1986, the Countach could quite well have been launched last week. It is still close to being the optimum supercar. The shape is as spectacular as ever (apart from that styling abuse, the rear wing) and apart from the fact that its cramped cockpit and poor rear vision is a little harder to tolerate this year than it was in 1974, the car's layout is still close to the supercar ideal.

The Ferrari Testarossa is a wholly smoother, more modern, more aerodynamic machine than the Lambo. It shows immediately in the drag factors: the Ferrari's is reasonable at 0.36, the Lambo's is an almost unmentionable 0.42 (without the wing, which must make it a lot worse, for all the stability it adds). What strikes you as soon as you see the Countach and Testarossa in company is the greater size of the Maranello car. It is nearly a foot longer at 177in, 2.0in longer in wheelbase at 100.4in, nearly 400lb heavier, more than 2.0in higher, similar in front track but nearly two inches wider in rear track. It is a big, big car. In overall length, the two-seater Italian is nearly three inches longer than a Sierra.

The Testarossa's basis, like the Lambo's, is a tubular steel frame. Some inner panels are glassfibre but outer panels are mainly alloy, except for the most vulnerable pieces, for example, the doors, which are steel. The suspension is by coil springs, unequal length wishbones and anti-roll bars at both ends. The rear has twin suspension units for each wheel and the brakes are big, vented discs.

Neither car has very good cockpits. The Countach's, right, is little better than kit-car-standard, and is cramped, with a poor driving position. The Ferrari suffers from poor switchgear and ugly instrument graphics

Whereas Lamborghini doesn't make encouraging noises about anti-lock brakes, Ferrari has already adopted the Teves system for its 412i, the front-engined two-door V12, and says it will be coming on the Testarossa, too. Steering is manual rack and pinion.

The Ferrari's 4.9-litre engine is the superb flat-12, now with its four camshafts driving 48 valves instead of the 24 this car's predecessor, the Boxer, had. The engine is mounted fairly high in the car because the gearbox and final drive are underneath. A clue to the fact that the powerplant's centre of gravity is a little high comes from the fact that Ferrari chose to widen its car's track to 3.5in more than the Boxer's, which used the same power unit and, in early versions particularly, lacked rear roll stiffness.

On the performance front, you'd expect the Ferrari's greater weight and size, plus its 390bhp, opposed to the Countach's 455bhp, would make it the slower car. That is not the case. The practical conclusions are that the Lambo is miles faster to 60mph (5.0sec against 5.9sec) because its first gear will actually achieve 61mph true if you pull the 7400rpm red-line. But after that, the Ferrari's better aerodynamics, and its more sensible second and third gear ratios redress nearly all of the balance. Both cars achieve 100mph in near enough to 12.9sec, a whisker short of the Ferrari's third-gear maximum (of 103mph) but well short of the 119mph the Lambo will achieve in third. After that, the acceleration continues unabated with the greater power of the Lambo unable to offset its much poorer aerodynamics. Both cars are doing 120mph in 14.5sec, as near as you can measure it, and they run on to top speeds of just about 180mph.

Practically speaking, each of these cars is as fast as you could wish. Squeeze the accelerator at more than 3000rpm in either car and any gear and it will go like mad. Over 4000rpm, each car delivers a mighty shove to the small of your back and you will discover that at least five rates of rapid acceleration are available, depending upon whether you squeeze, push, prod, shove or mash the pedal towards its stop.

But, really, it is the cabin environment and the driving factors which define most clearly the distinction between these two cars. We discovered, after complete familiarity had been established, that the two cars were like chalk and cheese, concrete and caviar, in the way they need to be driven.

The Testarossa is such a civilised car. It has a fairly soft ride which we felt was let down at times by extremes of surface roar and bump-thump from the Michelin TRX tyres. It is far firmer than a saloon car's ride, of course, but no more so than, say, a Lotus Excel's. There are times when, on undulations taken quickly, you could hope for stiffer damping – and in corners you are surprisingly aware of the car's body roll. But the pay-off is a level of comfort to your progress that won't be found in other exotic cars.

The steering is firm by saloon standards but needs no real muscle to manage. It is less direct than the Lambo's but provides a decent turning circle, which, combined with the excellent visibility (about the best there is in a mid-engined car) gives the Testarossa a real town capability. The brakes are light to use, too, but overservoed. You can't just stab them as you might a set of stoppers intended for constant serious use.

The gearchange isn't exactly foolproof. No lever which must transmit nearly 400bhp can be that. But it moves fluently about its open gate with the characteristic 'ker-snap' of other machines which use the same system. The clutch matches the rest of the car's efforts: it is light but a trifle woolly. But the Testarossa's twin-plate clutch unit does have the virtue of being a full inch greater

These were the two greatest supercars of their day. The Ferrari, above, is more cautiously styled and easier to master, but the Countach, left, is the more dramatic driving – and visual – experience

'THE LAMBORGHINI IS CLOSE TO A KIT CAR, TO BE BRUTALLY FRANK'

in diameter than the Boxer's. That will please the many earlier flat-12 owners who had to replace standard clutches in 10,000 miles.

Inside, the Testarossa is a leather lover's paradise. In the test car, the treatment was all tan with black dashboard (whose shiny top still reflected badly on the windscreen, just as the Lambo's did) and it looked luxurious, even given that this is a 15,000-mile car.

The leather bucket seats are comfortable and supportive of the body being conveyed at steady speeds, and their power adjustment combines well with the tilt-adjust (Fiat-supplied) steering column, to give a wide variety of driving positions. The driver sits higher than is usual in cars like this (because the car itself is a couple of inches higher than the norm). The car suits people of far above average height and there is plenty of legroom, too. Behind the seats there is a luggage shelf which can be used to accommodate £1000 worth of specially tailored luggage. Another 'Swiss millionaire' touch is the huge vanity mirror that pops up like a jack-in-the-box whenever you open the copious glovebox. But the Fiat switches and controls are cheaper items than the buyer of a £63,000 car is going to like, and the truly awful instrument graphics – nasty italicised figures in yellow on dark green dial faces – wouldn't do justice to a Toyota MR2. Same goes for the 'parts bin' digital clock and more dials, mounted in the ugly centre console.

The Lamborghini, once you've got over the look of it, is quite closely akin to a big kit car, to be brutally frank about it. Mind you, some people never get over the appearance. It is indisputably the more spectacular looking car of the two – we have the reactions of the crowds who surrounded it every time it stopped to go by. Invariably there would be a clump of half a dozen people gathered around the Lambo, discussing its outlandish lines. The Ferrari, in this company, rated hardly a glance, however cruel that sounds.

Inside, the dominating thing about the Countach is a lack of headroom and visibility. If you're more than about 5ft 10in, you have to slouch in the seat, bum forward, knees high, head retracted into the shoulders as far as is comfortable. The Countach's steering wheel, smaller in diameter, is on a column that is adjustable for reach, not height. Most drivers find that they do best to extend the column so that the wheel is quite close, clearing the rising knees. Then the car can be driven with elbows tucked comfortably into the sides. It sounds awkward, and is for some, but both Green and I found it comfortable enough for 200 miles at a time (which is about when you'll need to stop for fuel, anyway). Getting in and out isn't as easy as it is in a wide-entrance 'ordinary' car like a Testarossa, but there is a certain appeal in developing a way with the Countach's upward opening doors, and learning casually to insert one leg and your rump into the car before dropping into the seat and pulling your other leg in afterwards. The best thing is, as with so many aspects of this car, that it's different.

The rest of the interior is awful. If the Testarossa's is bad, this is

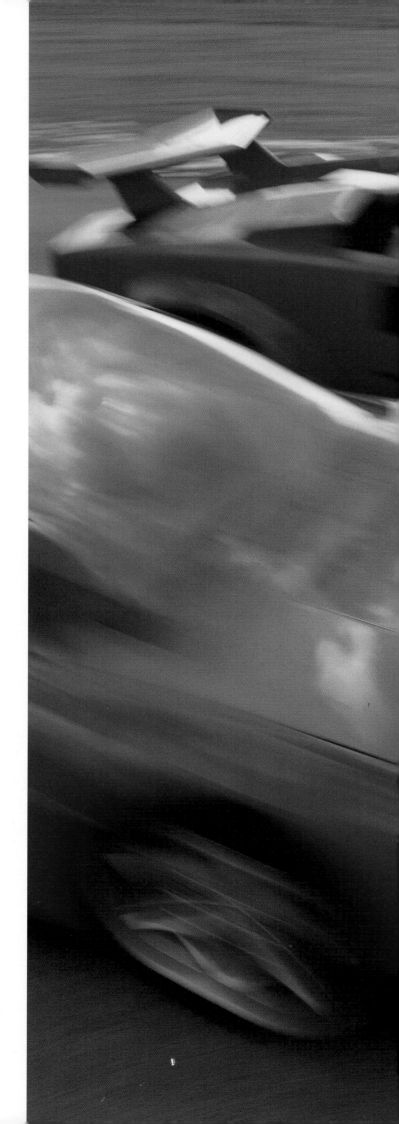

worse. Shiny black leather was the main trimming material of the test car and it just looked cheap, despite its undoubtedly hideous cost. If the Countach has aged at all, this is where it's most apparent. This, to be fair, is hardly the point of the Countach's excellence. The point of the Countach – the thing which spells its superiority over the Testarossa in my book – is the way it goes when driven at top speed, maximum effort, full noise. At Castle Combe, we found the Lambo's conclusive point of advantage.

Both cars did well. The Countach felt instantly at home, its heavy steering, gearchange and pedal efforts – and its compact driving position – suited the extreme loads of hard driving. But what told most was its superb capability over high-speed bumps and its marvellous handling balance. It turned in best, it stayed flat under serious provocation, it braked without dive and it steered quickly and with precision.

All around was noise, of course. The gears under the driver's elbow would scream in a way that would probably actually frighten the habitual driver of more staid machinery. But here it was: chassis and performance superiority from a car which should be

SPECIFICATION
FERRARI TESTAROSSA

Years manufactured: 1984 to 1992

Numbers made: 7177

Concept: mid-engined two-seat supercar, developed from its predecessor, the BB 512i. Powered by four-valve-per-cylinder version of BB's flat-12, generating 390bhp. Testarossa much wider than BB, in effort to overcome effects of high centre of gravity forced by engine location. Partially successful, but the Testarossa was always a slightly soft supercar, often appealing to poseurs rather than performance drivers

ENGINE
Layout: flat 12

Capacity: 4942cc

Max power: 390bhp at 6300rpm

Max torque: 361lb ft at 4500rpm

Power to weight ratio (per ton): 259bhp

Installation: longitudinal, rear drive

Construction: alloy heads, alloy block

Valvegear: four valves per cylinder, twin overhead camshafts per bank

Compression ratio: 9.2:1

Fuel system: Bosch K/KE-Jetronic

GEARBOX
Type: five-speed manual

Traction control: no

SUSPENSION
Front: double wishbones, coaxial coil springs and telescopic shock absorbers, anti-roll bar

Rear: double wishbones, coaxial coil springs and telescopic shock absorbers, anti-roll bar

BRAKES
Front: 309mm ventilated discs

Rear: 310mm ventilated discs

Anti-lock system: yes

STEERING
Type: rack and pinion

Assistance: no

TYRES AND WHEELS
Front: 225/50VR16

Rear: 255/50VR16

BODY
Construction: steel monocoque

Weight (kg): 1505

PERFORMANCE
Max speed: 180mph

0-62mph: 5.8sec

■ For Lamborghini Countach specification see page 52

outmoded. When the chips are down, the Countach is quicker, better handling, better braked, and nicer to drive.

After that, the Testarossa felt like a Ford Fiesta. Efforts required were light, it made less noise (but kept the pleasing ones prominent). It offered a nice, upright driving position and seemed almost airy in comparison with the Lamborghini. It rode better, too, but its steering didn't have the bite, it understeered more (before threatening oversteer with roll at the limit). Its seats lacked the proper degree of lateral support for maximum effort corners, probably in the case of easy entry and exit, and its brakes felt a little spongy after very much work. Its areas of clear superiority were its gearchange, not nearly as heavy as the Lambo's and twice as slick, and its engine throttle response. That by a whisker.

It would be easy enough to write a conclusion about horses for courses. The Ferrari is easiest to use, and still has towering performance with an excellent chassis to accompany it. But such a confrontation requires a decision, and it's quite easy to make. The Ferrari is probably the best car of the two, but the Lamborghini is undoubtedly the greater. Ferrari has shown how well it under-

stands what Americans are inclined to call 'the psychology of customer satisfaction', and the Testarossa shows how little Lamborghini thinks it matters. That will be a point in the Ferrari's favour.

But to us – to me, I suppose I mean – an exotic car is built for speed and handling and steering and going. Comfort and visibility are secondary. If you're going to have a silly car, you may as well have the silliest of the lot, especially if it is the quickest and the best-looking, by a conclusive margin.

Whenever we stopped, all eyes were on the Countach, the most outrageous looking car possibly there has ever been. Both cars have 12-cylinder engines, and both sound glorious at big revs, although the Countach's is gutsier

IN RETROSPECT

One of Ferrari's most flamboyant series production cars, the enormous Testarossa was always a bit soft for hard drivers, who preferred the better-handling Countach or, if they fancied something of more modest demeanour, the 911 Turbo. The Testarossa's problem was its high centre of gravity – because the engine sat over the gearbox - which made its high-speed handling tricky. It was also ludicrously wide. But Pininfarina's styling gave it real drama, and the flat-12 sounded like nothing else. The Testarossa has been one of Ferrari's most popular models, with over 7000 built up to 1992. The car then evolved into the 512TR, receiving major mechanical improvements, including a lowering of the engine, before finally metamorphosing into the F512M – again, essentially a fiddled-with Testarossa.

Death
IN THE AFTERNOON

At the back of the Lamborghini factory there was once a scrapyard. In it you'd find not the usual junk pile, but dead Miuras, Countachs and Urracos. So, savour this lot, and weep

By Richard Bremner

IT'S NOW MORE THAN A DECADE SINCE I VISITED Lamborghini, and stumbled across a small scrapyard tucked behind the factory. It made for a jaw-dropping sight. Instead of the battered and rusting carcasses of mundane family saloons, there were about a dozen dead Lamborghinis. Some looked remarkably complete, others were stripped, a few had been crashed. In the mud sat a Countach, bits of a Miura, several prototype Urracos, the prototype Espada, the shell of a Jalpa and a couple of the outrageous LM002 off-roaders. Fearing he'd be escorted off this shameful patch of land, snapper Tim Wren swiftly recorded the scene – you see the results here. Shortly after, Lamborghini cleared the site. A few of the cars were saved for restoration, but the rest got scrapped.

In the late 1960s, Lamborghini decided to develop a junior supercar that would sit below the Miura. Featuring a 2.5-litre V8, it emerged in 1972. The car you see above is the second Urraco prototype, which was handbuilt by Bertone. On the right in the foreground is New Zealand development engineer Bob Wallace's racing Urraco, behind that a standard Urraco and to the left, a Jalpa. Far right is the second Urraco prototype

A pile of Urraco prototypes, far left. Aluminium bonnet, left, is from a Miura. Below is Bob Wallace's race-prepared Urraco, on slicks, looking very complete. This car is believed to have been rescued and restored. The factory cat, called Lenin, lived in this Urraco prototype, and was fed by test driver Valentino, who features in the Diablo story on page 148

A technical tour de force, the 959 was a rolling demonstration of late '80s Porsche engineering. It had it all – twin turbos, all-wheel drive and astonishing pace – but lacked a soul

PORSCHE
959

By Gavin Green

ONE HUNDRED AND SIXTY MILES AN hour. Time to change into top. Move the stumpy gearlever, fitted with leather knob and gaiter, straight back into sixth. The engine pauses momentarily, then bursts back into life once the lever is safely secured into the bottom right corner of the double H-gate. And so the acceleration inexorably, relentlessly continues.

The German autobahn, once a wide motorway of hard shoulder, two distinct lanes, and a grass verge of central reservation, resembles a narrow country lane. Once straight, it now seems winding, tight. The pine trees bordering the road become an amorphous green blur. Corners that seemed a mile off are suddenly upon you. Alas, far ahead, is also a pair of lorries, labouring in the slow lane. You must back off, be circumspect. You were on the way to 300kph, 188mph – the fastest you've ever been in a car. If you had kept the throttle pedal hard down, you would soon have been there, for even at speeds above 150mph, this Porsche pulls in the horizon with unceasing vigour. But the thought of a lorry suddenly pulling out while travelling 140mph slower than you is too frightening. So, at just over a true 175mph, the right foot comes off the throttle and touches the brake. The whole car jolts slightly, as the big disc pads grip and the engine changes note, from an accelerative wail to a decelerative bellow. The Porsche still races past the lorries, doing a good 130mph.

It is not difficult to drive a Porsche 959 at these speeds. Far from it. It's as stable as a BMW at 70mph, and quiet, too. At more than 150mph, the engine – which growls and wails truculently under hard acceleration – is a distant drone. Wind noise is negligible. The tyres hum, quietly. There's no need to correct the steering to keep the rocket on path: no need to fight against side winds or minute bumps which may send lesser cars off course. In most supercars, you have to work hard at speeds over 150mph. In a 959, the most advanced and fastest production road car ever made, your role is merely that of controlling passenger.

The car does all the work, copes with most of the dangers, and transcends the limitations placed on machines with four wheels, an engine and a metal body. The effort needed to work the car up to 160mph or so, and stay there, is minimal. What you do need plenty of, though, is concentration. Daydreaming and 150mph on crowded autobahns are the stuff of nightmares.

Not only is the Porsche 959 fuss-free at high speed, it is an easy car to drive at low speed and around town. The complicated mechanical specification – electronically controlled four-wheel drive, six-speed gearbox, adjustable ride height and dampers, two sequential turbos – does not call for an unusual driving technique. Rather, the 959 is one of the easiest supercars to drive. The clutch, although firm, is far lighter than a Ferrari GTO's or Testarossa's. It is a gentle device, too, that has none of the hairtrigger snap of the normal 911's. The gearchange, gently spring-loaded towards the third-fourth plane, is short of throw, light and precise.

The steering has the same ratio as the 911's, and is servo-assisted. It is firm and sharp, yet can still easily be wielded by someone of slim build. But as with the Quattro, and other power-assisted all-wheel-drive systems, there is a curious deadness about it. The steering is sharp and responsive, but it doesn't sing in the palms of your hands in the way the steering of rear-drive sports cars, such as a GTO or a 911, does. It doesn't load up during fast cornering, follow the camber of the road, or kick back over sharp bumps. The steering, as with so many of the functions of this car, has been tamed. Similarly, the brakes do not need a particularly hefty jerk to be activated. There is almost no travel before the pads bite the four vast centrally ventilated and laterally drilled discs. Massive retardation follows. Further to help the 959's ability to putter in town, the view from the driver's seat is excellent.

Take up station behind the wheel for the first time, and a 959 does not feel intimidating. You don't sit particularly low; the car does not feel vast or heavy. The cockpit is narrow; passengers travel almost too close. The nose is not long: the front wings finish shortly in front of you. And the back of the car, crowned by an integrated rear wing clearly in view, is close behind. While the cockpit may not look very inviting – its tones are too sombre for that – it has a look of normality that many will find reassuring. There are no high-tech switches or electronic displays – the

'THE EFFORT NEEDED TO WORK THE CAR UP TO 160MPH AND STAY THERE IS MINIMAL'

Despite its extraordinary acceleration and the cruising capability of a light plane, the Porsche is fabulously stable, fabulously safe. The only problem is other traffic, which it bears down upon like a guided missile. Circumspection is a necessity

The 959 interior is remarkably similar to the 911's, but for the addition of a couple of gauges and switches. Cabin is comfortable, amazingly quiet at speed

interior is the least high-tech part of the car.

Behind the standard 911 wheel is a conventional 911 instrument binnacle, complete with familiar white-on-black analogue gauges. Only the calibrations – the speedo doesn't run out of numbers until 340kph – are unusual. Right in front of the driver is the tachometer – the largest gauge on the dash – which is red-lined at 7300rpm. There are gauges for water temperature (for the heads; the rest of the engine is air-cooled), oil temperature, oil pressure, fuel level and turbo boost. The only unusual instruments are a pair revealing the amount of lock in the two control clutches. One of these is at the heart of the four-wheel-drive system. The computerised control unit for the all-wheel drive draws on engine output (determined by boost pressure) and wheel speed (delivered by wheel sensors). It computes its findings, and sends messages to an electro-hydraulic actuator, which in turn varies the laminae pressures in the PSK control clutch, located between the gearbox and front differential. Thus, the amount of drive sent to the front axle is varied. In bald terms, when the front wheels need lots of grip, they get it. At constant speed, the front axle gets 40 percent of the drive; during full-blooded acceleration tests, the front gets only 20 percent of the drive force. The second PSK control clutch is mounted in the rear differential, for limited-slip traction-control purposes. All this may sound complicated but it needn't bother the driver. There is never any discernible hint of the drive altering between axles. All the driver need worry about is a column-mounted stalk, which tells the computer-controlled drive system what sort of conditions it is trying to master. There are four positions: dry road, rain, snow, off-road. The driver makes his choice, and the computer sorts out the rest.

There are two other unusual controls. One alters the damping, the other the ride height. Both switches are on the centre console, and each has three positions. The damping switch alters the firmness of the shock absorbers. In addition, the dampers automatically stiffen when speeds increase. The ride-height switch, which activates the hydropneumatic levelling, offers three choices of ground clearance: 120mm, 150mm and 180mm. Self-levelling

ensures that the car stays at the ride height selected, independent of load. At speed, however, the car will automatically lower itself, regardless. At more than 94mph, the 959 rides at 120mm (4.7in).

Apart from the four-wheel-drive control column stalk and the two rotary switches on the centre console, the remaining switchgear is prosaic. In typical 911 fashion, it is haphazardly arranged, and not of the finest quality. Lots of old-fashioned push-pull switches litter the dash. And the facia itself is skinned in unattractive black leatherette. Real leather clothes the door casings.

The seats are standard 911 – in this car upholstered in grey wool. Electric controls look after the driver's seat movement. Lateral support is poor: go around a corner quickly – as you're soon to do – and the tyres arrest any car body movement better than the seat controls your body. Two tiny rear seats, smaller than those fitted to the 911, snuggle behind the front chairs. Their squabs fold forward, providing the most effective stowage space in the car. The boot, in the nose, is too shallow to hold anything bulkier than a briefcase. It is noticeably smaller than the 911 trunk, owing to the intrusion of the larger fuel tank (18.8gal) and front differential.

Settle yourself behind the wheel. Feel the clutch (firm) and the gears (easily shifted). You sit quite square in the car behind a normal 911 screen and two faintly ridiculous (on a car so technologically advanced) conventional wipers. A Porsche engineer – we are at Weissach, the company's engineering nerve centre – explains the controls. 'The car is very straightforward. Have you driven a 911? Then you will have no problem. It is a very easy car to drive.' You're shown the unusual display which warns of tyre-pressure loss. The tyres are so wide, and of such low profile, that a driver may not be aware of a slow puncture: the Bridgestone rubber is of run-flat design. The fronts are 235/45VR17s, the rears 255/40VR17s. There's no spare, not even a rudimentary space-saver.

The door, of 911 design but of aluminium rather than steel, is shut behind you (it doesn't open as wide as do the doors on the 911) and the Porsche engineer, suitably clad in expensive watch and designer T-shirt, waves goodbye. The winding roads around Weissach, and beyond, beckon. No British journalist has driven

Twin switches on centre console, above, control stiffness of the dampers, and ride height. Instrument display, right, contains graphic indicating status of lock-up clutches between front and rear axles

'THERE'S AN ERUPTION BEHIND YOUR SHOULDER, AND THE 959 CHARGES'

Porsche's fastest, most expensive car, on a public road before. The gates open, and £145,000 worth of wunderwagen is let loose.

The engine, stuck out the back in typical Porsche style, wails in the normal flat-six 911 tone – although the twin turbos do soften its glorious roar. Hydraulic tappets quieten it further. First, actually known as the Ggear (for *gelande*, or super-low) is good only for 35mph; you can start the car easily in second, which stretches to just over 60mph. So far, everything is simple: you could almost be driving a Fiesta. The power, at low to medium revs, is not enormous, either. Porsche's sequential turbo system allows for one of the identically sized blowers to operate from low revs, when all the exhaust gas is directed to it, allowing it to build revs rapidly. At higher revs, the additional blower is engaged.

Below 4500rpm, a 959 feels fast, but not that much brisker than a normal 911. You can even be excused, as you drive smoothly and briskly over the twisting poorly surfaced roads around Weissach, for wondering what all the fuss has been about. Why have customers been waiting four years for one of these monsters, when a normal 911 – which costs almost only one-fifth as much, and has better panel fit and paint finish, and sounds better to boot – could be had tomorrow? Spin the engine to 4500rpm, and you find out.

Suddenly, an eruption behind your right shoulder interrupts the muted engine note, and the 959 charges violently forward. That second turbo comes in like an afterburner, and your back, nestling comfortably in the seat, is suddenly gripped by the backrest. Your head is forced rearward, too. The whole beast springs to life like a frenzied animal, surging forward with irresistible urgency. Seventhree on the tacho, change to fourth, the needle falls to just under 5000rpm and, after a momentary hesitation for the gearchange,

returns to the 7300 mark with impossible-seeming alacrity. Change into fifth, you've passed 200kph (125mph), and are going far too fast for a secondary road, so you back off. Your palms are sweating. Calm yourself, before the blast along the autobahn.

That's when the serious speed comes. That's when the silver Porsche, with a sharper, flatter nose than the 911's on which it's based, and the wider, squarer tail, will surge past superheated BMWs and Benzs and Golf GTIs and big Opels with crushing superiority. When the big powerful saloons are left behind – they disappear surprisingly quickly from the rear-view mirror – and when the road ahead is clear, it's time properly to exercise the fastest road car in the world. The 200kph at which you've been cruising becomes 210, 220, and the car is still surging forward, unerringly steady, pleasingly quiet, seemingly expending no real effort. At just over 250kph – 160mph – the red line says go no further, so you grab sixth and still the car thrusts onward. And it's still easy-going, still quiet, still accelerating strongly. This car seems to defy the laws of physics which impede lesser supercars. Every other fast car in the world struggles when grasping at higher velocities, gaining those extra mph slowly. And they've done so for the last 20 years. Not this one. This is a performance car on a different plane. At 280kph – 175mph – it is still surging ahead relentlessly, still handling its speed with unfussed confidence. You can still converse. The car remains stable, quiet. But the traffic ahead prevents you from reaching the magic 300kph. Sadly, poor weather and heavy traffic mean you never achieve it. Other magazines have, though. *Auto Motor Und Sport* clocked the 959 at 317kph, or 197mph. That's exactly what Porsche claims. Ferrari GTOs and Countachs just aren't in that league.

Wheels are made from magnesium for lightness, above. The 959's ability to bound along twisting roads like these is nothing short of astonishing

In standing-start acceleration tests, the 959 scores an even more emphatic victory over its rivals (if it has any). Helped enormously by its four-wheel drive, the Porsche can sprint from 0-62mph in 3.7sec, 0-100mph in 8.3sec, and 0-125mph in 12.8sec. It covers the standing quarter mile in 11.9sec. No other supercar even gets close. Off the autobahn, onto roads that wind through the Black Forest – roads that are beautifully cambered, wide enough to accommodate real speed, and fairly free of traffic. What traffic is encountered is dispensed with quickly. Apart from what the speedometer is telling you, other traffic is the only tangible measure of this 959's velocity. You approach slower cars like a closing missile, steering around the other vehicle at the last minute, and powering on down the road. The slower car almost instantly disappears from the mirror. And all this is accompanied by minimal wind or road noise, and a muted wail from the 2.85-litre flat-six. Even at big revolutions, when the second blower has settled into its rhythm, the engine note is nowhere near as noisy as an Italian supercar unit. You just don't get the delicious, inspirational noises that emerge from a Testarossa or Countach or 328GTB. Or even a 911. There's a growl there, but it seems distant, and restrained. The engine's relative quietness reinforces the high-speed missile impression of this machine. It's almost too good to be a normal car. It is so unlike any other ever made, in its power and in its roadholding capabilities, that it stops feeling like a car. This machine is beyond such limitations. It is an alien. It does things cars can't do.

Around large-radius, fast bends, its guided missile character is particularly evident. The 959 stays flat, its tyres avoid so much as a chirp, it handles neutrally, the steering feels strangely desensitised yet sharp, and the car just goes where it is pointed.

What it lacks is feedback. Sure, the steering is so responsive that a minor jerk would change the attitude of the car, a dab on the brake would wipe off speed almost as effectively as hitting a brick wall. Accelerate, and the car charges. Yet in steady-state fast driving the car simply goes. It doesn't send messages through the steering wheel that a camber is odd, or that the road is bumpy.

Rough patches of road are ridden with extraordinary aplomb – you feel eerily isolated from the road surface, compared with most sports cars where the slightest bump can make you wince. And then there's the quietness, of which we've already spoken. It all amounts to a strange feeling of isolation. To a feeling that this beast is so supreme a machine that the Porsche engineers have forgotten one vital ingredient: human involvement. Sure, you have to guide the machine, and you get the thrill of going safely at extraordinarily high speeds. But you don't enjoy the feeling of man and machine working together. Rather the machine does most of the work. You have to concentrate only to avoid running up the back of other cars and not falling off the road.

Obviously, some skill is needed to point the beast accurately when you're powering through sweeping roads at more than 100mph, going at least twice as fast as anyone else on the road. You need to have some idea about cornering lines, for instance. But you can let the tyres and traction take care of the grip, and the enormous torque and power of the engine take care of the go.

When you really take the 959 by the scruff of the neck, and ask it to give its all on tighter corners, you start getting a bit more attitude, and feedback. Pushed hard into a tight bend, the car will understeer quite discernibly. Back off, and the nose tightens its line, as weight is transferred up front. Forget about any nasty mid-

Porsche's detail design terrific: this silver mushroom, left, hides headlight washers. Engine, below, looks unprepossessing, but twin turbos ensure plenty of power

SPECIFICATION
PORSCHE 959

Years manufactured: 1987

Numbers made: 200

Concept: an ultimate supercar, and a demonstration of Porsche engineering. Based on the 911, the 959 had four-wheel drive whose computers governed the torque sent to each axle, electronically adjustable suspension and a flat-six spitting 450bhp – good enough to see the 959 to 197mph. Built in small numbers, the 959 was snapped up during the limited-edition supercar boom of the late '80s. A landmark of technical sophistication, but lacked the glamour of the contemporary F40

ENGINE

Layout: flat-six, air-cooled

Capacity: 2850cc

Max power: 450bhp at 6500rpm, 430bhp with catalyst

Max torque: 369lb ft at 5500rpm

Power to weight ratio (per ton): 310bhp

Installation: longitudinal, rear-mounted, rear drive

Construction: alloy block, alloy heads

Valvegear: four valves per cylinder

Compression ratio: 8.3:1

Ignition and fuelling: Bosch Motronic multi-point injection, plus twin turbos

GEARBOX

Type: six-speed

Traction control: electronically-controlled permanent four-wheel drive

SUSPENSION

Front: double wishbones, coil springs, anti-roll bar, electro-hydraulically controlled shock absorbers

Rear: double wishbones, coil springs, anti-roll bar, electro-hydraulically controlled shock absorbers

BRAKES

Front: 322mm ventilated discs

Rear: 304mm ventilated discs

Anti-lock system: yes

STEERING

Type: rack and pinion

Assistance: no

TYRES AND WHEELS

Front: 235/45VR17

Rear: 255/40VR17

BODY

Construction: steel monocoque, Kevlar exterior panels, aluminium doors and front panel, aramid engine cover

Weight (kg): 1450

PERFORMANCE

Max speed: 197mph

0-62mph: 3.7sec

corner snap, which can see a 911 charge off the road. Nonetheless you can still feel the car moving in relation to its tyres and you can feel it needing some correction. It's a pleasant experience.

Power again, and the car enters a controllable four-wheel drift, if the speed is high enough, with just a touch of oversteer. On the tighter turns, you can throw the 959 around. It is composed and stable and neat, though sideways driving is not really part of its behaviour. It lacks the handling exuberance of a GTO, even if it replaces it with handling excellence.

The 959 also lacks the design flair of the GTO. It is designed to be stable at high speed, and to cleave the air with maximum efficiency (its Cd is 0.31). It is not meant to look pretty, and it doesn't. Instead, it looks what it is – efficient, and rather soulless. The panel fit on our test car was poor, the paint finish not great. Production cars – there are to be 200 – will improve, Porsche says.

Between the axles the car looks almost identical to the 911, apart from the side skirts and the broader wheel-arches. The roofline looks the same, the glass area looks the same, the door catch is the same. To the 911 centre section are added the bits which distinguish this car from its lesser brethren: the chisel nose, the wide rear to house the engine. There are slats and ducts and holes all over. The starfish pattern magnesium alloy wheels look vast.

Open the engine cover, and visual disappointment continues. The spec sheet talks of 450bhp and twin turbos and titanium con-rods and forged light alloy pistons and Nikasil-coated cylinder barrels and four-valve water-cooled cylinder heads and quad cams and twin intercoolers. But when you open the lid, all you'll see are pulleys and belts and part of the induction system. The engine doesn't even look big, and it certainly doesn't look powerful. How

can such a little, ordinary-looking motor produce such wallop?

Efficiency, not ostentation. Speed, not thrills. Enormous competence, not character. Excellence, not extravagance. That's what the 959 is about. It is the finest fast car ever made, of that there is little doubt. No car ever built can boast its combination of speed and stability, of quietness and ride comfort. And no car has yet embraced this level of technology. Porsche, which is in the business of selling technology as well as selling cars, no doubt sees the 959 as its showcase. Look guys, this is what we can do.

Of course, the 959 is utterly magnificent. A car that vanquishes the Countach and the GTO. A car unlikely to be rivalled for years. Yet, on my way home, after a day experiencing a new motoring sensation – and of setting a personal best for maximum speed – I feel strangely unmoved. I don't really want one. Somehow, the car is too efficient, too tame, almost too good. It doesn't sing, dance, live and breathe in the way that the best Italians, and the 911, do. In its quest to make the world's greatest supercar, Porsche has forgotten to involve the bloke behind the wheel.

IN RETROSPECT

By the end of the '80s, supercar fever was at its height. Not since the early '70s had it mattered who built the fastest and most glamorous car. Porsche's contender was fastest (briefly) and remains the most sophisticated of all. No-one doubted the 959's 197mph top speed - Porsche's claims are invariably accurate - and no-one who drove a 959 said it was anything less than the finest fast car ever made. Nothing in the 10 years since this article was written has displaced it. But it did lack something. In 1987, a 959 cost £145,000. You'd pay the same today. A GTO has tripled in value. That's charisma for you.

F40

FERRARI

By Roger Bell

Perhaps the most extreme road-going
Ferrari ever, the savagely quick, limited-
edition F40 needs skill, circumspection
and bravery to give its electrifying best

AS MY FIRST TWO MINUTES in Ferrari's F40 were among the most harrowing, let's start this odyssey, at the beginning in Gifford Street, London N1, a stone's throw from the locos rumbling out of King's Cross.

This was not to be a grand-route extravaganza, or another test-track eulogy of derring-do. Those epics had been done before. Our mission: to boldly go in Ferrari's street-legal racer where no man – well, no humble scribbler, anyway – had been before. Could this car with such awesome power actually survive the frenzy of West End traffic? How would it cope with the roaring concrete of the M4 motorway, the mud-strewn B4040 to Chipping Sodbury, Castle Combe's notorious Quarry corner, the Exeter by-pass and rain-lashed Dartmoor? The fearsome speed of the 200mph F40 was not in question. We wanted to find out whether the world's fastest stock supercar, Enzo's final master-piece, could cope with the winter maelstrom of southern England, on roads we loved as well as loathed.

'I'll get you the keys,' said Stella. The nerve centre of Nick Mason's Ten Tenths operation, which commercially exploits his amazing collection of historic cars, is a huge, open-plan, steel-girdered office in the yard of a grim apartment block. Gifford Street is not one of London's more salubrious areas. The percussion instru-ments that have earned drummer Mason and Pink Floyd a bob or two in the past 21 years occupied one corner. Opposite, a RAM sin-gle-seater squatted on the carpet, next to a cluster of desks and PCs. At the far end, behind floor-to-ceiling shelves of a zillion model cars, mostly Ferraris, was the boss's lounge. Pink Floyd posters jockeyed for wall space with car memorabilia.

Stella's telephone call to Nick Mason at his Hampstead home was short. 'He won't be in for a while. Would you like to take the car now?' There were no special requests, no instructions. Just get in and go. It says something for the coolness of Mason that he was prepared to allow his latest acquisition – the first customer F40 to be delivered in Britain – to be placed in the hands of someone he'd never met. It also says something about the Ferrari F40 that a stranger can 'get in and go' after neither cockpit tuition nor perusal of the handbook – a four-language, copiously illustrated loose-leaf document that occupied half the cabin's stowage space.

There was enough room to thread a feeler-gauge between the

Roads like this, above, the F40 can bound along as if jet-propelled. Cockpit, left, like a Le Mans racer's: stripped out, simple and easy to get to grips with. Kevlar bucket seats clamp occupants in position

doors of the high-security lock-up and the Ferrari's flanks. Wouldn't someone else like to get it out? They wouldn't. The job was mine. I clambered over the wide, high sill – a sort of Kevlar RSJ which makes getting in and out very awkward – and took stock in the gloom. That didn't take long because there's not much to take in. Cockpits don't come much simpler than this. Blanket-grey cloth covers the dash, central tunnel and screen pillars, peppered plastic the roof. So much for the furnishings. The rest is bare metal and composites. Three familiar Fiat stalks handle most minor functions – lights, dip, flash, wiper, washer, indicators. Pressing the prancing stallion on the wheel sounds the horn. There's nothing special about the small, reflective instruments other than the calibrations of the 360kph (225mph) speedo and 10,000rpm tacho, red-lined at 7750rpm. Surprisingly, the boost gauge (about the last thing you look at when the turbo's blowing) gets prominence over the lubricant's temperature and pressure.

What's notable about the F40's workmanlike cabin is that it's so spartan, bereft of the fittings and equipment expected in a £16,000 car, never mind one costing over 10 times as much. To keep weight down (to less than 22cwt) there are no electric windows, no internal means of adjusting tiny outside mirrors that stare down black-hole air intakes feeding the voracious engine. There's no carpet, no interior light, not even door handles. Wire pulls release the catches. With good reason there is no radio, either.

The handbook indicates alternative lap-and-diagonal seat-belts, but Mason's car has a four-point harness that trusses your torso to a bright-red bucket seat that embraces so snugly from thighs to shoulders, it might have been poured into a body mould. Too bad if the chunky three-spoke steering wheel is a bit high: neither column nor seat are height-adjustable. Once strapped in, there's no shifting: limbs and head are free to move, but not by much.

Whirrrr. Pumps hummed from the aft bowels when I turned the key. Recalling the Ferrari 288GTO, I remembered not to twist it further but to stab instead at a rubber-faced starter button. The twin-turbo 2.9-litre quad-cam V8 fired instantly. There was no need to coax it into life with the throttle. Electronic management of ignition and injection made start-up and cold idle as dependable and untemperamental as switching on an electric shaver. The loud snarl behind my neck was steady, even, intimidating.

Another coat of paint on the mirrors and the garage doors would have scraped it off. With my left leg heaving on an edgy clutch, I crept into daylight, down a narrow alley, over a plank that prevented the snout grounding, and into the road. That was the tricky bit. Now for the excitement – and scares.

It took no more than the length of Gifford Street to appreciate the Ferrari's no-compromise competition heritage. This is no high-tech showcase like the Porsche 959. The F40 is a comparatively simple car, built simply for speed. Anything detrimental to the dynamics of performance and handling went out with the

door handles. You're immediately aware of it, too. The ride is as solid as an unsprung kart's. The stiff, all-wishbone suspension clattered and clonked on the pocked roads of London N1. Chippings sizzled against bare wheel-arches. The tyres – immense Pirelli P-Zero gumballs, outrageous 335/35s at the back – thudded and whooshed, amplified by the Kevlar sounding board.

In nose-to-tail traffic down the Euston Road, the engine – warm now, second gear just about engagable – continued to snarl malevolently with an all-eight smoothness that stop-start crawling was evidently not going to unsettle. Plug fouling is a thing of the past. In the lower reaches of its rev range, the 32-valve V8, hidden by its dominant induction system, is smooth, tractable and utterly docile. Alongside taxis it lugged without labouring at idling revs, cleanly and without stutter. The smoothness was that of flowing cream, the noise loud but not intrusive. Only on the over-run did the exhaust sound rumbly, occasionally whoofly.

Static thermometer readings indicated that the engine could take a lot more of this go-slow punishment than I. Frustration apart, the want of rearward visibility was worrying. I mistrusted the exterior mirrors' field of view and the inside one revealed more of the F40's rear superstructure than what lurked behind. The backbone of the rattly louvred plastic that passes for a rear window created a blindspot I was to curse. You change lane in an F40 at your peril. Better to be ridiculed as indecisive – humbling in the world's fastest road car – than to risk a scrape.

The A4, gateway to freedom, provided the quickest escape route. As the traffic melted, I zapped above 3000rpm for the first time. My God! The slingshot thrust was unbelievable. I slowed down and did it again. Holy Enzo! Expletives unfit for publication will help preserve the memory of that first burst of eruptive F40 power. In the blink of an eye it exploded open a 400-yard gap on

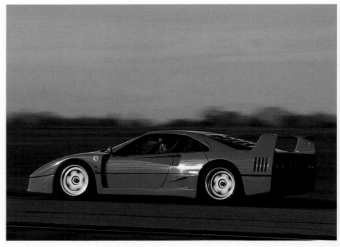

Dramatic, race-car influence in Ferrari's styling evident from any angle. Like a racer, F40 is stripped of all unnecessary equipment to limit weight

'I ZAPPED ABOVE
3000RPM FOR THE FIRST TIME. THE
SLINGSHOT THRUST WAS
UNBELIEVABLE'

'ON COUNTRY LANES
THE CAR FLOUNDERED.
A GTI WOULD HAVE
TROUNCED US'

a tail-crawling GTi. It was alarming in its ferocity, that acceleration. For a moment it felt as though the car had taken over, like an ignited rocket. Momentarily, I had an overwhelming urge to back off, just to confirm that my right foot was still in command. It was.

Fast-lane Cavaliers made shorter work of the M40 than the Ferrari. I ambled in fifth at a pace that wouldn't attract jam-sandwich attention. Besides, anything faster and I'd have needed earmuffs. The engine's smooth, deep wail was barely audible above the roar of the tyres. Catseyes sounded like kettle drums, ridges like rifle cracks. Over concrete, the F40 made the sort of racket heard in a tunnelled express with the windows open. At best it's unpleasant, at worst painful. Fully to appreciate a Jaguar's chassis refinement, you need to drive a car like the F40 which has none.

The cross-country rurals I traced from the M40 to Castle Combe began to reveal the naked truth about this formidable Ferrari. For a start, it needs space, like a combat fighter needs space. Muscle of this order demands plenty of room if it is to be flexed. On open roads and smooth tarmac (much quieter than ridged concrete), the F40 was simply sensational. By a huge margin, it is the most exciting, exhilarating car I have driven in 35 years. To reel in an empty ribbon of tarmac with nearly 500 obedient horses at your command is an unparalleled motoring experience.

Charging through the gears was heady stuff. There's no lost motion in the tall, rigid gearlever which clonks noisily through its six-barred gate. You punch it through from the shoulder, assisting weak self-centring with sideways pressure. First is out on a left-back limb, opposite detented reverse; fifth is straight through from fourth. With a practised hand the gears slot cleanly.

The F40's immensely stiff-bonded tub can handle all the power it harnesses. The steering is superb, the best I've encountered. Set the car in motion and the chunky wheel comes alive. It jostles and writhes, faithfully communicating every camber nuance, every hump and hollow, obediently responding to the lightest touch. Little effort is needed, though just occasionally, when the big tyres tramlined, it was prudent to grip the wheel tighter and nudge the car straight. Normally it would self-correct even when the wheel, delicately held to give it freedom, was flexing to and fro.

It was a different story on country lanes where vision was restricted and the verges tight. Here the car floundered, and me with it. A GTi would have trounced us, especially on sections which seriously rattled the F40's stiff suspension. Berserk kickback through the steering so jarred my wrists that I had to cling on with both hands; changing gear could wait. So great were the assailing forces that I slowed to a crawl. Composure was restored only on smooth tarmac. After that experience, I avoided roads like these.

Our pet race track was on the programme as much for photographic freedom as unfettered speed. Not that I had any intention of trying to set a benchmark time for the F40, insured by *CAR* for £350,000. By crashing that Jaguar XJR-9 at Silverstone, Jackie

Stewart did us testers a favour. He taught us a lesson in restraint. If the maestro can get it badly wrong, what chance mere mortals? Circumspection prevailed. Besides, after two exploratory laps, the brakes started to judder. Later, Nick Mason opined that the pads were too soft for track work, the cooling probably inadequate.

Without assistance, the brakes – iron-faced discs on ventilated alloy cores to contain unsprung weight – are inordinately heavy. At first I wondered if they were up to it, so feeble was their response to normal pedal pressures. Later, I learned to attack the pedal with resolution, and marvelled at their power. Only once – under deliberate provocation – did the front wheels lock on a wet road. There's no ABS, of course, but a heavy pedal, tolerant of indelicacy, is the next best thing. It also provides a solid pivot for heel-and-toe work, for which the drilled throttle was evidently designed. If it heightens driver satisfaction, Ferrari provides it.

It is perfectly correct and feasible to adjust one's cornering line at speed, by judiciously booting in more power or by withdrawing it: lift off, and the car eases onto a tighter line, still perfectly poised. It is something else, though, seriously to break the grip of

those huge rear rollers on dry roads: ensuing breakaway can be checked, but this is not a car that you naturally provoke into oversteer. If circumspection doesn't prevent it, plain fear probably will.

Wet roads are something else. Most cars can spin their wheels in first gear. The F40 will spin them in second, third and (though I hadn't the nerve to confirm it) in fourth gear as well, when the torque – all 426lb ft of it – peaks at 4000rpm. This surfeit of oomph over traction distances the rear-drive F40 from the 4wd Porsche 959, which translates power into rocketing acceleration almost regardless of what's underfoot. But let's not be sidetracked. Comparing an F40 with Porsche's wunderwagen is, on a lower plane, like comparing a Caterham Seven with an MR2. They are different sports cars, sharing ground only in what they do, not how they do it. The 959 is by far the safer, more forgiving machine, the F40 emphatically the more demanding and exciting.

Dartmoor was photogenic backdrop as well as testing ground. Getting in and out had become such a chore that I was instructed to stay put, cocooned within the Kevlar shell, while the tripod was arranged. Like the big sills, the winged seats are not shaped for

SPECIFICATION
FERRARI F40

Years manufactured: 1987 to 1989

Numbers made: 1315

Concept: mid-engined, twin-turbo Le Mans-style lightweight racer for the road. A limited edition built purely for speed and driving sensation – hence the absence of power steering and anti-lock brakes. Race-car construction ran to Kevlar central tub, composite body panels, all designed to enhance power-to-weight ratio

ENGINE
Layout: V8

Capacity: 2936cc

Max power: 478bhp at 7000rpm

Max torque: 426lb ft at 4000rpm

Power to weight ratio (per ton): 435bhp

Installation: longitudinal, mid-mounted, rear-drive

Construction: alloy heads, alloy block

Valvegear: four valves per cylinder, twin camshafts per head

Compression ratio: 7.8:1

Fuel system: Weber Marelli, twin IHI turbochargers

GEARBOX
Type: five-speed manual

Traction control: none fitted

SUSPENSION
Front: double wishbones, coaxial coil springs and telescopic shock absorbers, anti-roll bar

Rear: double wishbones, coaxial coil springs and telescopic shock absorbers, anti-roll bar

BRAKES
Front: 330mm ventilated discs

Rear: 330mm ventilated discs

Anti-lock system: none fitted

STEERING
Type: rack and pinion

Power assistance: none fitted

TYRES AND WHEELS
Front: 245/40ZR17

Rear: 335/35ZR17

BODY
Construction: tubular steel chassis, central tub in carbonfibre and Kevlar, composite exterior panels

Weight (kg): 1100kg

PERFORMANCE
Max speed: 201mph

0-60mph: 4.9sec

Twin-turbo V8 delivers a 478bhp belt in the back, above. Transparent engine lid is perspex, has louvres cut in it to disperse heat build-up

easy entry. Once you've wriggled into their cosseting embrace, though, they are supremely comfortable. So is the driving position. The slight offset of the huge, drilled pedals is not a problem, and there's a left-foot rest. Occasionally, I would drop my hands to the bottom of the wheel to relieve aching arms, but for serious motoring you adopt the classic 10-to-two position.

I read the handbook on Dartmoor, searching in vain for demisting instructions. None were found. From the three central outlets I could get volcanic heat as well as icy cool: air-conditioning is the car's only luxury. Two tiny knobs – one for temperature, the other fan speed – regulate the system. I could get nothing, though, from the dashtop swivellers, so the screen was prone to misting, a big problem when the window's shut. There's no other ventilation.

There were other irritations. The doors – locked with an absurd doll's-house key – needed a hefty slam. Access to the front 'boot' is a two-man job, so big and floppy is the hinged front body. It's the same with the engine lid: dipping the dry-sump lubrication system is not lightly done. The twin fuel fillers, feeding a single 26.4-gallon tank (good for more than 600 miles – the F40 can be surprisingly economical) are beautifully made but fiddly to unlock.

There's a nice snappy action to the three-stalk switchgear but it was too easy to extinguish (and lower) the headlights during routine night-time dipping. I did it several times. Homeward-bound, we lost the indicators and rear lights before discovering that a connecting plug had pulled out.

I barreled back to base on a gloriously clear night, cutting loose across country to the A303, turbo whooshing on the over-run like a chill wind through a chink. Dipped lights were indifferent, but main beam gave a decent range. That sprint along the A303, where the F40 was spatially in its element, was so uplifting I considered delaying its return until the following morning. I was hooked, addicted, already planning the next fix. Then I recalled how the car had snaked viciously under acceleration, catching me unawares on Dartmoor. There would be ice on the roads before the night was out. No, tonight, not *domani*.

With 950km added to the odometer I squeezed through the Gifford Street doors once again, with confidence this time. It is open to question who was most relieved to see the F40 safely tucked up – me, Nick Mason or *CAR*'s insurers. I switched off and pondered in the dark. What a magnificently absurd machine. It had thrilled and enthralled, worried and frightened like no other car in my experience. In the wrong hands, it would be lethal. Even in the right ones, it needs huge respect and understanding. As practical transport, it is seriously flawed by excessive noise, poor visibility and minimal luggage space. As raw entertainment it is the world's greatest sports car. Isn't that what Ferrari set out to make? Bullseye.

IN RETROSPECT

There were those, CAR among them, who said at the time of the F40's unveiling that it was a cynical exercise. It was a stripped-out racer that was never intended to race, not least because it probably would not have been competitive. Beside the likes of the Porsche 959 it was also mechanically crude. And it never had the sublime beauty of its predecessor, the GTO.

Its purpose may have been uncertain, but now it doesn't seem to matter. What matters is that the F40 was the first road car to top 200mph and, on the road, it served up a uniquely vivid thrill. It is now secure in the supercar hall of fame. No car says 'speed' more clearly.

IF YOU'RE VERY, VERY RICH, YOU ARE PROBABLY INSULATED from the effects of a recession that can cause serious problems for the merely very rich. How else can you explain the fact that people still buy supercars even when the financial climate is stacked right against them?

The boom of the late 1980s fizzled out as the next decade began, dampening demand for anything consumer-durable but failing to defeat the supercar. On the contrary, as the 1990s progressed, the 200mph club gained four new members. These were the production Jaguar XJ220, now powered by a twin-turbo V6, driven by two wheels instead of four and reduced considerably in the wheelbase; the Bugatti EB 110, similarly turbocharged but with twice the number of cylinders and driven wheels; the McLaren F1, as extreme and as expensive as a supercar has so far been; and the Ferrari F50, conceived (loosely) as a Formula One car for the road.

But then, maybe the McLaren is not so extreme. In an echo of the way Le Mans cars used to be road-usable – something which, ironically, fizzled out just as our mid-engined ideal supercar template was being set – endurance racing is now for cars of the GT1 class. These are very serious racers, but the rules dictate that there must be a certain number of road versions, too. So while the McLaren F1 quickly developed into a Le Mans-winning racer, companies such as Porsche, Mercedes-Benz and even Nissan have come at it the other way and devised racers with, of necessity, road-going examples as a spin-off. Supercars don't get much more super than this, as a drive in a Porsche GT1 will soon reveal.

There's been plenty else happening this last decade, though. Ferrari has recast the ill-handling 348 as the totally delightful F355, and Porsche has completely reconstituted the 911. Lotus has finally given the Esprit a V8, turbocharged for good measure, and perverse folk (like those at CAR) are now saying that the old four-pot car, particularly in purist GT3 guise, is much the better drive.

And, despite over three decades of exposure to engines mounted behind the driver, there's no sign of the front-engine layout falling from favour if the layout suits a car's concept. For example, the mighty Chrysler Corporation created the Dodge Viper, an 8.0-litre V10-powered, politically-highly-incorrect sports car to tap into the had-enough-of-do-gooding-greens mood that took root in the US a few years back; now there's a GTS coupé version, vastly better honed, and the Viper is absolutely not a joke. In a similar vein, Aston Martin gave the Virage the Vantage treatment (supercharging, this time around) with the earth-trembling results you would expect from 550bhp.

Even in Italy, the supercar's spiritual home, there remain adherents to the front-engine faith. Maseratis have been thus arranged since the early 1980s, all based on the Biturbo but encompassing vastly quick, twin-turbo-propelled coupés such as the V8 Karif and Shamal, and today's V6 Ghibli. The greatest of them all, though, are Ferrari's 456 GT and the Testarossa replacement, the 550 Maranello. A mid-engined supercar replaced by a front-engined one? If Ferrari reckons it handles better, then perhaps we should just go away and reassess our standards. Maybe the mid-engined supercar has been nothing more than a fantasy trip after all. If so, though, the trip isn't over quite yet.

THE Nineties

The Diablo succeeded Lamborghini's
Countach and gained entry to the
200mph club. Initially overshadowed
by the F40 and 959, it survives as the
most dramatic-looking supercar today

LAMBORGHINI
Diablo
By Brett Fraser

VALENTINO LOOKS AT HOME IN his office. The sleeves of his light-blue overalls are rolled up to his elbows, his sunglasses seem a permanent fixture, and he has a confident, relaxed air. And he's smiling. Not a face-cracking smile, but the contented smirk of a man who clearly enjoys his work.

Behind the smile you can see the concentration. He's a professional. And I'm pleased he takes things seriously, because I'm sitting beside him in his office and it's going pretty quickly. Around 165mph worth of quickly. On what wouldn't rate as an A-road in Britain. And I've just noticed the sign that warns of the cross-roads on the other side of the blind brow we're bearing down on. Valentino backs off slightly – we lose, oh, five mph or so.

Valentino is one of Lamborghini's development engineers and testers. His office, for today, a pimento-red Diablo. Tomorrow it could be the P140, the V10-engined replacement for the long-dead Jalpa. In the past he's worked on and in the Jalpa, Countach, and even the Miura. So I figure that if he's survived this long, in those sorts of cars, he must know what he's doing.

Despite appearances, my riding with Valentino has nothing to do with an application to join the Dangerous Sports Club. I'm at Sant'Agata Bolognese, a tiny village which lies in the sun-broiled agricultural lands between Modena and Bologna in northern Italy, home of Lamborghini, to collect the first right-hand-drive Diablo and drive it back to Britain. This car will become the Portman Lamborghini (the UK concessionaire) demonstrator, and Portman's sales director Peter Leonard-Morgan is here to sort the paperwork.

But, being Italy, there's a certain amount of confusion about the paperwork. And, being Lamborghini, our car isn't ready anyway. So Valentino is enlisted to make the wait more interesting, and demonstrate what it is about the Diablo that would make you part with £156,000.

And the demonstration is mostly about performance. Monster performance. Performance which shocks with its ferocity, startles with its force. Performance outside the realm of my previous experience. Even after a 911 Turbo or a Ferrari 348, the Diablo takes you to a new dimension. Those who know say the Countach seems tame in comparison (though those of us who know no better may well find it brisk enough). The Diablo's acceleration pins me to the thinly padded buckets, as the scenery turns to a multi-coloured blur. It's more like jet thrust than simple, internally combusted acceleration. And on the roads around the factory it's relentless, all the way up to 165mph. The Diablo just keeps going and going – Valentino claims it's easily possible on the autostradas

You can't see the bonnet from the cockpit, only the instruments and the road, which it gobbles at a ferocious rate. Cockpit, right, is confined for head and feet, but quite comfortable. Chrysler, which owned Lamborghini at the time, helped design cabin

to hit 185mph or so. The last 17mph to the Diablo's 202mph claimed top speed takes a bit too long to wind up on the public road, he reckons. Accompanying this moon-shot potency is a noise to make the earth vibrate. Going for broke, it fills your head with violent sound, pounds your eardrums to a fearsome beat. It doesn't serenade you, as would an Alfa or some Ferraris, but it seduces all the same. It commands, not asks for, your attention, and it can't be ignored. Up to 4000rpm it produces a promising rumble; there's a subtle undertone of American muscle car about it. Then the tone lowers, becomes menacing and beastly, building quickly into a hell-raising yell.

Snap gearchanges, which Valentino whips through 1000rpm shy of the 8000rpm red line (the torque's exhausted by then, and 'revving it harder does nothing for me'), have an astonishing effect. A mortar round, armed with the roaring of a jungle-full of wild animals, explodes behind your head. The explosions continue all the way up the 'box, and once you're over the shell-shock, your face bursts into an ecstatic smile every time one goes off.

Back at the factory, Valentino is proud of the engine that has excited, frightened and thrilled me. It's a development of the Countach's all-alloy 48-valve V12, increased in capacity from 5.2 litres to 5.7 litres by means of boring and stroking. Part of the reason for the growth in cube is the need to meet emissions regulations while still boosting power and torque. Two catalytic converters hide behind the longitudinally mounted engine under what looks like a bootlid; they and the sequential fuel injection do their bit for the environment, but take their toll on the engine's output. And, as Valentino says, there's no substitute for cubes.

From 5729cc, the vociferous quad-cam V12 knocks out a titanic 492bhp at 7000rpm, and 428lb ft of twist action at 5200rpm. On the road you can really feel that the torque peaks quite high, and the engine's change of tone confirms it. What isn't as immediately obvious is the pains Lamborghini has taken to ensure the Diablo isn't gutless lower down. There's a two-stage inlet manifold which promotes bottom-end torque – at 2000rpm it develops 206lb ft, enough to be going on with, even in a car weighing 1.6 tons.

More time-filling next, and a quick tour of the factory, guided by Lamborghini's grave PR boss and ex-world champion rally driver, Sandro Munari. Of special interest is the body assembly section, which, despite the institution of a proper assembly line, and a certain amount of robotisation, still relies on the traditional, time-consuming skills of hammering, filing and filling. Though assembled on jigs, Diablo bodies require a lot of handwork to get the many different sections to fit smoothly together. Therefore, each car is slightly different. The rear wings, in seven parts, doors, and front wings, are of light alloy, the roof and door shuts are steel, the centre tunnel carbonfibre, and the bumpers, sills, engine cover and (front) bootlid, a composite called Autoclave.

At the opposite end of the production process, Munari shows me the final preparation bay, where scores of Diablos, lined up like a *Boy's Own* fantasy, in every one of the 12 official colours (plus a couple extra) await last minute de-wrinkling. Although all engines are bench-tested, every car is subjected to a 90-mile test drive and shake down. So it's hard to understand why there are still some glitches stopping Leonard-Morgan and me taking our car away. Most serious is that the door mirror adjustment switch,

Diablo sits very low, left, has limited ground clearance. Makes a startling sight in any rear-view mirror. Bodywork, above, full of ducts and intakes, to feed the brakes, radiators, air-conditioner and catalytic converters

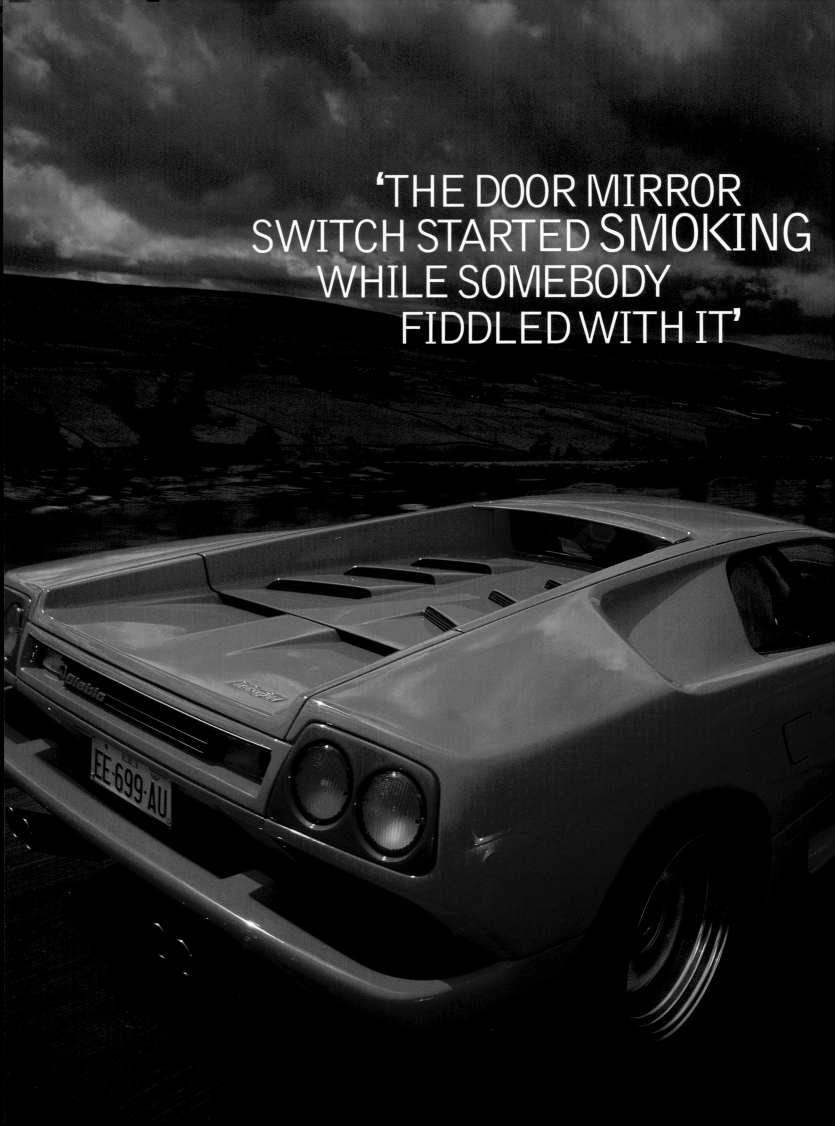

'THE DOOR MIRROR
SWITCH STARTED SMOKING
WHILE SOMEBODY
FIDDLED WITH IT'

mounted on the driver's door rest, started smoking while some-one was fiddling with it, then dropped deep down inside the door.

Still, there are worse places in which to be thumb-twiddling. Petrol-heads can get a buzz just from standing by the gates, watching completed, cling-film-wrapped Diablos scurry around the factory grounds. Gargantuan LM002s, Lambo's off-roader, occasionally appear, although production stops at the end of the year. There's a posse of Countachs, from all around Europe, standing outside, waiting to be serviced, and a time-scuffed Espada, in for restoration. Last time I was in Sant' Agata, I was 10, looking on agog as my father insinuated himself into a dramatic, waist-high wedge with upward-opening doors – the prototype Countach. Eighteen years on, it feels weird to be waiting to drive away in its successor.

Finally, late into the scorching afternoon, our Diablo is ready. There's urgency now, as one more piece of paperwork needs to be stamped at the customs office in Modena, soon to shut for the day. Quick march we chuck our modest luggage into the tiny boot, leap across the fat, leather-covered sills, and wiggle down

Diablo feels extremely securely planted at speed and in corners, left and below. Heavy unassisted steering lightens with speed. Mirrors, below, mostly reflect body

into the sparsely padded, but comfortable seats. Closing the doors – which open up, not out – requires a technique and brute force.

As we clear the factory gates, a large number of the workforce emerge to watch our departure. You'd think they'd be sick of the sight of the car, or at least bored by it, but their interest is genuine and enthusiastic. It's part of the magic of the Diablo – and we're to encounter it time and again on our trip across Europe – that people want to see it, touch it, hear it, learn about it. People feel good about it, which makes you, driver or passenger, feel good, too.

At Modena's customs office, and all around the immediate vicinity, business stops awhile, as people crowd round, ask questions, take photographs. As at the factory, the locals must see Diablos down here quite often, but it hasn't taken the edge off their fascination. Paperwork properly stamped, we strike out north on the autostrada towards Milan. I'd been warned by those who'd driven early left-hookers that, because the pedals were so closely spaced, I'd probably have to drive in my socks. But recent modifications have cured the ailment and I'm able to pedal the car in my Doc Martens. Other changes over early cars include sturdier door hinges, a revised instrument binnacle with a longer hood to shield the dials from reflections, a few small suspension adjustments, updated electronics, and a narrow, black-painted lip, running between the taillamps, to stop heat bleed scorching the paint.

Though the late afternoon is fast turning early evening as we lope along at a sedate 90mph through the flat farmland around Parma and Piacenza, the temperature is still 36degC. The steeply raked windscreen makes a fine sun trap, but fortunately the standard air-conditioning makes an equally fine fridge. However, it has to be run at its noisy highest setting to win the battle.

Much of the autostrada is concreted, yet surprisingly we aren't deafened by roaring rubber. The Diablo wears steamroller 335/35ZR17 Pirelli P Zeros at the rear, only slightly more modest 245/40ZR17s at the front. For the Swiss market it runs on Bridgestones, to comply with local noise regulations, but either our ears are less sensitive than the Swiss's, or they're just being silly.

The tyres may not roar much, but over joining strips on the autostrada they slap sharply, like rifle shots. The suspension – double wishbones all round, with transverse links and twin coils and dampers at the rear – adds to the clatter, for although it has quite a pliant ride for a supercar, it provides little vertical wheel travel.

As we strike one particularly knobbly section of road, which sends a jarring jolt through the unassisted steering, the low-tyre-pressure warning light comes on. A quick inspection of all four corners reveals nothing amiss, for which we're extremely pleased. There's no spare in the Diablo, not even a space-saver – just a can of emergency 'squirt and inflate.'

It's now so late, we decide to head into the hills between Milan and Turin to find accommodation for the night. Both these cities have an evil reputation for the theft of cars and their contents, so we're looking for a little hideaway. The small, and largely characterless, town of Biella provides a haven in the form of the Astoria Hotel, which has an underground car park.

After answering countless questions from the town's population about how much and how fast, we embark on the tricky business of getting the Diablo down the car park ramp. Tricky because the front spoiler has racetrack ground clearance, and it doesn't take much to crump it over even modestly high obstacles. You have to exercise great care negotiating garage forecourts, sleeping policemen, or any sort of debris in the road.

Early next morning we take our red devil to the nearby hilltop religious sanctuary of Oropa. The road up the hill is narrow and kinked into sharp hairpins, making it hard work in a car two inches wider than a Testarossa. In the tight corners the lack of power-assisted steering makes itself felt as a slight burning in my chest.

Apart from this weighting-up, the steering is superb, energetically direct and explicitly informative. A firm grip on the wheel is essential, though, as pot-holes can kick it out of loose hands, and the car has a tendency to tramline, owing to its clodhopping rubber. Another, more irritating, complaint concerns not the steering, but the steering wheel. No matter how you adjust the trunk-like column, which has a large range of movement for reach and rake, the fat, leather-rimmed wheel cuts the main dials in two. The short of torso will also have their view of the road ahead obstructed irritatingly by the towering instrument binnacle.

Another stamp is needed at the French-Italian border, at the mouth of the deep-throated Mont Blanc Tunnel, and therefore another stop. More questions, more photographs, more awe. Everyone's smiling; it's made a few people's day. Red Diablo, golden sunshine, French mountain pastures – it hardly seems to matter that, despite the engine's bench-testing, we've been advised to keep the revs to a maximum of 5000 for the first 700 miles or so. That's more than enough to be getting on with, and we're not in a hurry. We slink (90mph is slinking in this thing) down to Lake Annecy, to admire the scenery and watch dayglo-clad dudes ripping along the water on their windsurfers.

Then, on the outskirts of Annecy, calamity. The power drops suddenly, there's a soft, metallic buzz, a muffled bang, and a much louder, rattling clatter. The 'right side engine' warning light comes on. Uh-oh, time to coast over to the hard shoulder. Tentatively, we raise the engine cover, lean over the wide wings, and peer in. The right-hand exhaust pipe of our metal devil is glowing like the fires of Hades. The aluminium heat shield surrounding it in the bay has melted (aluminium melts at 660degC), and molten blobs trace the glinting trail of our manoeuvre across the carriageway.

As we wait for the Mondial Assistance truck to take the car to Geneva – site of the nearest Lamborghini dealer – we're joined by throngs of people. We're there a long time, so answer a lot of questions. Nobody cares that the thing's broken down, nobody sneers

'RED DIABLO, GOLDEN SUNSHINE – EVERYONE'S SMILING. IT'S MADE A FEW PEOPLE'S DAY'

or laughs, as they would if the motionless vehicle were a Porsche or BMW. One family brings a video camera and poses by the car; on the opposite carriageway there's a minor karump, as someone stops in the outside lane for a better look. Leonard-Morgan and I make alternative travel arrangements.

Swiss Air takes us back to the Diablo a few days later. Factory troubleshooters have diagnosed and fixed the problem. There are two engine-management systems, which each look after a bank of six cylinders. If there's trouble on one side, you're still left with a straight-six to get you home. Because a wire had fallen off one of the Lambda probes for the cat, the right-hand side of our engine was closed down by the chip – hence the power loss. But it seems the fuel wasn't cut off at the same time, and as it reached the exhaust it ignited inside the pipe. At the same time as curing this the engineers have sorted out the tyre pressure warning light, and replaced a faulty electric window switch, which lowered the side glass of its own accord. But the interior lights still have a life of their own, and the brake warning light continues to cry wolf.

No dawdling this time. It's already 11am and we want to be home this evening. On clear stretches of French autoroute we cruise at 140mph, an easy gait for the Diablo. Were the laws different and the roads less densely trafficked, this car feels as if it could chew up entire continents in a day. It's reassuringly stable (and at this speed it's nice to be reassured), and hardly rolls in the long sweeping bends that channel us away from the Alps.

Before long, rain as heavy as last week's sun was hot, turns the autoroute into a cheerless grey canal. In the deeper puddles, aquaplaning kick-starts the adrenaline gland. The massive, single wiper looks like a marvellous piece of engineering, with its carbonfibre foils that are supposed to keep it in touch with the screen. But it only kisses a small patch of the glass, fortunately in front of the driver. On the passenger side, it hovers like a gull over a cruise ship.

We arrive at the gateway à l'Angleterre seven hours after leaving the Swiss capital, having stopped only for fuel. An inaccurate fuel gauge has meant we've stopped more often than necessary – the tank holds 26.4 gallons. Despite cruising at three-figure speeds, and the occasional blast to allow the engine to kick in our eardrums, the Diablo has averaged 15.3mpg over 1000 miles.

SPECIFICATION
LAMBORGHINI DIABLO

Years manufactured: 1990 –
Numbers made: 970 to end of 1993
Concept: mid-engined, two-seater V12 supercar, available with closed and roadster bodywork. Available with two-wheel drive, four wheel drive (badged VT) and in two-wheel drive lightweight specification (badged SV). Dramatic style conceived by Marcello Gandini and refined by Chrysler (the American giant owned Lamborghini during the Diablo's development) which also designed the interior.

ENGINE
Layout: V12
Capacity: 5707cc
Max power: 492bhp at 7000rpm; SV 500bhp at 7100
Max torque: 428lb ft at 5200rpm; SV 428lb ft at 5200rpm
Power to weight ratio (per ton): 312bhp; SV 333bhp
installation: longitudinal, mid-mounted, driving rear wheels
Construction: alloy heads, alloy block
Valvegear: four valves per cylinder, twin camshafts per head
Compression ratio: 10.1:1
Fuel system: Lamborghini LIE multi-point injection

GEARBOX
Type: five-speed manual
Traction control: VT has permanent four-wheel drive
SUSPENSION
Front: double wishbone, coil springs, anti-roll bar, electronically adjustable shock absorbers
Rear: double wishbone, coil springs, anti-roll bar, electronically adjustable shock absorbers
BRAKES
Front: 330mm ventilated discs; SV 355mm
Rear: 284mm ventilated discs; SV 335mm
Anti-lock system: none fitted
STEERING
Type: rack and pinion
Assistance: no
TYRES AND WHEELS
Front: 245/40 ZR17; SV 235/615 18
Rear: 335/30 ZR18; SV 330/675 18
BODY
Construction: square-section tubular steel, alloy, steel, composite skin panels
Weight (kg): 1575
PERFORMANCE
Max speed: 202mph; SV 205mph
0-62mph: 4.1sec; SV 3.9sec

Oh, the ignominy. Overheating trouble – the Diablo finishes its journey on a truck. Right, more problems: a sheared gearlever knob

A couple of weeks after we drive through the 'something to declare' (a low, wide, red car, officer) channel at Dover, I'm back behind the wheel of the Diablo. Co-driver this time is deputy editor Bremner. We're off to the Yorkshire Dales. But the journey doesn't start well. As we leave Portman's central London showroom, the air-conditioning blows out warm air on its lowest setting, followed by clouds of steam that immediately fog up the windscreen. Soon steam is billowing from the Diablo's external vents. We turn the air-conditioning off. Getting out of London illustrates how cumbersome the Diablo can be. Its enormous circumference, the rear blind spots, the gravel-grazing front spoiler, and the strong-arm low-speed steering make it impossible to nip around town. You just have to go with the slowest part of the flow, and never mind 492 horsepower.

Away from scrums of holiday caravans, the roads over the remoter parts of the Dales offer the chance to let loose all those horses. The car's run in now, so they're free to stampede. Being at the reins makes the Diablo even more exhilarating than it was sitting beside Valentino. I still can't believe how fast it goes, how viciously it accelerates, but revel in the fact that it does. Hanging tightly to the writhing steering wheel, feeling every bump and dip in the road surface through the seat, watching distant objects zoom into sharp focus through a screen which denies you a glimpse of the bonnet, listening to the explosive eruptions of the engine, is both frightening and addictive. Jump out and you'll be quivering slightly, but rapturous.

The fun stops when the leather-topped gearlever snaps, just below the polished aluminium gate. The change, with its dog-leg first gear, had always been quite stiff and even awkward. After much head-scratching, we effect a temporary fix by removing the gate, plonking a socket over the lever stump, and using a couple of socket extension bars as a makeshift lever. This permits use of second and third, both being in the same vertical plane, but not reverse, first, fourth or fifth. Still, it's good for 120mph or so.

Eventually, the clutch starts smoking and we again need the assistance of Mondial. For the second time in three meetings, I watch the Diablo head into the sunset, piggybacking aboard a lowly flatbed truck.

Not a good record for a car which costs as much as a healthy hunk of real estate. But I can't dislike it, or harbour many negative emotions beyond mild annoyance. I've never known an Italian supercar which hasn't had its share of problems. It's almost to be expected, to my mind, at least.

When the Diablo's going, it's shattering. And when it's not, it still has the power to brighten people's lives. Practical? Nope. Reliable? Nope. But who cares? Your £156,000 isn't buying a car, it's buying a fantasy, one that others can enjoy along with you. It's like meeting your favourite film star face to face – you don't worry too much about the warts. If any other car had let me down as badly as the Diablo, I would have stabbed it with the poison pen; as it is, I feel honoured to have made its acquaintance.

IN RETROSPECT

It's astonishing to think that, when Lamborghini decided to replace the Miura, favoured coachbuilder Bertone managed or better its drama with the Countach. Both were designed by Marcello Gandini, who designed the Diablo too. Perhaps it was too much to expect that this third generation should be as startling, when the Countach did so much to define the look of the modern supercar. But we would defy anyone not to stop and stare when confronted by a Diablo – it has astonishing presence. It also meets modern crash and emissions regulations, as well as moving the genre on, not least by adding four-wheel drive to the mix, and by busting 200mph.

Few modern cars are as sculptural as a Diablo, above. It's a wide car, and wider at the rear, partly to accommodate the cooling system and the huge twin catalytic converters. Doors scissor aloft, just as they did on the Countach. To see when reversing, open door, sit on sill, stretch legs and steer

Bugatti, probably the world's greatest pre-war sports car manufacturer, was resurrected – in name, if not in spirit – when the EB 110 was unveiled in the early '90s

BUGATTI
EB 110

By Brett Fraser

BY THE END OF OUR SECOND day in northern Italy, we'd seen two car production plants. One produces 20 million units a year, the other, when it reaches full capacity, will construct a few hundred a year.

It's not just the scale of their unit capacities that differentiates the two Italian companies, but the scale of their products. One builds cars at 1:1. The other makes replicas, in a variety of scales from 1:87 to 1:18. One is called Bugatti, the other Bburago.

The name of Bugatti will probably be more familiar than Bburago, but chances are you'll have had more first-hand experience of the latter. Think of those beautifully detailed, well proportioned, large-scale model cars that wink seductively at you when you pop into a big petrol station. You'll likely own one or two; they're irresistible for the 12 or 13 quid they cost. My personal collection is comfortably into double figures. But that didn't stop me last Christmas from asking for a couple more of these 1:18 scale beauties – the Lamborghini Diablo or the brand-new, and

Adjustable tail spoiler helps high-speed grip. The Bugatti's looks aren't to everyone's tastes, but there's no denying the car's on-road presence, nor its speed – it will exceed 200mph and, in its day, vied with the Jaguar XJ220 for the 'fastest car in the world' tag, before the McLaren F1's entry

extremely rare, Bugatti EB 110. Santa fronted with the Diablo on the day, but by the New Year I knew my collection would be incomplete without the Bug.

Quite why I'm so captivated by the EB 110's shape is hard to fathom. When it was launched at the 1991 Paris Show I thought it as ugly as a Vietnamese pot-bellied pig. It's heavy of flank, ungainly at the rear, too aggressive at the front. Bugattis are supposed to be elegant. The EB 110 (so called because if Ettore had still been alive at the time of the car's launch, he would have been 110 years old) has the visual drama of Bugs of old, but none of the grace.

And yet the looks of the darn thing have grown on me. Especially its slightly demonic, ground-sucking front profile. The original concept for the car was drawn up by Marcello Gandini (who also has Countach and Diablo-shaped notches in his belt), and it was honed by design consultant Giampiero Benedini. Maybe those two are right; perhaps elegant is out, ugly is in. As Bburago has already sold more than 190,000 models of the EB 110, with little attendant publicity, there must be hordes of others out there who agree. Well, if Santa won't bring the model to me, I'll just have to go to the model. And what better way to go to it, to the place where it's made, than in the full-size version. It's the perfect way to check the model for accuracy, and the real thing for its supercar credentials.

Bburago's works is in the outskirts of Milan, the city in which Ettore Bugatti was born on 15 September, 1881. It's easy to forget he was an Italian because his name will always be linked with Molsheim in Alsace, France, where he spent most of his life and established his factory. When the new Bugatti factory was set up in the supercar heartland of Modena, the purists began to mutter: how could Bugattis be built anywhere other than hallowed Molsheim? Easy, really. You want ready-made expertise in supercar design, engineering and manufacture, then you pitch shop where there's the greatest concentration of talent.

We're met at the Campogalliano factory by Simon Wood, a Brit who worked previously for Lotus on the Esprit SE Turbo and Lotus Carlton projects. He's now vice technical director, design and advanced studies at Bugatti. Wood lets slip how nice it is to be working for a company where money isn't an issue. He isn't forthcoming about where, exactly, all that cash comes from, but the official line is that a group of enthusiasts are responsible for the revival of Bugatti the car maker, and for part of the finance. They were aided by the French government, several other investors, and supported by Messier-Bugatti, the aeronautics company that has kept the famous name alive since it ceased making cars in the early 1950s. But one has only to look at the size, the facilities, the modernity and the expensive decor of the factory, and the quali-

Final inspection at the end of the production line, below. Quality could have been improved, when writer Fraser visited the Campogalliano factory. Thundering through a village near Modena, right, the city that is the heartland of the Italian supercar industry

ty of the staff, to begin pondering the wisdom of making such an investment in a project that promises only moderate returns.

To make sense, the firm needs to sell some cars. Which means it needs to make some, and for an agonising time after launch there was little evidence of that. But 40-odd have now been delivered and today we see 10 more being built. That's not many, I grant you, and the pace of the 'line' is unlikely to worry even Morgan; still, there are cars. And there's a chance for fairly close inspection, as the cars are in various stages of build. At the far end of the line we catch a glimpse of machines receiving their final screws and widgets; at the start each EB 110 is simply a flat-bottomed black carbonfibre honeycomb tub, reinforced with solid carbon in areas of high stress. The 280lb tubs are made by French aeronautical giant, Aerospatiale, and arrive fully prepared, all mounting plates and bushes already moulded into position. Body panels, which are attached at a later stage, are made of aluminium by the local *carrozzeria*. But before the alloy skin is draped over the tub, the rest of the EB 110's mechanical skeleton is fitted. Down the line we have a clear view of the metal bones. In the case of the exhaust, probably too clear. The pipework is a botch of crudely welded metal. Equally tatty is the silver heat shielding between tub and exhaust, which appears to have been recycled after covering somebody's Sunday roast. Both are apparently being attended to.

While the exhaust system appears shabby, what it's attached to is as dapper and beautifully crafted as can be. Central to the appeal of the EB 110 is its 3.5-litre quad-cam quad-turbo 60-valve (five per cylinder) 60deg all-alloy V12. And what a mighty meaty motor it is. Its outputs put the fear of the devil into even the Diablo. From just the 3.5 litres, Bugatti has conjured up 553bhp (at 8000rpm), and 451lb ft of torque (at 3750rpm); the Lambo makes do with but

492bhp and 428lb ft of torque, and requires 5.7 litres to do it. By stumping up with the compelling figure of 158bhp per litre, Bugatti has broken one of the golden rules of engine design, the one which says there ain't no substitute for cubic inches. The substitute in this instance is a foursome of tiny turbos from the Japanese company IHI. Their primary virtue is in their low mass impellers which give speedy response, but they're also reliable and, because they're made in large numbers, inexpensive.

Turbocharging, controlled by a well-tuned engine-management system, allows an engine designer more options to fiddle with the torque curve than does normal aspiration. In the EB 110, for example, the torque curve is manipulated so that above 2400rpm, there's never less than 339lb ft available, a figure not so far short of a Ferrari 512TR's peak. Impressive. The longitudinally mounted engine is noticeably offset from the car's centre-line, because the gearbox casing is cast integrally with the cylinder block. This arrangement saves weight and, more important, allows room for the gearbox to lie parallel with the engine. This keeps down the height of the powertrain, leaving the car's centre of gravity – critical to handling – as low as possible.

Four-wheel drive might also look voguish, but that's not why the EB 110 uses it. There are a fair few horses lurking beneath the Plexiglass engine cover, and the best way to tame them is to split the responsibility between each of the wheels. The Bugatti apportions its torque 27 percent to the front, 73 percent to the rear, and features a Torsen diff at the rear to make sure the torque goes to the wheel that can make best use of it.

When the EB 110 was wheeled out a couple of years ago, its all-wheel drive was unusual in the supercar market. Now Lamborghini has introduced the 4wd Diablo VT, thereby elimi-

Cabin is neither opulent nor stylish, not when you consider the price. Trim quality wasn't all that brilliant, either, when writer Fraser took the wheel. Handling, however, is very sure-footed, helped by the terrific grip of the 4wd system. The EB 110 is a deceptively fast car, and a brisk ground coverer

'ITS MIGHTY MOTOR PUTS THE FEAR OF THE DEVIL INTO EVEN THE DIABLO'

nating one of the EB 110's unique selling propositions. The suspension is by double wishbones all round. At the rear there are twin coil/damper units, and at the front the springs act via racing-type pull-rods. Both ends have adjustable spring platforms to set ride height and corner loadings.

As the roller door at the end of the assembly line clatters upward, the outside world throws in a bright bolt of light, illuminating our steed. Though its silver colour isn't flamboyant, it doesn't lessen the visual impact of the EB 110. Even the line workers take time out to stare. Pushed out into the daylight, what's particularly striking about the car is its relatively compact size. Smaller than a Ferrari 348, it is dwarfed by its leviathan rivals.

Bburago's EB 110 requires a fingernail hooked under the bottom edge of the doors to get them to scissor upwards. It's trickier in the real thing, as you have to fumble about under the lower edge of the door's swage line to find the handle. When you do, inevitably it's covered in dirt.

However, the doors swing open high, leaving a yawning hole through to the leather-wrapped cocoon of the cabin. To reach your seat, you must first vault the stylish Bugatti kick-plates and a chubby sill, then slide your legs down into tight footwells. The door's an upward stretch, so close it before you buckle up. It shuts with a gratifying ker-thunk. So we're encased in a legend. What, tangibly, does that mean? Luxury, certainly, in the form of tree and

hide, but merely standard-grade luxury, Lotus Esprit-grade, MVS Venturi-grade. I'm expecting something more opulent, more innovative, more stylish. The EB logo embossed on the seat backs isn't enough in a car which aims to be a cut above the average, however high that average happens to be. Furthermore, the cabin isn't all that well made. Definitely not £343,100-worth of well made. And this is Bugatti president Romano Artioli's own car. Some of the leather is poorly finished, trim panels don't align, air vents rattle, the wood veneer is too flimsy.

The seats will suit the corpulent, but for the rest of us, the tombstone buckets don't provide sufficient lateral support for the exceptional side forces the EB 110 generates. They don't follow the curve of the average spine very well, either, and the electrically adjustable lumbar support is unable to compensate. Supercars aren't renowned for generously dimensioned cabins, and this one succumbs to the tendency. You sit a fair way inboard, and the fat A-post curves up just to one side of your straightahead sight line, mating with the roof panel only slightly above your left temple. Your feet are hemmed between the wheel-arches and the transmission tunnel. There's not much fore and aft movement for the seats, either, and I suspect folk on the beanstalk side of six feet could find the cabin cramped.

Will the EB 110 live up to its extraordinary mechanical specification? Or is it just a designer-label supercar? Twelve small cylin-

Doors open upwards. Some agility is required to vault the wide sill and kick-plates before the driver can squeeze himself in. It's worth the effort, though, to experience the EB110's mindwarp speed

ders gurgle into life. Their sound is soft, restrained, harbouring none of the menace implicit from a Diablo at idle. Blip the throttle a couple of times. Nothing much happens. The pedal is mushy and long of travel. Tread harder. Snar-yowl, snar-yowl. Ah, that's better. It still doesn't sound like you'd expect a V12 to, but it's more than stirring enough to set your sap rising. Imagine the ferocious cat-call of a Porsche 911, drop the tone a couple of octaves, and you get the idea. Grab fat-rimmed, leather-covered Nardi steering wheel in left hand, grasp fat-topped leather-covered gearlever in t'other, snick into the first of the six forward ratios, ease out the modestly weighted clutch. Unlike big butch supercars of old, there's not a moment's worth of worry about stalling in front of the assembled throngs; the EB 110 has taken a leaf from the Honda NSX book of user-friendliness, and is intended to be a cinch to punt around the plaza. The clutch feeds in smoothly, the brakes (huge drilled and vented discs, serviced by race-spec Brembo floating calipers) are servo-assisted, the gearbox synchronised.

Yet you're not mollycoddled: you still feel in touch with the driving process, even at low speed. Left out of the factory gates, we kiss the outskirts of Modena and Bologna. Every couple of hundred yards or so, someone flashes their lights, toots the horn, waves, sticks their thumb up. Urban dawdling is a doddle. Not only are the controls manageable, but the ride quality, the bane of the brawn brigade, is remarkable. It's smoother than some executive saloons. Sure, there is bump-thump, but only over surfaces where it would be hard to avoid in any car. Precious little din is generated by the tyres, a staggering achievement when you look (and gasp) at their size and profile, colossal 325/30s mounted on 18x12 BBS alloy rims at the rear, 245/40s on 18x9 rims up front. With such a large patch of rubber on the deck, you'd expect road roar like Concorde on full afterburner, but the only time you're the least bit troubled by it is on concrete-surfaced motorways. The slender sidewall profile of these thumping great tyres makes

the ride quality all the more impressive.

The road clears. Until now the EB 110 has seemed almost sluggish. The long-travel throttle robs it of about-town perkiness, and despite the free-spinning nature of its turbos, and the robust stature of its torque curve, it's indolent at low revs. Still, the thought of 553 horses corralled behind my cranium suggests any flexing of the right foot should be tentative. I probably overdo the caution, for on the first blast up the road, the Bugatti is swift, but not breathtakingly so. As I'm about to discover, this is because a) I haven't booted it hard enough, b) the engine's refined and well soundproofed, and c) the four-wheel drive is a sensation sapper. The speedo reveals the Bug was going pretty fast after all. But not as fast as it's a few seconds away from doing. It's a bit of an effort to get the accelerator down to the carpet, but the effect is devastating. There's a small delay while the engine gathers its full resources, then reality is suspended for as long as you dare keep your clog on the gas. Pilots being catapulted from aircraft carriers must be used to the sensation, but this thing takes road car thrust into a new dimension. Fast cars are often described as pushing you back into your seat; the Bugatti slams you into the backrest and pins you there until you relax your right foot. The German magazine *Auto Motor und Sport* has recorded a 0-100kph (62mph) figure of 3.6sec, 0-180kph (112mph) in 10.8sec, and 0-200kph (124mph) in 14.0sec. The action doesn't really begin until the crank's spinning at 3500rpm, but from then on it's all go, go, go. The red line becomes earnest only on the forbidding side of 8000rpm. Start chasing the rev limiter, and you'll suddenly find the road isn't as long as it looks. Out of the side windows, trees and buildings are leaning back at jaunty angles; the world's a blur. The conquest of the red line becomes a challenge and, it has to be said, a test of nerve. For the novice, it's mind-warp stuff – you hang onto the wheel for all you're worth, effectively a passenger.

As the hills rise slowly out of the flatlands, the roads narrow and

SPECIFICATION

BUGATTI EB 110

Years manufactured: 1992 to 1996
Numbers made: 153
Concept: two-seat, mid-engine, supercar intended to be a technological ultimate (before the McLaren F1 came along). Sophisticated four-wheel drive system powered by 60-valve, quad cam, quad turbo V12 via six speed gearbox. Carbonfibre composite and light-alloy body. Originally to have hydraulic suspension, but coil sprung for production. Gandini-designed bodywork. Killed by Bugatti's failure to stay afloat.

ENGINE

Layout: V12
Capacity: 3500cc
Max power: 553bhp at 8000rpm
Max torque: 451lb ft at 5000rpm
Power to weight ratio (per ton): 341bhp
Installation: longitudinal, mid-mounted, four-wheel drive
Construction: alloy heads, alloy block
Valvegear: five valves per cylinder, twin camshafts per head
Compression ratio: 7.5:1
Fuel system: Bugatti-Weber injection, four IHI turbochargers

GEARBOX

Type: six-speed manual
Traction control: no

SUSPENSION

Front: double wishbones, coaxial coil springs and shock absorbers, anti-roll bar
Rear: double wishbones, coaxial coil springs and telescopic shock absorbers, anti-roll bar

BRAKES

Front: 332mm ventilated discs
Rear: 332mm ventilated discs
Anti-lock system: yes

STEERING

Type: rack and pinion
Power assistance: yes

TYRES AND WHEELS

Front: 245/40 ZR18
Rear: 325/30 ZR18

BODY

Construction: carbonfibre understructure, carbon bulkheads, aluminium skin panels
Weight (kg): 1620

PERFORMANCE

Max speed: 209mph
0-62mph: 3.6sec

urge restraint. Though compact by supercar standards, the EB 110 is still more than six feet broad. As the route climbs it begins to meander, gently at first, and then it turns more switchback. Then, a deserted section of serpentine tarmac, and time for some exploration. Much grip, little inspiration, is the outcome of this hillclimb session. Its natural tendency is to understeer in tight corners, if you can get it to relinquish its grip at all. It can be encouraged to let go by a big dose of throttle, yet even then, it's the front end that slips away first. During all this, the steering is a well-weighted ally, if not an especially crisp or talkative one. And now the gearshift is turning against me, grating and obstructing.

Morning of day two, and we're off to Bburago. A downpour has turned the miserably drained autostrada into an aquaduct. No problem for the Bugatti, though, as its stability in standing water is impeccable. Around Michelin's wet-weather test track, the EB 110 is the quickest car ever tested. Cruising at 100mph, noise in the cabin isn't a problem. It's not all that quiet, but it's pleasing. The Bburago factory is sited in the town of Burago (single B) Molgora. The second B is for the family that owns the company, headed by president Mario Besana.

The arrival of the Bugatti momentarily stops work at the factory. Not for long, though, as the plant has highly automated and swift lines: get distracted and you could quickly end up neck deep in unpainted bodyshells. It's quite a spectacle watching bodyshells spewing from the machines (which operate 24 hours a day, although the human workforce doesn't). The castings are of excellent quality and require no hand finishing, merely sand cleaning to rid them of any grease before painting.

Assembly doesn't take place at the factory. Components go to scores of outside piece workers, and finished models are crated back into the plant for packaging. Before we leave, we watch father and son Besana take turns to blast up the road in the Bug. Each returns smiling, chattering animatedly about what happens when the tacho hits 3500rpm. I wonder if Bugatti has another customer or two for the EB 110. Me, I'm slightly bewildered as to whether I like this car or not. Its power and performance are intoxicating. The memory of its cataclysmic thrust will stay vivid for many years. The fine ride quality is an unexpected bonus. But I'd prefer it to act more like a supercar more of the time, and I suspect there are those at Campogalliano who would, too. Why else would they be working on the 600bhp Supersport version? A rethink of the interior and better quality control wouldn't go amiss, either. Yes, I do like the EB 110, but I don't yearn for it. It doesn't arouse the emotions the way an F40 or a Diablo can. Unless it's 1:18 scale. And yes, my Bburago collection is now bigger by one.

IN RETROSPECT

The attempt to relaunch Bugatti was a huge folly – the surprise was that the folly got as far as it did. Funds were raised. Eminent people were hired. An extraordinary factory got built. Launch parties were held. And a car did appear. Trouble was, though hugely plausible in many respects, the EB 110 was neither particularly eye-catching, nor particularly attractive. Given that the cars of the original Bugatti were notable for their grace and beauty, this was a big disappointment. Orders were limited, further choked-off by a recession. Teething troubles stalled deliveries, and eventually, the banks foreclosed. Sadly, the Bugatti rebirth will be better remembered than the car.

Romano
ARTIOLI
■ 1932 -

ROMANO ARTIOLI HAD A DREAM – TO SEE THE REBIRTH OF ONE OF MOTORING'S MOST FAMOUS LEGENDS. AND SO, IN 1987, BUGATTI WAS BORN AGAIN, BASED NOT IN FRANCE AS BEFORE, BUT IN ITALY, NEAR MODENA AND FERRARI. A MONEY-NO-OBJECT VENTURE (AND FEW KNEW QUITE WHERE THE FUNDS CAME FROM), BUGATTI DID, EVENTUALLY, PRODUCE A CAR – THE EB 110. VASTLY LESS DRAMATIC THAN THE EVENTS SURROUNDING IT, THE EB 110 STRUGGLED, AND SO DID ARTIOLI, HIS GRAND PLAN FINALLY DYING IN 1997

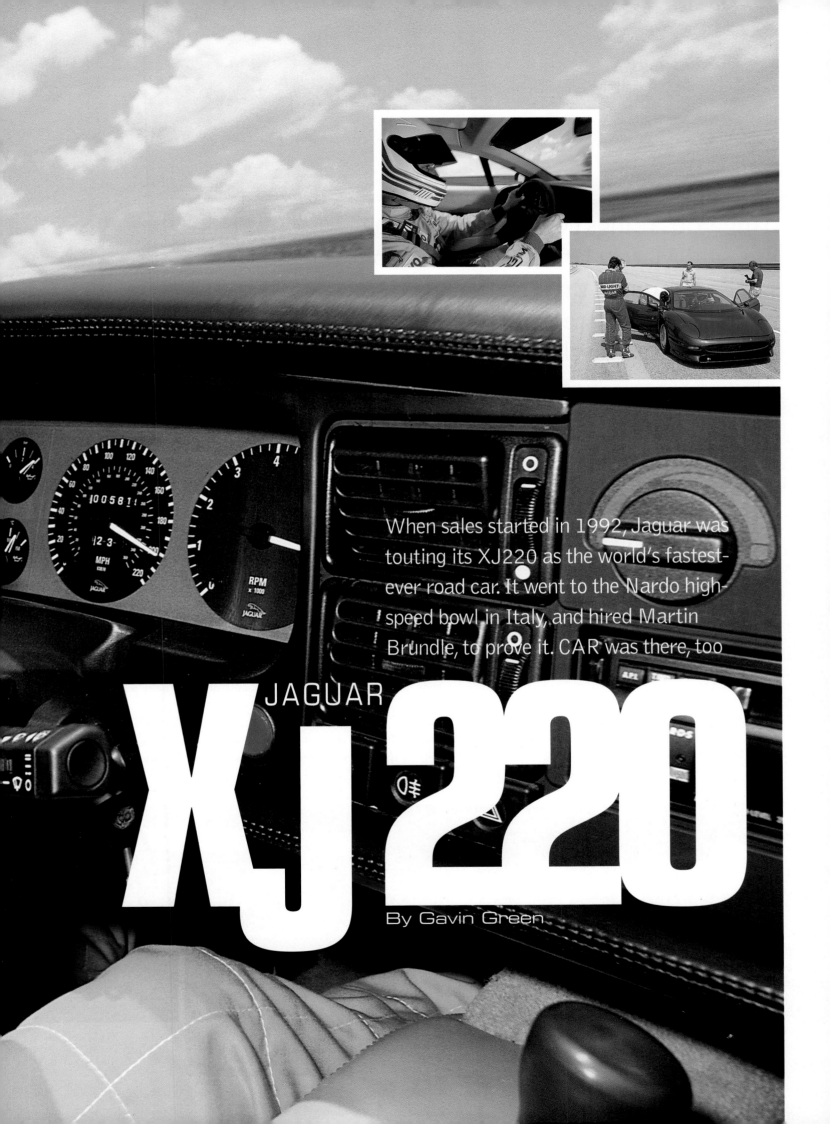

When sales started in 1992, Jaguar was touting its XJ220 as the world's fastest-ever road car. It went to the Nardo high-speed bowl in Italy, and hired Martin Brundle, to prove it. CAR was there, too

JAGUAR

XJ220

By Gavin Green

'THAT'S ONE OF THE MOST dangerous things I've ever done in my life,' said Martin Brundle, an hour or so after he'd just proved the XJ220 to be the world's fastest production car. I'm glad he came clean after the run.

Had he told me before we – yes, I mean we – had climbed inside the Jaguar cockpit at the Nardo proving ground in Italy, I might have been reluctant to help. If, that is, riding shotgun with Martin Brundle, doing absolutely nothing except, if it came to it, holding his hand as we launched ourselves off the banking, Thelma and Louise fashion, can be deemed help.

'If a tyre had blown, part of the car broken, or there had been any failure, there's no way that Armco barrier would have held the car. We'd have gone straight through it. In F1, you're inside a composite shell that's massively strong, and there are medical facilities – including a mobile operating theatre – on hand. Here,' he said, gesturing towards the parched outfields of Nardo, 'there's nothing'.

The whole thing was pretty crazy, really. In a nutshell, Jaguar was keen to see how fast its new XJ220 could go, just before deliveries started. There are only two circuits in the world on which a fast car can be driven at over 200mph: Fort Stockton in Texas and Nardo in Italy. The XJ220 had already recorded 212.3mph at Fort Stockton, which is faster than any production road car has gone.

The hope was that Nardo might yield a still higher velocity. The goal – and the expectation, too – was 220mph, which obviously would tie in well with the model name, and the pre-launch publicity, which spoke about a top speed of 'over 200mph'.

Martin Brundle, Benetton Formula One driver and former Jaguar sports car racer, was to do the driving. The theory was that he might be able to eke out a few more mph than Jaguar's test drivers, if for no other reason than that he's probably braver.

Fiat owns Nardo (now there's a surprise), the site chosen because it's apparently the driest area of Europe. Rain, and high-speed testing, obviously don't go together. On the Sunday when Brundle was going for glory, it was hot and dry, with just a hint of a breeze. The track itself is completely featureless – which is what you want when you're doing over 200. It's a 7.86-mile circle of constant radius, mildly banked, and four lanes wide. Two titchy pieces of Armco, one on top of the other, stand between the tarmac and eternity. 'That Armco wouldn't hold a Golf doing 120mph, let alone a big Jaguar doing 220,' said Brundle afterwards. I have no idea what lies on the other side of the barrier and, as far as I know, no-one has discovered. The Jaguar technicians and test drivers had been in Nardo since the Wednesday, finishing their durability tests. They had two cars, chassis numbers 007 and 009. Brundle, who arrived just after we did on the Saturday evening, would use 009 for the glory run.

The plan, on the Sunday, was for Brundle to do a few laps in the car in standard trim, to check the car's road-going maximum speed. Then I'd get to ride shotgun, after which photographer Ian Dawson would take my place in the passenger seat (to give you a view of what I saw). Then the Jaguar's mechanics would remove the car's catalytic converters, thus adding about 50bhp to the XJ220's already substantial corral of 542 horses. Free of any obstructive green things in the exhaust, or of any hefty passenger, our man Brundle would go for the 220.

It was all done in an unstructured, unofficial way, more for the hell of it than for any meaningful reason. There were no independent witnesses – no *Guinness Book of Records* judge, for instance

Mechanics working on car at Nardo; cats were removed for the final run. Brundle, in yellow overalls, then a Benetton F1 man, did the driving

– apart from two journos (self and John Lamm from America's *Road & Track*), Dawson and a TV cameraman. And none of us understood how the testing equipment worked. There was no minimum distance over which the speed had to be held, no attempt to repeat the feat in both directions to compensate for any wind, no hard-and-fast rules, no official laws or regulations. And, of course, taking off the cats instantly made the car non-standard, and thus non-production. Irrelevant it may have been (does a road car that can do 220mph matter these days?), yet we all knew that we were witnessing something of great moment.

Two pieces of timing equipment, both on board the car, would measure the runs. One activated an on-board print-out; the other was telemetrically linked to a computer back in the base, in the centre of the Nardo bowl.

Brundle's first run, then – with the engine and exhaust in standard trim and no passenger on board – would be the most representative, inasmuch as your average XJ220 owner could in theory do the same thing with his car. Decked out in his United Colors of Benetton yellow overalls, and looking very much at ease (this sort of thing must be a doddle for a bloke used to driving wheel to wheel against Senna and Mansell on Sundays), Brundle got down to business.

I watched from the trackside, with the JaguarSport engineers and mechanics. A far-off but very muted roar, sounding a little like a jet aeroplane, presaged the car. Then we caught sight of it, high on the banking, metallic green and looking lovely in the bright midday sun. It fairly belted by, trailing a great whoosh, and a muted but truculent engine note. Apart from the noise, which gave you some idea of the sheer hell that the engine and the tyres and the other mechanical bits must be going through, and the sheer visual speed – you turned your head quickly, as your eyes followed the car – the whole thing looked uneventful. The car was tracking as straight as a bullet, and going not much slower.

Next time around – two and a half minutes or so later, on this track of almost eight miles – he pulled in, and the mechanics opened the boot, where the on-board speed print-out was sited: 211.2mph maximum, said the little piece of tape. 'I could have gone faster, but the engine was bouncing on the rev limiter in top,' said Brundle, matter-of-factly. The limiter comes in at 7400rpm. Later, for the non-cat run, it was increased to 7900.

Back in the garage in the middle of Nardo, near the big control tower, the print-out from the telemetric timing kit on the car recorded the maximum at 212.3mph, exactly the same as the top recorded at Stockton, which can't just be a coincidence. 'Which

Timing beacon catches the big Jag whooshing past, above. Our man Green, in grubby grey overalls, rides shotgun with Martin Brundle on one of the record runs. The much-publicised (by Jaguar) 217mph record run was done with Brundle driving alone, with the rev-limiter increased and the catalysed exhausts replaced by big straight-through shotgun pipes

speed reading is the definitive one – the read-out in the car, or the telemetric one?' I asked of an engineer. 'Whichever is the higher,' he said with a grin.

My turn. Garbed out in my old Renault 5 Turbo racing overalls – the fastest they'd been was probably about 130mph – and a rather scratched old Bell helmet (put it this way, when I stood next to Brundle, you could tell who was the pro and who was the hack), I slithered into the passenger seat. Headroom is at a premium in an XJ220, and my bash-hat was kissing the glass sunroof.

Strapped in with a four-point harness, one hand clutching the centre console grab handle, I was soon propelled out of the central workshop area down a service road, heading for the speed bowl. Behind me, the engine sounded a bit feeble. There was none of the bellowing growl that so distinguishes an F40 or a Diablo motor. The XJ220's note was too high, too anaemic. Its bark is a lot worse than its bite. 'The production cars will sound different, apparently,' said Brundle, yelling through the slot in his full-face helmet. When the turbos started to influence events, the engine note deepened, as progress jumped.

Out on the bowl – just like a four-lane motorway except that it's banked and deserted – Brundle gave the Jag some welly and the car sprang around to 180mph on the speedo very easily. The acceleration was ferocious, my backbone wedged into the thick leather seats, hanging on hard to the grab handle, Brundle still talking but fast becoming inaudible. I told him I couldn't hear him – the engine and wind noise were overwhelming – but he couldn't hear me, so kept talking. I wish I could have heard him: I'm sure what he said, as we edged up to 207.4mph, was interesting.

It wasn't actually that dramatic. Sure, the kilometre posts were disappearing very quickly, it was hellishly hot inside (the air-conditioning was turned off, the air vents were shut, and the glass roof and the vast screens at the front and rear of the cabin were turning that cockpit into a hothouse), and it was mightily noisy. But the car felt so stable, so safe. The ground effects seemed to suck it down, clamping it firmly and safely to the tarmac, never mind that the road was flashing by underneath at a quite insane speed. The bumpiness of the circuit surprised me. Look at the surface, from the trackside, and it seems glass-smooth. Drive on it, at

SPECIFICATION
JAGUAR XJ220

Years manufactured: 1992 to 1994

Numbers made: 280

Concept: mid-engined, two-seat supercar. Produced in their spare time by a dozen Jaguar personnel (called the Saturday Club), the original XJ220 was four-wheel drive and powered by a 500bhp 48-valve Jag V12. Adopted by Jaguar a month before its '88 NEC show debut, it cost little to make because component suppliers contributed expertise for nothing. It was manufactured by TWR, but as a two-wheel drive V6 twin-turbo, changes that led some owners who'd signed up in 1988 to sue Jaguar. Most wanted out because the market for supercars had collapsed, but either way, the XJ220 never quite fulfilled its promise

ENGINE
Layout: V6

Capacity: 3498cc

Max power: 542bhp at 7200rpm

Max torque: 475lb ft at4500rpm

Power to weight ratio (per ton): 374bhp

Installation: longitudinal, rear-drive

Construction: alloy heads, alloy block

Valvegear: four valves per cylinder, twin overhead camshafts per bank

Compression ratio: 8.3:1

Fuel system: Zytek digital engine management, two Garrett turbochargers

GEARBOX
Type: five-speed manual

Traction control: no

SUSPENSION
Front: double wishbones, pushrod actuated coil springs and telescopic shock absorbers, anti-roll bar

Rear: double wishbones, pushrod actuated coil springs and telescopic shock aborbers, anti-roll bar

BRAKES
Front: 330mm ventilated discs

Rear: 300mm ventilated discs

Anti-lock system: no

STEERING
Type: rack and pinion

Assistance: no

TYRES AND WHEELS
Front: 255/45ZR17

Rear: 345/35ZR18

BODY
Construction: honeycomb and machined aluminium alloy understructure, aluminium skin panels

Weight (kg): 1470

PERFORMANCE
Max speed: 217mph

0-60mph: 3.9sec

Brundle about to set off for his solus, record run. He subsequently said it was probably the most dangerous thing he'd ever done. The in-car speed read-out, right, showed a maximum of 216.0, but another readout, in the Nardo garage, showed 217.1. Naturally, Jaguar chose to promote the latter

200mph-plus, and the tiniest pimples kick the car's suspension, in turn kicking you. My helmet was rattling against the glass roof, as it bobbed up and down, at one with the car's tortured springs.

Brundle didn't do lap after lap at 200-plus, gently coercing the last mph out of the car; far from it. He would slow down and speed up regularly. On a normal lap, the speed from the surprisingly accurate speedo (200 is apparently a true 199), varied from about 150 to 200. Accelerate at 150, and the car would surge forward. Even at 180 – at which speed the car is particularly comfortable – the XJ220 jumped when Brundle so demanded. From 180 to 200 in an XJ220 feels like 80 to 100 in a Golf GTI.

Over 200, more patience was needed, the engine's power trying to break free from the massive drag. The speed rose only gently after that, and the bumps became bigger and much more violent. There is one particularly bad one at Nardo, and every time we hit it, the car – just fleetingly – felt like it might be brushed off course. Other than that, the XJ220 just went around as though guided by rail. Dawson went next, camera poised. He didn't have a helmet, which concerned him. 'Don't worry,' said Brundle. 'If we crash at

200, a helmet's not going to do you much good. Besides, I'm here as well, and they don't come much more chicken than me.'

Chauffeur driving out of the way, it was time for the serious part of the day. While Brundle and I had lunch next to the Nardo pool, the mechanics reset the high-rev cut-out, and took off the catalysed exhausts, replacing them with a pair of straight-through shotgun-like pipes.

An hour later, now screaming like a racer, the XJ220 once again took to the bowl. He did only one flying lap ('I didn't need any more'), and the sight of that car streaking by, screaming like a tormented monster, whooooooshing by like a low-flying jet, waves of disturbed air and dust trailing in its wake, will live with me forever. It looked much faster than before, and we all cheered and wowed in awe at the sight of that green Jaguar which quickly disappeared from sight.

Brundle trundled in next lap. The front bonnet now stood about an inch proud of the body; the front hinges had bent at speed from the enormous pressure. He said the car felt faster but didn't feel 220mph fast. 'The speedo showed 220, so it's probably 215 or 216.' The boot read-out confirmed it: 216.0mph maximum. The telemetric read-out, we later discovered, showed 217.1. It looked faster, if anything can possibly look faster than 217 miles an hour.

The JaguarSport guys must have been disappointed – they all really wanted to see 220, as a final reward for four years of graft. Yet they now knew, with even more clarity than before, that they were about to launch the fastest production car to hit the road.

The Japanese Bridgestone men, on hand but always discreetly in the background, said that Nardo had 1.1deg of scrub all the way around – so a car never steers dead straight, and that palpably hurts top speed. Apparently, you should add three percent to the Nardo figure, to get the real top, as would be achieved on a long, long straight. Add three percent to 217.1mph, and you get 223.6.

So we proved that, on some theoretical straight road, driven by someone as good as Martin Brundle, in weather conditions like southern Italy's, with minimal wind and the cats taken off, the XJ220 could probably do 220. Which means we didn't prove much. No matter. I know I witnessed history. There may never be a faster road car than this one. It's a day I know I'll never forget.

IN RETROSPECT

The XJ220 had a rather confused identity. Conceived by engineering chief Jim Randle, and developed in his (and his team's) spare time, the XJ220 was originally a much longer V12 4wd supercar. By the time it reached the road – after being 'productionised' by TWR's Tom Walkinshaw – it featured twin-turbo V6 power and rear-drive. Alas, by then, the world's economy had turned bad; it was not the moment to try to market a £415,000 car. Many who'd ordered it, tried to cancel; values nose-dived. The XJ220, although undeniably fast and handsome, was vast and mechanically unsophisticated. It is now regarded as something of a second-rate supercar.

XJ220 ON THE ROAD

Fast, in a straight line, the XJ220 undoubtedly was. But there was much about its dynamics which were suspect. Its V6 turbo engine, although gutsy, was vibratory and had an anaemic note – unsatisfactory when cheaper rivals from Ferrari and Lamborghini sounded so superb. In a supercar, the music is part of the magic. The handling was also slightly leaden, not helped by the car's vast size. On the road, the car just didn't deliver the delicious communication that was expected.

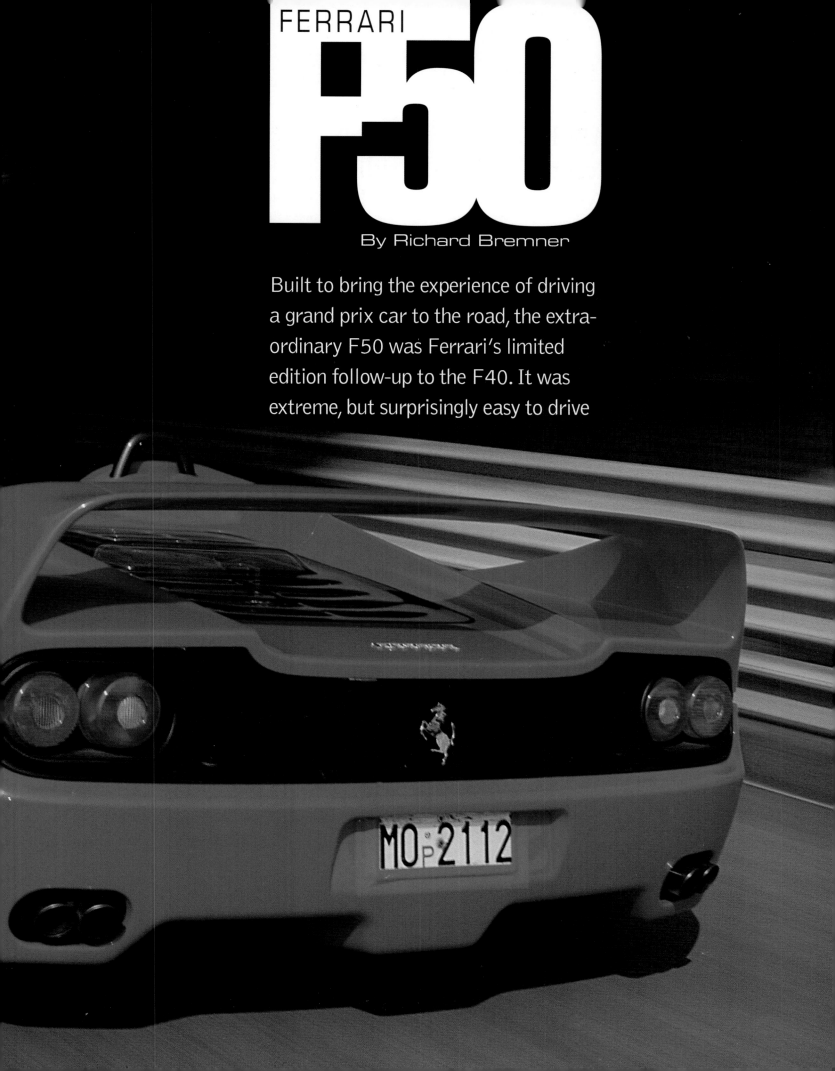

FERRARI
F50

By Richard Bremner

Built to bring the experience of driving
a grand prix car to the road, the extraordinary F50 was Ferrari's limited
edition follow-up to the F40. It was
extreme, but surprisingly easy to drive

MO·P·2112

IT'S HOT, DAMN HOT. BUT THIS IS heaven, not hell, even if the devil is riding at my shoulder. And he's grinning. Why?

Because he has just slip-slithered a Ferrari F50 through a mighty tight turn, power-skating this howling red monster into a drift so fluent that it almost feels lazy. The monster isn't even straight when he glances at his passenger for approval. And he gets it. It's stupid, but I'm almost laughing at the lunacy of it. This man is throwing around a car that costs the price of a house. He's stretching the engine to the rev-limiter in almost every gear (almost, because if he tried it in sixth, we'd be in orbit) and stamping on the brake pedal as if he hates it. This isn't abuse, but it's close.

And who is this devil? It's Dario Benuzzi, Ferrari's famous rubber-burning test driver. But even a ride with Benuzzi around Ferrari's Fiorano test track doesn't match the exhilaration of circumnavigating it yourself. So belt yourself into this F50, and be my passenger. I will be much, much slower than Benuzzi, and I might frighten you, but hell, any F50 experience is better than none.

You don't look elegant when you get into the F50, because there's that fat sill to step over, and you kind of fall into the seat because it's a long drop down. But you'll find it comfortable once you're in because it's well padded, and reassuringly tight-fitting – the hip bolsters must be almost six inches deep. You probably won't notice this as much as the heat, though. It's searing in this carbon-fibre cockpit, even with the roof off and the windows wound down. It's like stepping into a boiler room.

Ignition on. Instruments lit. Fuel pumps a-whirring. Hit the go button – that's the rubber bellows below the key – and hear the starter motor go live. The starter's clunk-clang sounds like it's belting the engine into life, dealing a kick up the V12's crank. The motor fires, whoops, and idles busily.

When I push the carbonfibre-capped gearlever into first, I'm unsure of what to expect. Will this be a white-water raft of a ride, a half-lost battle for control? Will it be a wrestle for supremacy with wheel, pedals, gearlever and 520bhp? Or will I just stall the engine in the Fiorano pits? Well, it won't be the latter because – whoops – the clutch is clenching, the engine is revving and we are moving, rather suddenly, onto the main straight.

I'm going for second early – you don't go flat chat first time out in a car like this if you like living – and vaguely register that the lever moves more easily than expected. Vaguely, because noise is drowning thought and because a tight corner's rushing up. There's time for third before pressing the middle pedal – hard – because it seems to need big effort to produce an effect. The F50 slows comfortingly; I blip the throttle in an attempt to match revs to cog speeds, and fail. I should have tapped the accelerator more forcefully, because the revs drop fast – the flywheel must be light.

I jink the wheel left, and then haul it right for this tight right-hander and get a bit of a surprise – there's understeer, and a pressing need to use the full width of the track. Hmmmmm. Or rather hm, because there's no time to ponder this now. Press that satin-action, alloy throttle and feel the engine gag a little before it climbs

Clean sculpture of F50's nose typical of designer Pininfarina. Bodywork shaped to generate aerodynamic downforce. Car comes with removable hardtop, as well as a soft removable roof. It's surprisingly draught-free at speed when roofless

the power curve, only to be knocked back because we're into another curve, a left-hander and now a right, a long one this, not quite visible, so I back off because a spin would be embarrassing, and yes, the nose is tucking in which is handy because the Ferrari's trained on the apex again. Now we're into a left, quite tight like the last two, and there's a straight, longish, where you can feel the force of the power before taking third and, boy, does this thing go, and boy, is that 90-degree right coming at us fast. Brake brake brake, second gear; no understeer this time and now we're climbing the flyover that crosses the main straight, into third, over the crest, BRAAAAKE, it's another tight right, down the hill, into third, jink left, a short straight and here's another 180-degree turn, swinging left. The commotion subsides with our speed, I take second, swivel the wheel, feel myself pressed into the side of the seat, feel the heat, tread the throttle – gently – straighten the wheel, press harder and, here's that hammering roar. Into third and there's a gentle right-hander. Let's be bold and keep accelerating, feel the seats tingle as the revs soar; brake for the sharpish left, power on, it's running wide and the camber's against us but we're onto a straight, another gentle right, into fourth, glance at the instruments, can't read them, heavy braking for the 180 left, edge through, short straight, mild right, under the bridge and go go go, third fourth fifth; this is the main straight and I've no idea how fast we're going but it feels great and phew, that's a lap and we haven't met our gods.

That was a sweaty but supreme experience. Time to collect thoughts and a cooling Coke. And reflect on a few surprises. For instance, we didn't get the world's most expensive vibro-massage. And we didn't get our hair wrenched out by the roots. And it wasn't an uncontrollable beast. And (not so surprising, this) I want to do it again.

Vibro-massage? Well, if you bolt your 520bhp 12-cylinder motor direct to the tub and bolt the chairs direct to that, it wouldn't be unreasonable to expect some fizz and zizz when the engine comes on strong. Hold out for the full 8500 revs that it will pull – and you don't have to wait for very long – and you will feel a bit of a tingle through the chair, and another buzz through the throttle pedal. But it's so mild that you have consciously to look for it. And there are plenty of other distractions, such as where you're going, and the noise, and the heat. We might be driving it roofless, but you don't even feel a mild breeze of progress in this Ferrari, let alone the whip and tug of wind skimming across your pate.

This is because Ferrari has put huge effort into quelling turbulence around the cockpit, and in keeping air heated by the radiators from jetting straight into your lap. Look at the front of this F50 and you'll see that air funnels through the front grille, to be ejected shortly afterwards via those two huge channels cut into the bonnet. Beneath those scoops are twin radiators, and they certainly heat up the air for the short time that it's in them. It's passed out at the bottom corners of the front screen, to be tripped by a pair of deflectors mounted on the trailing edges of the quarterlights. They make a valiant effort to direct it from the cockpit, but your Häagen Dazs isn't going to last long.

The F50's back in the pit. Its fans are whinnying, ejecting Vesuvial gusts through that gauze tail panel. The thing seems alive, and the motor isn't even turning. Back in the hot seat, and a pause to survey the cabin. It's mainly black – the red cloth of the seats provides

Dashboard, far left, features exposed carbonfibre. LCD instruments colourful, but hard to see in sun. Rubber button below key is starter, left. Spacious cabin, above, has grippy race seats

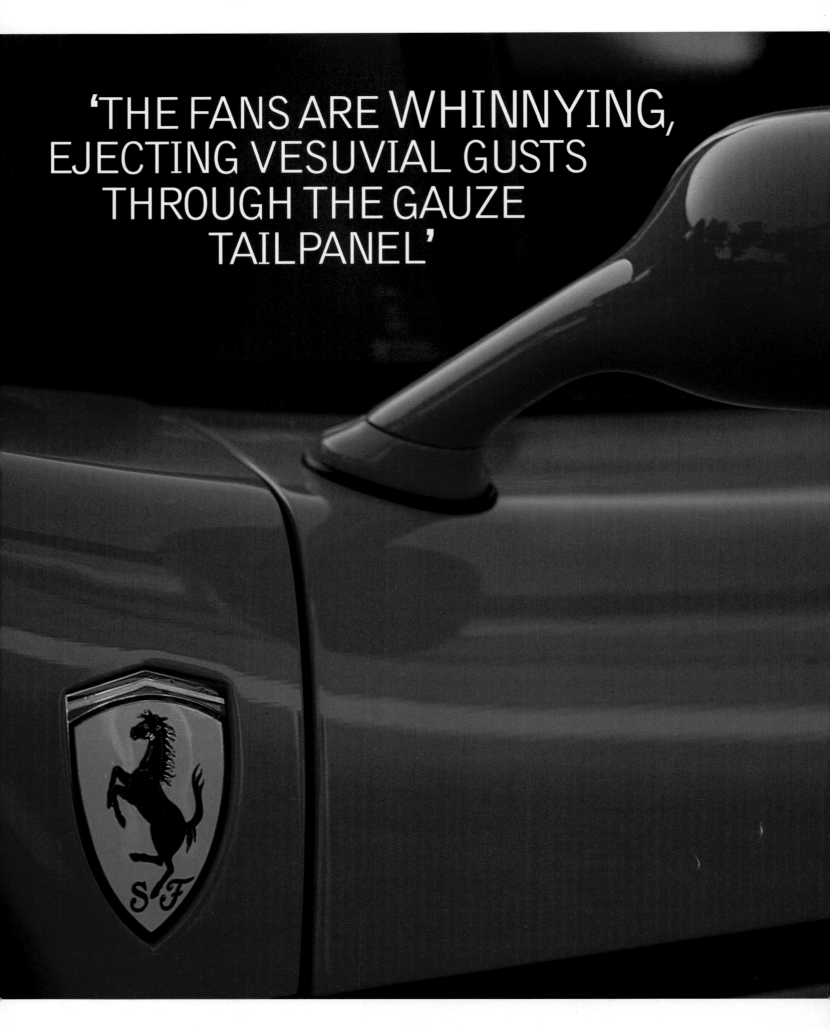

'THE FANS ARE WHINNYING, EJECTING VESUVIAL GUSTS THROUGH THE GAUZE TAILPANEL'

Mesh tail panel, right, enables followers of F50 to see into engine bay and admire V12, pushrod suspension. Engine cover, below right, is perspex. One of the roll-over hoops, below

the only contrast – and at first sight it looks simple to the point of crudity. The dashboard, a no-nonsense horizontal structure, could have come from a car of the '50s. Its lower half is exposed composite, the upper section dressed in black Alcantara suede. In the centre are a trio of those twin flap air-vents found in Alfa 33s. To their left is the ignition key and, below it, the starter button, and left of this, hidden by the wheel, are two further buttons. One cycles the trip computer (conventional, except that it can reveal the intensity of the instrument lighting – useful, eh?), the other enables the car's management computer to communicate with Maranello via your portable phone in the event of trouble. The instruments themselves consist of a speedo, which runs to 360kph, or 224mph, a 10,000rpm tacho, temperature gauges for oil and water, and oil-pressure and fuel gauges. In the middle of the speedo is a gear-engagement indicator. The binnacle is black until the ignition is switched on, the dials being LCD, which is why they wash out in bright light. On the far left of the dash are three plastic paddle switches (from the 456GT) controlling ride height (for kerbcrawling, so to speak), fog lamps and hazard flashers. The column stalks control the usual functions, but they're special for their velvet precision and the marvellous electro-technoid 'plink-plink' of the indicators. Mind you, that can only just about be heard, even at idle.

The cockpit is divided by a simple carbonfibre tunnel from which sprouts the gearlever; complete with famous alloy gate, and aft of that, a pair of rotary knobs controlling the air-conditioner, whose efforts seem easily overwhelmed. Behind this are the handbrake and part of the boot – a small storage tray containing a plug-in torch that doubles as interior light. This and a trio of Connolly leather pouches Velcroed to the rear bulkhead are the F50's only stowage space. So your dirty weekend really will be, unless the butler is tailing you in the Range Rover.

The seats are fabulous. They have composite chassis for lightness, and they're sleeved in cloth and Connolly leather. The backrest supports your torso with extravagant flying buttresses, and has cut-outs for a race harness (although a hole in the cushion is curiously absent) while the base is flanked by those bulky bolsters mentioned before. The chairs slide and recline (via a cool, smooth rotary alloy knob) but there's no height or lumbar adjustment. No matter. The driving position's good, if slightly long-arm, short-leg, and there's plenty of space for a full, limb-flailing work-out. Should you be one of the 349 who are going to buy an F50, you can have the drilled alloy

TURNING RACER INTO ROAD CAR

Ferrari says the F50 is a Formula One car for the road. But a Formula One car is designed to blaze around a race-track as fast as possible while complying with a set of technical rules, and we won't be seeing F50s attacking the Formula One Championship. Instead, these cars will be driven on real roads by folk of less than superhuman ability.

So, how do you make a road car feel like an F1 car? Or, more particularly, how do you make it feel as you think an F1 car might feel, but still be tolerable on the road? The purest way is to develop your car with your own F1 team, incorporating F1-derived componentry. Thus the F50 is based around an immensely rigid structural tub built from the same Nomex and carbonfibre composites as an F1 car's, to which the F1-derived V12 engine is rigidly attached. Then there's the

pushrod suspension (bolted directly to the engine/gearbox assembly at the rear), the rubber-bag fuel tank, the downforce-creating aerodynamics – and, a road-car first, the use of telemetry to hone its handling.

Telemetry is a science beloved of today's F1 pit lane. Of course, most modern cars are developed using computer data gathered from strategically placed sensors. Zoom around a test track, and see what the sensors have sensed. But F1 telemetry is different.

Here, the sensors transmit data as it is gathered, in what computer buffs call real time. When you might get just one chance at a super-quick qualifying lap, you want to learn as much about that lap as possible, quickly. And a moving picture always tells you more than a series of stills. So why not use this potent tool on a road car? Not only

would it speed development, but it would also hone it further. Even better, if you're trying to create an F1 car for the road, you can use the F1 data already acquired from the track, and apply it to your new project.

Of course, it would only work if the F50's suspension moved like an F1 car's, and so it does: real race-car pushrod suspension with springs operated by rocker arms. The idea behind such a suspension is to keep the springs out of the airflow around an open-wheeled car; so it's hardly necessary in the enclosed F50. But in a Formula One car for the road, this is the way it has to be.

pedal pads adjusted to suit your hooves. In-car entertainment? Don't be silly – that's provided by you and your 4.7-litre V12.

Let's get back on track and answer a few more questions. For instance, does the F50 feel like a Formula One car? Well, the answer is I don't know, for I've never driven a Formula One car, but project engineer Amadeo Felisa (who hasn't driven an F1 car either) points out that the F50 does not have 700bhp and weighs rather more than Alesi's transport. We shouldn't be too disappointed, because it certainly feels dramatic – any car that can top 200mph and hit 60mph in 3.7 seconds is going to make an impression. Yet the F50 is no wild animal. It makes a lot of noise, it makes you hot and it gets you about rather briskly, but this is not one of those heart-in-mouth-every-minute supercars.

Why not? Because it's so controllable. The steering, which is unassisted, is not particularly heavy, and neither are the rest of the controls. The gearchange is lighter and more direct than in other Ferraris and of the pedals, only the brake needs firm action, but that makes it easy to modulate, and easy for the driver to perform jerk-free heel-and-toe manoeuvres. Because the V12 is normally aspirated, it isn't the slightly flighty device that the F40's engine is.

If you merely want to edge your speed up slightly, you can. True, the engine does fluff a little below 3500rpm – the real venom comes beyond – but this is an ex-F1 engine, remember, and it certainly doesn't jerk sulkily at the drivetrain when it's puttering.

But best of all is the F50's handling. We'll get to that tight-turn understeer shortly, but through any other kind of curve the F50 feels so composed that you don't realise what an achievement its fine manners are. It feels utterly stable, true to its line even when you throw it about. Which is what you'll be doing after a few laps, it's so benign. It doesn't seem to roll at all, and as you pile on speed you begin to feel it working, and sense little jinks and spasms through the seat, the kind that tell you the car's being stretched.

Use more revs and you discover that seamless gearchanges are easy, so well cushioned is the clutch, and that the brakes are as dependable as Big Ben. Indeed, they're so strong that decelerating is almost as much of a thrill as accelerating. It can easily get a bit too exciting – I got carried away, and locked some wheels entering a tight turn (there's no ABS, for that would deaden the feel), but a rubbery shriek and a momentary slither were the F50's only reaction – there was no surrender to instability.

At low speeds, the F50 is happy to slide at whim. It probably is at high speeds too, if you've got the nerve – its handling is supremely controllable

And that understeer? Well, it's undeniably there, but according to Benuzzi, Ferrari's F1 cars run wider still. And understeer is certainly preferable to oversteer; a characteristic that might have been a dominant part of the mix when you consider that 58 percent of the F50's weight sits over its fat back wheels.

So Ferrari has certainly satisfied one of its objectives: that the F50 should be an easy machine to drive hard and fast – easier than the F40 ever was. And it is, on the track. For the road, we still don't know. It's a wide car, and that will limit the opportunities for full-throttle blasting (throttle-stretching moments don't come often even at Fiorano) and we don't know how it rides, either, because the track is caramel-smooth. But Ferrari's suspension engineers are claiming great things for their electronic suspension. In any case, it's hard to imagine the F50 being anything other than supremely exhilarating, utterly addictive and a great way to sweat off excess weight. It's like a big Caterham for rich boys. The Renault Sport Spider and the Lotus Elise will probably have a little of what it's got, too. They're very similar, after all – minimalist, immensely fast, and built for undiluted entertainment. I mention them because they're the closest most of us are going to get to this kind of magic. Ferrari reckons it will have no trouble shifting all 349 (at 350,000 ECUs apiece – that's £342,700 – this currency chosen to eliminate exchange-rate fluctuations) and it's never going to build a car like this again. Why? Because, explains Ferrari chairman Luca di Montezemolo, forthcoming legislation will make it impossible to homologate a two-seat F1 car for the road again. So that's it – Ferrari's celebration of 50 years in GP racing. Not a bad substitute for popping a few champagne corks.

IN RETROSPECT

The F50 is one of the rarer Ferraris – there are only a third as many as there are F40s – and it may well be the last slightly mad car Ferrari ever does, because legislation makes it so difficult to build cars like this. Though the F50 delivers a scintillating on-road experience, it is more likely to be remembered for being astonishingly easy to drive than for emulating the sensations offered by an F1 car. In truth, it doesn't, even if its V12 produces over 500bhp and its suspension is similar to a GP car's. Nor is it likely to be remembered for its looks – it's no beauty. But it is a glorious, glorious folly.

SPECIFICATION
FERRARI F50

Years manufactured: 1995 to 1997
Numbers made: 349
Concept: mid-engined two-seat supercar designed to provide the sensation of driving a Formula One car – V12 engine even based on 1990 race car's. Like an F1 car, bodywork shaped to generate downforce, tub and body panels made from Nomex and carbonfibre composites, suspension is pushrod-actuated, rear suspension bolted direct to drivetrain, and chassis developed using telemetry, a first for a road car

ENGINE
Layout: V12
Capacity: 4699cc
Max power: 520bhp at 8500rpm
Max torque: 347lb ft at 6500rpm
Power to weight ratio (per ton): 423bhp
Installation: longitudinal, rear-drive
Construction: alloy heads, alloy block
Valvegear: five valves per cylinder, twin overhead camshafts per bank
Compression ratio: 11.3:1
Fuel system: Bosch Motronic 2.7DME

GEARBOX
Type: six-speed manual
Traction control: no

SUSPENSION
Front: double wishbones, pushrod-activated inboard coil springs, electronic shock absorbers, anti-roll bar
Rear: double wishbones, pushrod-activated inboard coil springs, electronic shock absorbers, anti-roll bar

BRAKES
Front: 355mm ventilated discs
Rear: 335mm ventilated discs
Anti-lock system: no

STEERING
Type: rack and pinion
Assistance: no

TYRES AND WHEELS
Front: 245/35ZR18
Rear: 335/30ZR18

BODY
Construction: Nomex and carbonfibre tub and skin panels
Weight (kg): 1230

PERFORMANCE
Max speed: 202mph
0-60mph: 3.7sec

F50's detail design, left and right, is attractive, but overall it's not the prettiest Ferrari, above and right, its shape dictated by cooling and aerodynamic demands

'SUPREMELY EXHILARATING,
UTTERLY ADDICTIVE – A
GREAT WAY TO SWEAT
OFF EXCESS WEIGHT'

Twenty years after Ferrari followed
rivals and built mid-engined
supercars, it went back to a front-
engine layout for its new ultimate
road car. The result is magnificent

FERRARI 550
Maranello

By Richard Bremner

THIS ISN'T AN ESPECIALLY
long stretch of road, but it is straight and it is clear. So I slow the Ferrari, almost to walking pace, until it is ambling at 1500rpm in second. And then I sink the throttle, abruptly.

There's no drama at first. No snatching drivetrain, no smoking, scrabbling wheelspin. The rising noise level nets your attention instead, but only momentarily, because now you must concentrate on the persistent gathering of pace. The Ferrari settles slightly on its rear springs as it spears forward, bounding its way to a corner barely visible in the distance. The V12 is stretching hard as it worries the tachometer needle around the dial.

The Ferrari's speed builds with authoritative zeal to 3500rpm, at which point it appears to decide that it is not being impressive enough and musters yet more effort. The V12 turns truly strident and the 550 squats still harder on its haunches, catapulting us forward with startling ferocity. Are backs being crushed into seats? They are. Are eyes widening in surprise? Indeed so. Will it soon be time to brake? Absolutely. As it nears the 7600rpm rev limit, the Ferrari makes a final, frantic lunge, the V12's note sounding more urgent, as if warning that you must change up. So I do, knowing now that this Ferrari is really, truly fast.

But without wishing to underplay the minor details that this 550 Maranello will fling you to 60mph in under 4.4 seconds and kiss 199mph (actually 203mph, but Ferrari quotes 199mph because it sounds a little more PC), this was kind of what I expected. The

Less ostentatious than its mid-engined predecessors, the new 550 Maranello is nonetheless a great looker. Ferrari boss Luca di Montezemolo reckons that thrusting, aggressive machines are now passé

tight. By the time it's undergone the pendulous effects of swerving from right to left to right again, the body's built up a bit of roll, and you can, if you're going fast enough, feel the rear of the car getting a bit edgy, a development sensed mainly through the seat.

But in the end, hurtling around Fiorano can only tell you so much. It's a smooth track, and deceptive in that it tends to diminish a car's performance. Time, then, to nose past the factory gates and into the real world. In short order you're struck by two things. First, this Ferrari is easier to see out of and, as a result, far easier to manoeuvre in confined spaces than its overblown Testarossa, 512TR and F512M predecessors. And second, it seems to ride rather well. I head for the hills – the Apennines in fact – where I will find out whether this car can deliver a great drive. The 550 Maranello has something else to prove, too. Which is that a front-engine, rear-gearbox configuration is now the path to supercar nirvana, as opposed to the mid-engined arrangement favoured for the Testarossa and most other supercars built over the past quarter of a century.

The main advantage of a midships configuration is the low polar moment of inertia that stems from having the heaviest part of the car concentrated around its middle. That makes it hang onto a corner for longer, although it can turn fractious once adhesion is lost. Mid-engined usually means flamboyant styling (Boxer, Testarossa, Countach, Diablo), poor visibility, a ropey gearchange and limited practicality. The idea behind the Maranello – apparently hatched by Ferrari boss Luca di Montezemolo after he'd been to a 250 GTO club meeting – is that it should be easier to drive, more practical, less ostentatious (the moment's passed,

reckons Ferrari, for unsubtle machines like the Testarossa) but, as before, damn fast. Having been lucky enough to drive a Ferrari 250 GTO one heady day, I can certainly say that's an easier car to drive hard with confidence than the Testarossa and its clones ever were. The GTO is a car in which one can take an adventurous approach to cornering, at least if one can forget how much it's worth, whereas the Testarossa was always intimidating.

The potential drawbacks of the 550's layout include poor traction, low grip and unbalanced handling, a worrisome combination in a 485bhp car. Fixing the weight distribution (it's 50/50 with driver aboard) has been achieved by mounting the gearbox at the rear and shifting the engine as far back as possible in its bay, while a short wheelbase heightens agility. But the main advance, says Ferrari, is the 550's huge tyres, specially (and independently) designed for it by Pirelli, Bridgestone, Goodyear and Michelin.

As our silver-grey 550 ascends the foothills, I have reason to feel intimidated. The sky has turned to the colour of the Ferrari's centre console and suddenly splits to soak car and road. The tarmac looks as slithery as freshly waxed linoleum, prompting me to come over all yellow and leave the traction control on.

Inviting electronic intervention turns out to be less easy than anticipated, because the Ferrari just seems to hang on, despite having garden-roller tyres that look as if they'd rather surf over puddles than sink into them. More provocation is required. It's not hard to deliver either, because the Ferrari, though not exactly small, is a wieldy thing. It pours into bends with at least as much commitment as many mid-engined cars, a sensation heightened by steering that is weighted just so. After a few miles of second-

Cockpit is classy and unpretentious and helps the driver get the maximum from the car. Compared with the 456GT, the Maranello has clearer instruments and better seats, as well as characterful drilled alloy pedals. Handling delivers in all conditions, from swoopy A-roads to tight secondaries, and is secure in the wet. It's even okay in heavy traffic

gear, rain-sodden, sinuous twists, I find myself reaching for the traction control switch and triggering the 'sport' button, which stiffens the dampers' resolve.

And now, here's a moment for some tail waggery: a tight uphill hairpin. Clack-clunk into second (yes, it's the usual Ferrari gearchange), whirl the wheel, tramp the throttle and, yeeeees, the tail swings sideways before snapping back into line on a released throttle. We dip and twist higher, faster. The 550 is wonderfully fluent even over roads that favour GTIs. It's unwilling to let go, stable, unbothered by bumps and a great resister of understeer.

It's less easy to get the hang of gearchanging. The shift is mildly obstructive, if less so than those of some Ferraris past, and the engine's light flywheel means that blipping the throttle is not enough to match crankspeed to gearspeed – the revs have died before you've reeled in the ratio. You must prod the throttle for longer, and that means heeling and toeing with finesse.

On the other hand, this is a car with more engine braking than most, allowing you to trim its speed on a trailing throttle before a turn. That's satisfying too, because there's less need to break the rhythm of progress with stabs on the (very effective) brakes. And

---

SPECIFICATION
FERRARI 550 MARANELLO

Years manufactured: 1996 –

Numbers made: 600 to October 1997

Concept: the ultimate series production sports Ferrari. Two-seater, designed as ultimate driver's car. Unusually, has front engine and rear-mounted gearbox; for more than 30 years, the optimum layout has seen the engine mounted in the middle, as per the 550's predecessor, the Testarossa. Advancing tyre technology is a major reason for the switch. Exterior and interior design by coachbuilders Pininfarina.

ENGINE

Layout: V12

Capacity: 5474cc

Max power: 485bhp at 7000rpm

Max torque: 420lb ft at 5000rpm

Power to weight ratio (per ton): 287bhp

Installation: longitudinal, rear-drive

Construction: alloy heads, alloy block

Valvegear: four valves per cylinder, twin camshafts per head, chain driven

Compression ratio: 10.8:1

Ignition and fuelling: Bosch Motronic multi-point injection

GEARBOX

Type: six-speed manual

Traction control: yes

SUSPENSION

Front: double wishbones, coil springs, anti-roll bar, electonically controlled dampers

Rear: double wishbones, coil springs, anti-roll bar, electronically controlled dampers

BRAKES

Front: 330mm ventilated discs

Rear: 310mm ventilated discs

Anti-lock system: yes

STEERING

Type: rack and pinion

Power assistance: yes

TYRES AND WHEELS

Front: 255/40 ZR18

Rear: 295/35 ZR18

BODY

Construction: tubular steel chassis, aluminium bodywork

Weight (kg): 1690

PERFORMANCE

Max speed: 199mph

0-60mph: 4.4sec

so it is that I'm hurtling through the gloom, revs rising and falling off as bends approach and recede, brake lights flaring into corners hidden by the overhang of dripping tree branches, the V12 beating harder as I pick off the occasional ambling Fiat and Renault.

I do mile after mile like this, almost mesmerised by an advance that seems so swift and secure. More secure, indeed, when the shockers are asked to behave sportily. In their normal mode the 550's ride is remarkably unruffled, the main disturbance being the sound of all that rubber surmounting rough stuff. But pile on the power, as you surely will, and you notice a certain floatiness, which can instantly be quelled by switching to 'Sport'.

It's early the next morning that I discover just how fast this car is. We're on wider roads now, bathed in an early autumn sun, and the Ferrari simply consumes them, vaulting from curve to curve with an almost lazy insouciance. There's power everywhere, so much that if you can't be bothered to downshift, you can almost certainly surge past merely by treading the throttle in fifth. Even in sixth, there's enough effort for overtaking, though this gear is really meant for cross-continent cruising. Cruising is something the Maranello manages consummately too. You expect the utter

Maranello is a magnificent cruiser; it's much quieter and more composed than the Testarossa or Boxer, helped by a long-striding sixth gear

effortlessness conferred by all that torque, and this advantage is exploited with excellent seats, that supple ride and minimal wind noise. If this recipe sounds strikingly similar to that which the elegant 456GT serves up, you'd be right. If anything, the 550 rides better. But there's no question that it is more the driver's car of the pair. It's the more tactile, especially through seat and wheel, it changes direction more keenly, it goes harder, feels more compact. Its cabin is no-nonsense, from the clearer instrument markings to the drilled alloy pedals and more heavily bolstered seats. It is built to deliver; and it succeeds, over a whole range of conditions – tight twisties, swooping A-roads, motorway cruises and even urban crawls. That's hugely impressive. But the best news of all is that this is an ultimate supercar you can really drive hard. It's been too long since you could say that of Ferrari's top road car.

IN RETROSPECT

Ferrari has come full circle with the 550 Maranello, returning to the front-engine, rear-drive layout that it deserted in 1973 with the mid-engined Berlinetta Boxer. Modern tyre technology enables the Maranello to achieve levels of roadholding and traction that would have been impossible in the early '70s – so does the ideal 50:50 weight distribution, effected by placing the engine well back, and the gearbox at the rear. Electronic traction control helps too. Whether the Maranello is the precursor to a wholesale swing back to the front engine remains to be seen, but there can be no question that it is hugely effective and, unlike its predecessors, easy to drive hard.

Luca di
MONTEZEMOLO
■ 1947 -

LUCA CORDERO DI MONTEZEMOLO HAS TWICE WORKED FOR FERRARI. IN 1973, WHEN JUST 25 YEARS OLD, HE WAS MADE FORMULA ONE TEAM MANAGER: FERRARI WON TWO WORLD CHAMPIONSHIPS DURING HIS THREE SEASONS. HE RETURNED IN 1991, AS FERRARI'S CHAIRMAN. SINCE THEN HE HAS REVITALISED THE AILING FORMULA ONE TEAM, AND OVERSEEN THE RENEWAL OF ALL THE ROAD CARS, LAUNCHING THE 456GT, F355, F50 AND 550 MARANELLO

'No compromise' is now a marketing cliché.
But that's precisely what the McLaren F1
was: a money-no-object attempt to build the
world's ultimate road-going supercar

McLAREN

F1

By Roger Bell

XP5

MY MIND IS BLOWN, MY soul corrupted. Absolute power has cast its spell. Solo or *ménage à trois*, I don't mind. Put me back in the middle behind the central wheel of the world's fastest driving machine. I need more, another fix.

Two days on the loose in McLaren's three-seater megacar, and I'm hooked. You would be, too. The 627-horsepower F1, which humbles all previous slingshot exotics, is just what design director Gordon Murray pledged it would be: the ultimate motoring experience, the closest sensation yet to a street-legal grand prix car. Forget Porsche's 959, Ferrari's F40, Jaguar's XJ220, Bugatti's EB 110. They're overweight, underpowered pussycats compared with McLaren's blockbuster. The F1 not only trounces them emphatically, but does so with spine-tingling sound-effects.

The F1 is more than mere hedonistic plaything. We knew already that it was the fastest, most powerful road car we were ever likely to test: Jonathan Palmer's 231mph at Nardo had put the McLaren firmly on pole for straight-line speed. We knew it was the most expensive, too: at £540,000 plus VAT, nothing else gets close for outrageous extravagance. That the F1 was the lightest, least compromised of the great modern supercars was ancient history. We knew all these things and much, much more. What we didn't know was what the F1 was like to drive. No-one outside the company bar a few prospective customers had driven an F1, never mind driven one in anger. *CAR* would be the first to do so.

There would be no demonstration run, no inhibiting company minder, no strings other than to sign a rather frightening indemnity. My brief was to be at McLaren's pristine Woking headquarters by 8am, have Jonathan Palmer, McLaren's marketing director, show me around the car, and then get in and go. Destination: Wales, via a circuitous route that would take in several favourite roads.

My departure was delayed by a small technical hitch with XP5, the fifth F1 prototype which is representative of customer cars dynamically, but not in finish. While the snag was sorted, I boned up again on the car's design.

To dismiss the F1 as a rich man's toy is to sell it short. Compromise was not in Murray's script. Perfection and cutting-edge technology were. To provide the ultimate, uncorrupted driving experience, Murray decreed a three-seater, with the driver in the middle, sitting well forward as in a racer. Anything that diminished driver pleasure, the car's *raison d'être*, was out. The definitive adrenaline pump would have minimal front and rear overhangs, and all masses – engine, transmission, fuel, occupants, luggage – would be contained well within the long wheelbase to avoid a 'dumb-bell' weight distribution. Low moments of inertia, regardless of load, were essential. So were a low centre of gravity and light weight.

Murray is obsessed by weight. His ambitious target of 1000kg (2200lb) – which was nearly achieved – meant compact dimensions and ruthless paring. Not for the McLaren masterpiece the gross obesity of a Jaguar XJ220 or Ferrari Testarossa, both of which weigh hundreds of kilogrammes more. It also dictated Formula One carbon-composite construction for the body/chassis unit.

Packaging was the key to the F1's success. Get that right and the rest would fall into place. Fashion would have little to do with the car's timeless styling. Ground-effect aerodynamics, a cab-forward driving position, spinal air-intakes... these and other considerations dictated how designer Peter Stevens would shape the car.

Central driving position was the McLaren's major oddity – it worked well, although overtaking and entry to the cabin could both be a bit awkward

'231MPH PUT
THE McLAREN FIRMLY ON
POLE FOR STRAIGHT-
LINE SPEED'

Another Murray edict that raised eyebrows was that there would be no turbo motor. Only the linear delivery of a big, high-revving, normally aspirated engine would do for a car that was to be the fastest in the world, and civilised with it.

McLaren talked to several engine manufacturers before accepting BMW Motorsport's proposal to build a 6.1-litre 60-degree quad-cam V12. Awesome though it is, this purpose-built 48-valve powerhouse, which yields considerably more torque than a Formula One engine (more than 479lb ft from 4000-7000rpm), draws heavily on existing BMW technology: variable valve timing from the M3 six, for instance.

Drive to the rear wheels is through a slimline six-speed gearbox. There's no traction control, for that would diminish driver involvement, not to mention add weight. Ditto power steering, anti-lock brakes and adaptive damping. There's not even a servo to assist the brakes – huge, cross-drilled ventilated discs clamped by four-pot calipers. Nothing has been allowed to diminish the tactile relationship between man and machine.

In eschewing such modern aids, the F1 is in several respects a simpler, less complex machine than many uprange executive saloons costing a fraction as much.

Jonathan Palmer interrupts my browsing: 'It's ready, you can go'. I sense a twinge of apprehension. Then I recall a Palmer throwaway: 'Really, it's just another motor car, Roger'. Of course it is, I kid myself. Getting into the driver's seat is certainly not for the elderly or infirm. Push-buttons on the rear wings release the amazing dihedral doors, pivoted on ball-jointed hinges. Gas struts waft them into the gadfly position.

Never mind being after-you polite – the driver gets in first. A handbook picture sequence suggests a bum-leading technique. Palmer favours the single-seater approach: lean back on both arms, swing your legs over the obstructive spar, then do a buttock-launch into the central bucket. It's an awkward manoeuvre which immediately exposes the only major objection to a central driving position: getting in and out. Shutting the door is a little awkward too – a long and fairly strong arm is needed.

Once the driver is in – from the nearside, to avoid a nasty accident with the phallic gearlever that sprouts from the offside spar – passengers can step aboard without contortion. As a three-seater, the F1 works brilliantly, not least because passengers are so comfortably ensconced.

At last, I'm on my own in the world's fastest road car. The slimline seat looks less inviting than the flanking passenger ones, but its embrace is tight, its contours perfect. There's no power adjustment (too heavy), and the pedals and steering wheel need time and a spanner to alter. Owners get a special fitting. I adjust for reach, strap in (customer cars will get a handier harness) and feel perfectly at ease with XP5's compromise settings.

There's nothing intimidating about the straightahead controls.

Styling, by ex-Lotus designer Peter Stevens, was pleasingly uncluttered. Not only was straight-line performance awesome, but the F1 was marvellously fast and stable on the twisty Welsh secondaries encountered during the test

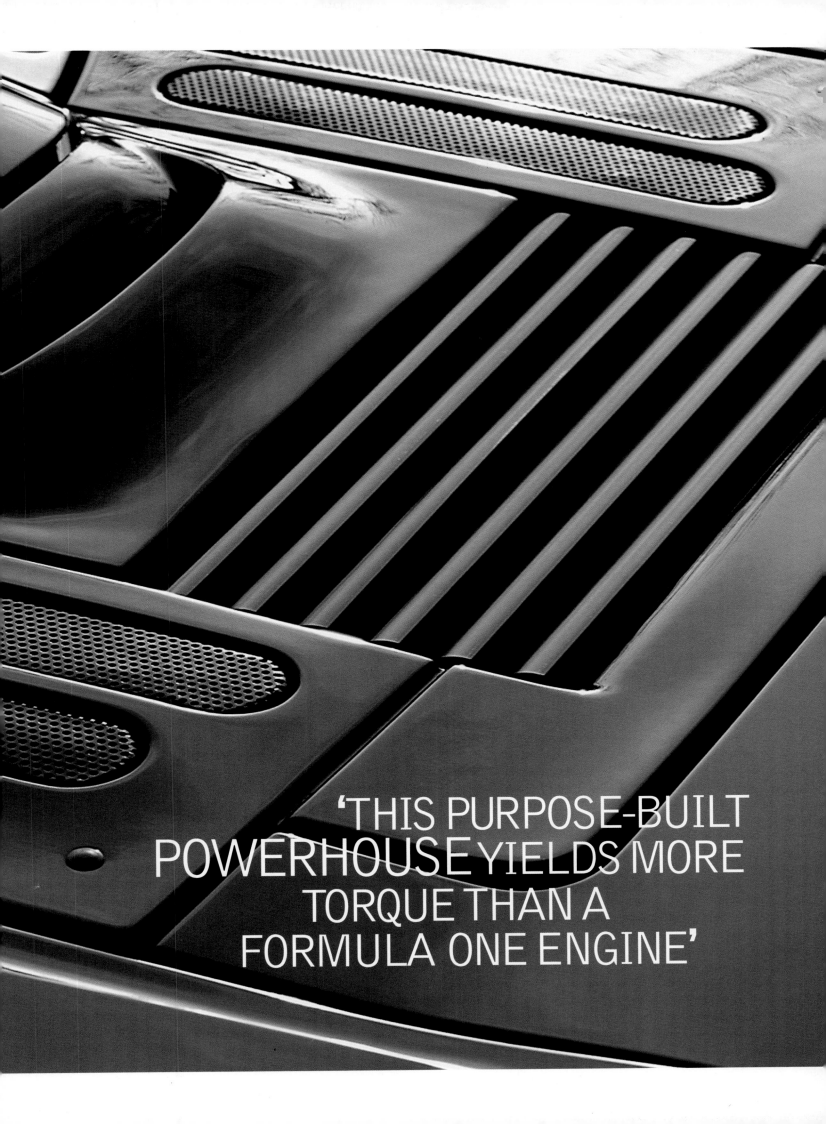

'THIS PURPOSE-BUILT POWERHOUSE YIELDS MORE TORQUE THAN A FORMULA ONE ENGINE'

'THE V12 IDLES WITH THE SMOOTHNESS OF FLOWING CREAM, PURRING SOFTLY, EVENLY'

'THE HUGE MUSCLE OF THE V12 CAN BE SWITCHED ON AND OFF LIKE A LIGHT BULB'

Flanking the thick-rimmed Nardi steering wheel are familiar (BMW) stalks for turn/dip and wash/wipe. Tucked behind the spokes are short-stroke fingertip levers which, through an infra-red system, work the flash and horn – a pathetic tooter. You've guessed: a strident air horn was rejected on weight grounds.

The rev-counter, black-blobbed at 7500rpm, dominates a light-faced instrument cluster. The speedo is relegated to a small, secondary dial, which is so finely calibrated (to 400kph – 249mph – in XP5) I couldn't read it. Other 'driving' switches – lights, fogs, spoiler, hazards, screen heating – are within a handspan of the wheel rim. Everything else is deployed on the two carbon-composite spars that flank the driver's torpedo-like tub. Buried down in the footwell, on view to passengers, are exquisite floor-hinged pedals. You could hang them on the wall as engineering art.

Let's go. I turn the ignition key on the right-hand spar down by my shin. There's a whirr of fans, the sound of mating crickets, a brief electronic buzz and lots of flashing red lights – information displays on a small, hard-to-read checkout. All's well. I fire the engine (foot off the throttle to let the management system do its thing) by punching a flap-protected red button.

The V12 idles with the smoothness of flowing cream, purring softly, evenly. To blip the heavy throttle – yeeow yeeow, like a Rottweiler's bark – is to reveal the ferocious side of the engine's dual personality. The immediacy of the response is down to the minimal flywheel inertia demanded by Murray. The carbon clutch is much lighter than I expect, but the short-throw gearlever is quite stiff into first – top left, as in a conventional gate (a lock-out slide prevents the inadvertent selection of reverse, which requires an even heavier hand, better still two). I lower the small, effective handbrake, which normally lies flush, to extinguish the last of the red-alert lights. There's a hint of judder as the sharp clutch bites, a whooshy rumble from the tyres and a classy whine from the powertrain. We're off.

The central driving position felt perfectly right and natural from the moment I clambered inside the F1. There's a small visibility problem when overtaking but by leaning to the right, you can see around it, especially as the car is not monstrously wide. The view forward over the low scuttle through a huge, electrically heated (and solar-insulated) screen is panoramic, despite the low, semi-reclined driving position. Reversing is tricky because you can't see directly behind (the dorsal intake gets in the way), but the mirror views aft, all four of them, leave no serious blindspots when you're solo. Three up, you see only mug-shot reflections of your passengers in the interior mirrors.

It's late. I abandon the favoured route to Wales and aim instead for the A4. The F1 is a doddle in traffic. It skims along quietly at low revs in a high gear, the patter of rubber overwhelming the rustle of the engine, its note gently oscillating like a draught through a chink. Fifth gear at 1000rpm, even sixth, causes neither hiccup nor pinking. There's no need to change down. Squeeze the throttle, and BMW's percussion section strikes up with a hard-hammering boom, as if from an echo chamber deep in the car's bowels. Docility gives way to ferocity as a brutal slug of raw, mountain-moving torque wells the car forward.

Long before I'm beyond urban limits, I realise where the mighty F1 is going to score over all its distant rivals: no matter what gear you're in, or what the revs, the huge muscle of its fabulously potent and tractable V12 engine can be switched on and off like a light bulb. It's that immediate, that accessible. No wonder Murray eschews the lag-prone turbo. The harder you squeeze the F1's throttle – and there always seems to be more movement, more revs, more decibels in reserve, so huge is the car's performance envelope – the greater the ferocity, the more strident the noise. No Ferrari V12 gets close for aural uplift, never mind for sheer, pulverising power. The world's greatest road car engine is right here, behind my back in the F1.

It was the McLaren's maximum that made the headlines, but it's the car's breathtaking acceleration that frightens and thrills.

Nothing, but nothing, gets anywhere close to this car, which has the world's best power-to-weight ratio. Even now, I'm not sure which is the more addictive: the slingshot thrust when you slash through the gears, left leg and right arm pumping like pistons, or the breathtaking sound-effects that go with it, terminating in a Formula One-style demented yowl.

Murray says the noise is perfectly natural, not technically orchestrated. What makes it all the more enriching is that it's throttle-induced, lending aural excitement only when it's required. Back off and the decibels subside, so you can cruise – and cruise fast, with barely a murmur from the engine. Trouble is, the drone of the tyres, which slap Catseyes and cracks with the rata-tat of a machine gun, denies the F1 cruise quietness.

It rained in Wales. Wet roads merely underlined the F1's colossal grip, though. Beyond initial first-gear getaway, there's no wheelspin in the dry, just stupendous acceleration that pulls 100mph in less than eight seconds with three gears to go (in round figures, intermediate maxima are 65, 95, 125, 150 and 180mph). What impressed in the wet is just how much power you can deploy

SPECIFICATION
McLAREN F1

Years manufactured: 1994-97

Numbers made: 100

Concept: intended to be the ultimate supercar, with no expense spared – and it wasn't: an F1 cost £634,500, including VAT. Conceived by ex-Formula One designer Gordon Murray and styled by ex-Lotus man Peter Stevens, the F1's weight was pared with fanatical zeal, to maximise the power of its specially designed BMW engine, which propelled it to a record-book-busting 231mph. Only the best materials were used – a fine layer of gold on the bulkhead, to dissipate heat, for instance. Just one of its many unusual features is the seating layout, which places the driver centrally, his two passengers either side. McLaren intended to sell 350, but in the end managed only 100. The car has had more success as a racer than as a commercial venture, winning Le Mans in 1995.

ENGINE
Layout: V12

Capacity: 6064cc

Max power: 627bhp at 7400rpm

Max torque: 479lb ft at 5600rpm

Power to weight ratio (per ton): 534bhp

Installation: longitudinal, mid-mounted, rear-drive

Construction: alloy block, alloy heads

Valvegear: four valves per cylinder, variable valve timing

Compression ratio: 11.1:1

Ignition and fuelling: multi-point injection

GEARBOX
Type: six-speed manual

Traction control: no

SUSPENSION
Front: double wishbones, pushrod-activated coil springs and telescopic shock absorbers, anti-roll bar

Rear: double wishbones, pushrod-activated coil springs and telescopic shock absorbers

BRAKES
Front: 332mm ventilated discs

Rear: 305mm ventilated discs

Anti-lock system: no

STEERING
Type: rack and pinion

Assistance: no

TYRES AND WHEELS
Front: 235/45ZR17

Rear: 315/45ZR17

BODY
Construction: carbon fibre composite chassis/body unit

Weight (kg): 1140

PERFORMANCE
Max speed: 231mph

0-60mph: 3.2sec

Engine, clearly visible under the rear cover, is a bespoke BMW V12 which writer Bell rated as the best supercar engine he'd ever experienced, as well as the most powerful. Carbonfibre scoops (top) helped feed air to the motor. Push-buttons on rear wings (above) release the amazing dihedral doors

without breaking traction. To avoid all risk of wheelspin, you simply opt for a higher gear and torque your way out of trouble. Who needs traction control, after all?

Who needs anti-lock brakes, for that matter? Passengers gasped at the way the F1 stopped in its tracks, as though arrested from behind by some mighty elastic hawser. Little did they know how hard I was heaving on the pedal. Never mind. The heavier the brakes, the easier it is to modulate them. Heel-and-toe downshifts are also facilitated by a solid brake fulcrum. Unless you look out for it in the mirror, the levitating rear spoiler – a brake and balance foil in McLaren-speak – that pops up to stabilise the car under high-speed braking goes unnoticed. It's the only surface-breaking aerodynamic aid on the F1, which achieves downforce via a fan-assisted ground-effect system.

Initially I was disappointed with the car's steering. It's wonder-

fully tactile and accurate, but not nearly as sharp as I'd expected. A Porsche 911's is decisively sharper. You certainly can't drive everywhere with your hands locked in the classic quarter-to-three position, as in a racer. Not with 2.8 turns from lock to lock. On fast corners, the wheel is perfectly weighted. On slow ones, worse still on manoeuvres, it's pretty heavy: 235/45 rubber takes some swivelling without hydraulic assistance. I was to change my mind about the steering, though. Familiarity bred respect for such a communicative system of unerring precision. To miss an apex by more than an inch is to cuss your clumsiness, not the car's.

Jonathan Palmer was anxious to know what I thought of the chassis, particularly its user-friendliness. The ride? Firm and jiggly – but never less than controlled and composed. So I got the tail out, did I? What gear was I in? Third, fourth? He's serious. I was actually in second (good for 95mph). You'll have to ask Dr Palmer what it's like to powerslide at three-figure speeds, but I dare say it's feasible. Know your F1 well and you know a forgiving car of fathomless ability. No mere mortal, though, is going to explore the outer limits outside the confines of a racing circuit.

Day two started badly – with an engine that wouldn't start. It fired, only to stop again down the road. The pattern became familiar: go, stop, go, stop. Alerted to the probability of an electronic glitch, the McLaren back-up machine swung into action: mechanics were diverted to the Brecon Beacons, a helicopter was scrambled from Woking. Boffin and black box were on the way. Why not? McLaren promises its customers unparalleled after-sales help. After some electronic surgery, all was well.

The delay meant ambling back to Woking on a dark, wet night – the sort of conditions that make for hell-hole driving in some supercars. Not the McLaren. I didn't think much of XP5's lights and its tyres are very noisy. But Murray's two major concessions to cockpit comfort – a lightweight Kenwood CD (but no radio) and air-conditioning – work well. Otherwise, my cruise down the M4 was as relaxing as in a BMW saloon.

End of story? Not quite. I made copious notes while driving the F1 but referred to none of them when writing this piece. The unforgettable, etched in the mind, needs no aide-memoire. Murray disliked my tape recorder, anyway. It weighs 10 ounces.

IN RETROSPECT

The aim was simply the ultimate driver's car; the headline-grabbing figures – the £540,000 (plus taxes) price and the 231mph top speed – were almost incidental in technical director Gordon Murray's quest to provide the biggest motoring high. Few have disputed that McLaren achieved its targets. Even now, three years after CAR first drove the F1, there's no sign that anyone is even trying to match it. Ignore cars like the Porsche GT1. Race-bred monsters like that are tamed just enough for a limited production run. The F1, on the other hand, was a road car – nothing race-raw about it – which happened to make a fine track machine.

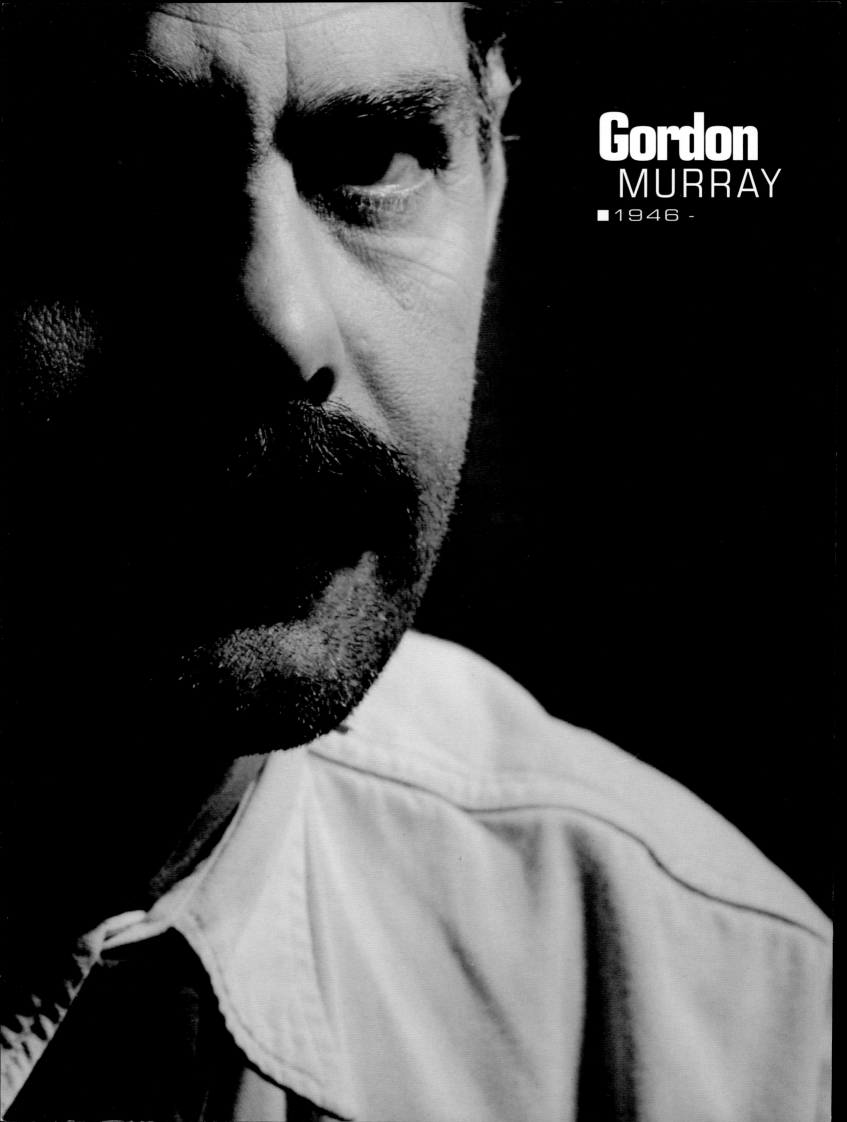

Gordon
MURRAY
■ 1946 -

GORDON MURRAY DESIGNED FORMULA ONE RACING CARS BEFORE HE DESIGNED A ROAD CAR, INCLUDING RACE-WINNING BRABHAMS AND McLARENS. BUT, BORED WITH THE FORMULA ONE WORLD, HE PERSUADED McLAREN TO LET HIM BUILD THE ULTIMATE SUPERCAR – THE F1. PRECONCEPTIONS, AND A BUDGET, WERE THROWN AWAY, BUT NOT DISCIPLINE – AMONG MURRAY'S MANY STIPULATIONS WAS A WEIGHT LIMIT OF 1000KG. HE JUST MISSED. COMMERCIALLY, SO DID THE CAR, FAILING TO SELL IN THE DESIRED NUMBERS. BUT THERE HAS BEEN NO GREATER, OR FASTER, SUPERCAR. EVER

THE NEED FOR SPEED

NEVER SAY NEVER. WHEN WITNESSING A JAGUAR
XJ220 at 217mph in 1992, Gavin Green thought that there
would probably never be a faster production car. Yet two years
later, the McLaren F1 had gone quicker – a startling 14mph
quicker, to be precise. No supercar has topped the F1's
231mph, the Ferrari F50 and 550 Maranello that followed
having much lower top speeds. Times have changed, and selling a car that tops 200mph looks irrelevant and anti-social
– the supercar makers have tempered their aims. But not all
of them. Don't expect them to stop making cars that accelerate faster, grip harder, stop faster and, better still, deliver a
more dramatic sensation behind the wheel. And don't rule out
the possibility of a production car breaking 231mph either –
it's still possible. Because there will always be someone who
wants to go faster. The supercar story is not over yet.

Richard Bremner
Associate editor, CAR Magazine

	0-60mph	Max speed
McLAREN F1	3.2	231
FERRARI 550 MARANELLO	4.4	199
FERRARI F50	3.7	202
JAGUAR XJ220	3.9	217
BUGATTI EB 110	3.6*	209
LAMBORGHINI DIABLO	3.9*	205
FERRARI F40	4.9	201
PORSCHE 959	3.7*	197
FERRARI TESTAROSSA	5.8*	180
FERRARI 288 GTO	4.9	190
ASTON MARTIN VANTAGE	5.2	170
BMW M1	5.8	161
FERRARI BERLINETTA BOXER	5.7	176
PORSCHE 911 TURBO	4.5*	180
MASERATI BORA	6.5	174
LAMBORGHINI COUNTACH	4.2	190
FERRARI DAYTONA	5.5	174
FORD GT40	NA	154
LAMBORGHINI MIURA	4.5*	177

*0-62mph

CREDITS AND ACKNOWLEDGMENTS

COVER AND SPEEDOMETERS TIM ANDREW. END PAPERS, FRONT: MERVYN FRANKLYN, REAR: TIM ANDREW. CONTENTS: PAUL DEBOIS. LAMBORGHINI MIURA: TIM WREN. FERRUCCIO LAMBORGHINI: GRAHAM HARRISON. FORD GT40: MARTYN GODDARD. BLACK & WHITE GT40 PICTURE: QUADRANT PICTURE LIBRARY. HENRY FORD II: FORD ARCHIVE. FERRARI DAYTONA: COLIN CURWOOD. ENZO FERRARI: UNKNOWN, BUT THANKS. LAMBORGHINI COUNTACH: PHILIP SAYER. MARCELLO GANDINI: RICHARD FAULKS. MASERATI BORA: TIM WREN. PORSCHE 911 TURBO: TIM ANDREW. BUTZI PORSCHE: STUART REDLER. FERRARI BOXER: MICHAEL BAILIE. BMW M1: COLIN CURWOOD. ASTON MARTIN VANTAGE: COLIN CURWOOD. FERRARI 288 GTO: TIM WREN. FERRARI YELLOW: KIEREN PHELPS. REDS: COLIN CURWOOD. DEATH IN THE AFTERNOON: TIM WREN. PORSCHE 959: MARTYN GODDARD. FERRARI F40: IAN DAWSON. LAMBORGHINI DIABLO: IAN DAWSON. BUGATTI EB 110: MARTYN GODDARD. ROMANO ARTIOLI: ROBIN BARTON. JAGUAR XJ 220: IAN DAWSON. FERRARI F50: TIM WREN. FERRARI 550 MARANELLO: TIM WREN. LUCA DI MONTEZEMOLO: COLIN CURWOOD. McLAREN F1: RICHARD NEWTON. GORDON MURRAY: MERVYN FRANKLYN. THE NEED FOR SPEED: ALEX PUCZYNIEC

EDITOR: RICHARD BREMNER. ART DIRECTOR: NICK ELSDEN.
ADDITIONAL WRITING: JOHN SIMISTER, PETER TOMALIN. SUB-EDITORS: RACHEL BUTLER, CHRIS TURNER.
ARCHIVIST: STEVE BLOOR. PRODUCTION: HELEN CRAIG. EDITOR-IN-CHIEF: GAVIN GREEN. PUBLISHER: MARK JEFFERSON.

PRINTED BY ST IVES (ROCHE) LTD, CORNWALL. COLOUR ORIGINATION BY HIGHLITE TECHNIQUES, RAYLEIGH, ESSEX
SPEEDOS: GARAGE ON THE GREEN, PARSONS GREEN, LONDON. MARANELLO CONCESSIONAIRES, EGHAM, SURREY. McLAREN CARS, WOKING, SURREY.